PENGUIN BOOKS

THE MODERN AMERICAN NOVEL

Malcolm Bradbury is a novelist, critic, television dramatist, and professor of American Studies at the University of East Anglia. His novels include *Eating People is Wrong* (1959); *The History Man* (1975), which was made into a major TV series; *Rates of Exchange* (1982), which was shortlisted for the Booker Prize; and most recently, *Doctor Criminale* (1992). Critical works include *No, Not Bloomsbury* (1987); *Ten Great Writers* (1989); and *From Puritanism to Postmodernism* (1991). He has edited *Modernism* (1976); *An Introduction to American Studies* (1981); *The Novel Today* (revised edition, 1990); and *The Penguin Book of Modern American Short Stories* (1987).

THE MODERN AMERICAN NOVEL

NEW EDITION

MALCOLM BRADBURY

PENGUIN BOOKS

PENGUIN BOOKS
Published by the Penguin Group
Penguin Books USA Inc., 375 Hudson Street, New York, New York 10014, U.S.A.
Penguin Books Ltd, 27 Wrights Lane, London W8 5TZ, England
Penguin Books Australia Ltd, Ringwood, Victoria, Australia
Penguin Books Canada Ltd, 10 Alcorn Avenue, Toronto, Ontario, Canada M4V 3B2
Penguin Books (N.Z.) Ltd, 182-190 Wairau Road, Auckland 10, New Zealand

Penguin Books Ltd, Registered Offices: Harmondsworth, Middlesex, England

First published in Great Britain by Oxford University Press 1983
Published in the United States of America by Oxford University Press 1983
Revised edition published in Great Britain by Oxford University Press 1992
Published in the United States of America by Viking Penguin,
a division of Penguin Books USA Inc., 1993
Published in Penguin Books 1994

THE LIBRARY OF CONGRESS HAS CATALOGUED THE HARDCOVER AS FOLLOWS:
Bradbury, Malcolm, 1932–
The modern American novel/Malcolm Bradbury.
p. cm.
Originally published: Oxford [England]; New York: Oxford University Press, 1983.
"OPUS."
Includes bibliographical references and index.
ISBN 0-670-84515-9 (hc.)
ISBN 0 14 01.7044 8 (pbk.)
1. American fiction—20th century—History and criticism.   I. Title.
[PS379.B67   1992b]
813′509—dc20   92-54084

Printed in the United States of America

Two bodies of modern literature seem to me to have come to the real verge: the Russian and the American . . . The furthest frenzies of French modernism or futurism have not yet reached the pitch of extreme consciousness that Poe, Melville, Hawthorne, Whitman reached. The Europeans were all *trying* to be extreme. The great Americans I mention just were it. Which is why the world has funked them, and funks them today.

D. H. Lawrence, *Studies in Classic American Literature* (1923)

Preface to the Revised Edition

And so I say one can have at any moment in one's life all of English literature inside you and behind you and you do not know if there is going to be any more of it. However very likely there is, there is at any rate going to be more American literature. Very likely.

Gertrude Stein, *Lectures in America* (1935)

THE revised edition of this book covers the hundred years of the American novel from the 1890s to the 1990s: the crucial period, that is, from the early beginnings of modernism to what seems to be the end or fading of postmodernism. The book has been very substantially revised, to do fair justice to the important new fiction that has come out since it was first conceived, to reflect my own altering sense of the contemporary directions, and my own changes of emphasis and critical judgement. Therefore the whole text has been fundamentally reworked and enlarged, the two original last chapters (Chapters 6 and 7), have been totally rewritten, and two extended new chapters have been added, to bring the story up to the immediate present and alter the balance and emphasis of the whole plot or argument. Postmodernism has always considered endings provisional, and had a taste for changing them. It seems very reasonable that I should apply the same principle to postmodernism itself.

A hundred years is a long time in the history of the novel, especially when that period is also one of massive change in American culture and history—and when the change has affected not just the nature and spirit of the American novel itself but the direction of fiction everywhere. Indeed the move of American fiction to its late modern power and influence is an essential part of the story. It should be remembered that the novel was a fairly late (and a virtually illegal) immigrant to new and pristine America: Jefferson condemned it as a European phenomenon, Noah Webster saw it as dangerous and encouraging to vice. Not till around 1800, with the work of Charles Brockden Brown, did it really settle on American shores, and then in the fashionable form of Gothic. And not until the 1820s did it become a widespread form, when James Fenimore Cooper, the 'American Scott' (though he was more than that), developed the historical, social, and frontier romance. In the 1830s Edgar Allan Poe established the American short story, still a form of great prestige and importance in the USA. But it was really in the 1840s and 1850s—when the novel was prospering anew in Europe in the hands of Dickens and Thackeray, Stendhal and Balzac, Gogol and Pushkin—that it truly established itself with authority in America. As is evident today in retrospect, it was Nathaniel Hawthorne's *The Scarlet Letter* (1850) and Herman Melville's *Moby-Dick* (1851)—and some would say Harriet Beecher Stowe's *Uncle Tom's Cabin* (1852)—which suddenly gave significant and radical expression to the idea of the American novel. It still remained largely a Gothic and romance fiction; not really until after the great break of the Civil War of 1861–5 did the dominant European movement of realism arrive amongst American novelists. The major figures of that movement—Mark Twain, William Dean Howells, Henry James—are those who dominated the American novel to the close of the century, and so to the point where this narrative begins.

'Modern' American fiction may have emerged in the 1890s; but not with any great confidence. American literature was still largely seen as an offshoot of British literature. There was little sense of a national tradition (Melville died in virtual neglect in the early 1890s) and Henry James, like others of his contemporaries and indeed successors, preferred to practice their serious art in the capitals of Britain and Europe. Not until the 1920s did a major new generation emerge in the American novel—Anderson, Fitzgerald, Hemingway, Sinclair Lewis, Faulkner, Dos Passos—with the power to impress their international contemporaries. In 1930 Sinclair Lewis was the first American novelist to win the Nobel Prize for Literature; Theodore Dreiser was a close contender. By now American fiction was beginning to have significant impact on European reading and writing, winning the admiration of European contemporaries, D. H. Lawrence, for example. In fact it was clear Americans were major contributors to the modern movement. By the 1950s its influence, if not domination, in twentieth-century writing was unquestionable. Gore Vidal once observed that writers in powerful countries usually get more attention than they deserve, but the influence reflected more than the fact of American superpower. The energy of American writing, the force of its response to modernity and history, the range of its forms, the power of its visions, images and metaphors, have shaped writing and reading on an international scale. Today, American fiction is simply inescapable; and it has influenced us all.

As American fiction acquired its modern authority, it became necessary for the critics to construct—and indeed to deconstruct, in recent disputes about the nature of the American canon— traditions and heritages. This was partly to explain what came increasingly to be seen as its difference, its peculiar, self-made distinctiveness; later the issue became that of whose tradition the American tradition was. In the 1950s, as it became more and more the world literature of a superpower, a number of important books appeared explaining its peculiar history: Richard Chase's *The American Novel and Its Tradition* (1957), Leslie Fiedler's *Love and Death in the American Novel* (1960, rev. edn., 1967), which he described as a novel in itself, Marius Bewley's *The Eccentric Design: Form in the Classic American Novel* (1959), and so on. These studies emphasized (in some cases over-emphasized) what marked the American heritage: the importance of a Gothic tradition, the relative absence of the social novel in its European sense, the importance of nature and solitude, the tendency to see history less as process than myth. It will be seen as this book goes on that a similar process has taken place *within* American novels themselves, as they too attempt to construct a tradition, change the canon, imagine a past, define or obliterate the rules of genre, aspire to the role of a supreme fiction, or an ethnic legend. American fiction is still preoccupied with Gothic and the novel as romance ('A Gothic Western', Richard Brautigan subtitled his *The Hawkline Monster*); it is still mixing and matching the genres, still inventing itself. The only danger of many of these approaches and interpretations is that, in emphasizing what was and still is particularly American about these fictions, they often ignore the fact that much of the sense of tradition, much contemporary influence on American writing, comes from elsewhere as well as from within. American fiction is undoubtedly the product of the history, the material conditions, the consciousness, the philosophical modes of perception, of the American culture and indeed the post-culture in which most but not all of it has been made. But the novel is an international form, and especially in the United States. So it is also the product of a larger history of fiction in a changing international world, as well as in a multicultural society which has been particularly open to foreign influence—and seems all the more modern for being so. This explains the double approach of this book—which is concerned with the story of American fiction on native grounds, but also with its links to, influences from, and powerful place in, international literature.

The history of the novel can perhaps be described, grandly, as a history of cultural epochs expressing themselves as forms. Or, to put it differently, the novel proceeds through generational aesthetic change to conduct an ever-shifting inquiry, internal and external, into the way life is and the way it can best be perceived and expressed. Sometimes it is reportorial, sometimes psychological; sometimes it is dominantly realistic, sometimes predominantly experimental or surreal. I have told this story in terms of the general historical and formal stages of modern writing—through the development of naturalism and impressionism, the growth of modernism, the attempted return to social realism in the 1930s and to liberal realism in the 1950s, the emergence of a new 'postmodern' experiment in the 1960s, and the development of the present, rather more amorphous, scene we see now as our own century closes. Looking at tendencies, I have also tried to look in some detail at the work of individual authors—especially those I most respect, or consider of inescapable importance. Canons are unfashionable just now, and critics quarrelsome, but in every artistic form there lies a significant history. This is an endeavour to construct that changing and important history—one fundamental not just to American writing on its own soil, but to our understanding of the richness and potential of the modern, postmodern and indeed postpostmodern novel generally.

Parts of this book draw somewhat on materials I have explored elsewhere: in *Modernism, 1890–1930*, edited with James McFarlane (1976; rev. edn., 1991); in *An Introduction to American Studies*, edited with Howard Temperley (1981; rev. edn., 1989); in *From Puritanism to Postmodernism: A History of American Literature*, written with Richard Ruland (1991); and in other places. In different form, pieces of this book have appeared as essays or reviews in *The Sunday Times*, the *New York Times*, the *Washington Post*, and *Encounter*. I am greatly indebted to Catherine Carver for her editorial work on the first edition, and to Christopher Butler, Catherine Clarke, and Robert Ritter for their influence on the making of this new one. Other debts are many, especially to colleagues who have discussed newer American fiction with me in many seminars and congresses over recent years: my appreciation goes to Guido Almansi, Christopher Bigsby, Dominic Bradbury, Melvyn Bragg, Hans Bertens, Christopher Butler, Marc Chenetier, Jon Cook, Maurice Couturier, Haideh Daragahi, Regis Durand, Raymond Federman, Winfried Fluck, William H. Gass, Ihab and Sally Hassan, Gerhard Hoffmann, Alfred Hornung, Hartwig Isernhagen, Jerome Klinkowitz, Paul Levine, Hermione Lee, David Lodge, Richard Martin, Helen McNeil, Penny Perrick, Sergio Perosa, Janice Price, Jonathan Raban, Richard Ruland, Lorna Sage, Anthony Thwaite, Kristiaan Versluys, Mas'ud Zavarzadeh, and Heide Ziegler, as well as several of the writers mentioned in the text. And I owe much to the University of East Anglia for its ever-contemporary emphasis and its supportive climate.

M.B.

Norwich, England, 1991

Contents

THE MODERN

AMERICAN

NOVEL

1

Naturalism and Impressionism: The 1890s

I'm not in a very good mood with 'America' myself. It seems to be the most grotesquely illogical thing under the sun; and I suppose I love it less because it won't let me love it more. I should hardly like to trust pen and ink with all the audacity of my social ideas; but after fifty years of optimistic content with 'civilization' and its ability to come out all right in the end, I now abhor it, and feel that it is coming out all wrong in the end, unless it bases itself anew on a real equality. Meanwhile I wear a fur-lined coat, and live on all the luxury my money can buy.

W. D. Howells, letter to Henry James, 1888

His mind took a mechanical but firm impression, so that afterward everything was pictured and explained to him, save why he himself was there.

Stephen Crane, *The Red Badge of Courage* (1895)

1.

IN 1893 the American historian Henry Adams sat down amid the novel machinery on display at the World's Columbian Exposition, that great celebration of American resources held in the new skyscraper city of Chicago, and contemplated the modern process. Four hundred years after Columbus, the United States of America was becoming a world power, very likely to dominate the twentieth century. The architecture of the White City built for the fair was itself a bewildering expression of the age, a confusion of Renaissance styles and frank modernity. Beyond lay Chicago, the emblematic American 'shock-city', the city of sudden growth—a village of 250 inhabitants in 1833, it was now the 'Second City', its population over a million, its high business skyscrapers rising in celebration of American industrialism and corporatism. It was the railhead of the plains, the hogbutcher of the world, the centre for new immigration from Southern and Eastern Europe, the typification of new America. Two great American motions met here: the westering motion to the frontier, and the urbanizing motion toward the modern metropolis. For all the celebration of American technology and ingenuity, this was a year of economic panic, so not only European immigrants but migrants off the land—forced off their homesteads by recurrent agricultural depression and mortgages—flooded into the factories, stockyards, and ghettos, increasing the social problems and demanding a new social interpretation of the nation. The Exposition itself was aimed to display the great promise of the American future, and technological marvels and corporate achievements everywhere were in evidence—along with such figures as Buffalo Bill, mythicizing the lost frontier. And all this made Henry Adams sit down in what he called 'helpless reflection', to consider the processes driving American culture and the modernizing future itself.

'Chicago', wrote Adams in his ironic, self-doubting, and third-person autobiography *The Education of Henry Adams* (1907), 'asked in 1893 for the first time the question of whether the American people knew where they were driving . . . Chicago was the first expression of American thought as a unity.' A new process and a new age of history were evolving, he said, with America at the centre; so new theories—based on laws of accelerating forces, exponential development, and the rules of entropy—were needed to explain it, displacing all nineteenth-century educations, including Adams's own. The Exposition was intended to express American optimism; William Dean Howells's utopian novel *A Traveler from Altruria* (1894) sees it as 'a foretaste of heaven', based on the American principle of competition. Others, like Howells's fellow utopian novelist Edward Bellamy, were less confident: 'The underlying motive of the whole exhibition, under a sham of pretense of patriotism, is business, advertising with a view to individual money-making.' For Adams it was the end of an American era, distancing the American past. Apocalyptic feelings about the direction of history are common enough as the end of any century approaches;

and such anxieties—accelerated by the Darwinian legacy that replaced the religious and humanistic world-view with one of rising process and power—were particularly strong in the United States, where modernization was most accelerated, where technological innovation and social change were advancing at an unprecedented rate. Yet the excitements, too, were many: the United States, born as a nation only a century earlier, was now a transcontinental, coast-to-coast power which outstripped in industrial production Great Britain and Germany combined. Pessimism and optimism, American doubt and American promise, combined in Adams himself as he contemplated what he called the new 'multiverse'. His *Education of Henry Adams* is a work of novel-like power, extraordinary images and contrasts, visionary prospects and ironic self-effacement, and a remarkable attempt to relate—as many subsequent American writers would—the world's, and especially America's, proliferating material power and energy, and the capacity of the mind and culture to master and unify them. For, Adams saw, great changes in the historical process generate corresponding demands on human consciousness. They require, indeed, new forms of education, knowledge, and expression.

This was also apparent in the cultural aspect of the World's Columbian Exposition. Writers and thinkers, architects and historians, were summoned in large numbers to the fair. (The Exposition motto was 'Make Culture Hum!', and it had its own poet laureate, Harriet Monroe, later founder of *Poetry (Chicago)*, who wrote a patriotic Columbian Ode for five thousand voices.) Here the historian Frederick Jackson Turner advanced his famous thesis on the significance of the frontier in forming the American national character—as it happened, just at the time when the frontier officially closed, and the new frontier shifted to just such cities as Chicago itself, where a fresh American character was being formed in the urban melting-pot. Here the new American philosophy of pragmatism was expressed, questioning traditional American idealism and gentility and looking to a changed relation between consciousness and the so evidently material world. Here Hamlin Garland—one of a new generation of scientific and realist writers (he called himself a 'veritist')—

came to lecture on 'Local Color in Fiction', and attempted to bridge the double regionalism of America: the agrarian West, the new cities of the plains. Garland acknowledged, as the fair itself did, that the power of the old East Coast patriciate, and the domination of New England in matters of culture, were fading. Himself a self-educated populist and a determinist, bred on Darwin and Haeckel, committed to reform, Garland looked to the Midwest and West to provide a new American writing, which somehow bridged the American world of plain and prairie and the world of technology, science, and skyscrapers in a single vision. The solution, for Garland, was some form of scientific realism. Ever since the revolutions of 1848, European fiction had been moving increasingly towards realism, growing ever more representational, concerned with common life and the record of the age. In American fiction the symbolist spirit of Poe, Hawthorne, and Melville had died after the Civil War, replaced by a more factual and detailed record of ordinary American life. 'Is it true?—true to the motives, the impulses, the principles that shape the life of actual men and women?' asked Howells, the great spokesman of realist ideals. For ideals they were: ideals of democratic fidelity, popular sentiment, commonplace experience that illuminated his 'foretaste of heaven'. Yet already that realism was becoming more anxious, more depressed, more deterministic, and above all more scientific, concerned with the systems that governed the age of process.

Since the Civil War realism had prospered in many guises. There was the local-colour realism of local writers like Edward Eggleston (*A Hoosier Schoolmaster*, 1871); Mary Wilkins Freeman (*A New England Nun*, 1891); or Sarah Orne Jewett (*The Country of the Pointed Firs*, 1896). There was the novel of progressive social indignation, like Henry Adams's *Democracy* (1880) or Garland's own *A Spoil of Office* (1892). There was the vernacular Western or Southern realism of writers like Bret Harte or Mark Twain, and the moral realism of Henry James. Chicago itself became a realist capital; Garland himself moved there and wrote of the city. A new business-novel prospered: Henry Blake Fuller wrote novels of Chicago skyscraper-life like *The Cliff-Dwellers* (1893), Robert Herrick tales of modern commerce like *The Web of Life* (1900). They would soon be followed by the powerful new naturalism of Theodore Dreiser (*Sister Carrie*, 1900) and Upton Sinclair (*The Jungle*, 1906), in part influenced by the rise of the new 'Chicago School' of urban sociologists and the researches of the Muckrakers into corporate corruption. However, the notion of realism was, as in contemporary Europe, also coming into question. Old realistic ideas of reporting ordinary life were under challenge from new processes. Science and Darwinism threatened the old teleological order, progressivism and socialism questioned the individualist spirit, psychology and behaviourism challenged the notion of the independent moral self. Fiction was becoming less the portrait of a commonplace reality all could acknowledge, more a response to the uncommon realities and processes underlying modernizing life. New languages drawn from sociology and biology explained these processes and the displacement of the individual from the centre of existence. The structures of expression, the images of consciousness, put fiction itself under radical strain. As Adams in Chicago saw a world of new powers, Garland at the same fair saw the need for progressive new form in the novel. In both of them we observe the old ideas of nineteenth-century America coming into question, in a novel age of American process and power. It all meant a great re-shaping, not just of American subject-matter, but of the very principles of composition and literary form. Just as the last years of the century generated new technologies, new scientific, social, and psychological theories to account for modernity, so they generated fresh notions of form and consciousness, pointing to the new structures that would transform the novel in the twentieth century.

2.

As the 1890s started, three novelists dominated American fiction in reputation and influence. All had started their work in or just after the Civil War; all represented different aspects of the realist tradition; and all now seemed to enter an artistic crisis in the shifting atmosphere of the end of the century. Mark Twain, America's most powerful novelist, had begun as a frontier writer, his vernacular prose insistently mocking the genteel pressures, the formal styles and ideals of 'civilization'. His major novels were written on the East Coast after the war, but they explore the world of the frontier West before it. His main subjects were the Mississippi Valley in that river's key years as the central American artery, and then the movement west—themes that carried enormous moral force, for they evoked the innocent morality of a life beyond social rule and genteel convention. The central book was *The Adventures of Huckleberry Finn* (1884), according to Ernest Hemingway the book with which American fiction started—a fundamental myth of self-creating American freedom, a vernacular vision of spontaneous open morality won on a river raft despite the enslaving pressures of life beyond. But Twain wrote too of post-war America, in a mixture of violent satire (*The Gilded Age*, 1873, with Charles Dudley Warner) and celebration of American technological potential. The ambivalent tone is summed up in *A Connecticut Yankee in King Arthur's Court* (1889), which displaces a Hartford, Connecticut, machine-shop superintendent back in time to King Arthur's sixth-century Camelot, now a late Victorian wonderland, to bring to its world of feudalism, monarchy, and slavery the modern American blessings—democracy, technology, know-how, and advertising. But the book ends in horrifying irony: Hank's machinery outruns its creator and murderously destroys all life with a mechanical holocaust, in a dark predictive image of modernity. That darkening vision spread through Twain's work of the 1890s and, though often explained as the result of personal crises, it clearly also derived from the intellectual crisis of the age—his growing doubt about the power of 'innocent' morality, his reading in the new texts of determinism. *Pudd'nhead Wilson* (1894) reverts to Twain's classic subject-matter, Mississippi Valley life before the Civil War, but sees it now through the eyes of 1890s pessimism and determinism. So an old story-book fable of two children of different backgrounds exchanged in the cradle is turned into a plot of devastating ironies. One child is white and 'free', the other black and a slave; Twain develops the plot to challenge all notions of freedom, showing that all his characters are slaves to something, to heredity or environment, and cannot assert an independent identity or sustain a moral intent. And that bitter irony dominates the yet bleaker works that follow: *The Man That Corrupted Hadleyburg* (1900), the philosophical tract *What Is Man?* (1906), the unfinished *The Mysterious Stranger* (posthumous, 1916).

'I have lost my pride in [Man] & can't write gaily nor praisefully about him anymore,' Twain wrote in 1899 to William Dean Howells, another Midwesterner who had penetrated the East Coast citadel by becoming editor of the *Atlantic Monthly*, where he powerfully urged his case for an egalitarian American realism which dealt with the 'smiling aspects' of American life. Howells had become the exemplary American realist, producing something like a novel a year, from morally acute, photographically precise works dealing with what he called 'the life of small things' to utopian romances. To a degree rare in American fiction, his characters were members of family and community, living out ordinary lives amid the contingency and moral pressure of place, time, and custom. His best-known book, *The Rise of Silas Lapham* (1885), deals with a simple Boston paint manufacturer who rises in the post-Civil War industrial boom, but is drawn into corruption. Scruples intervene, and his social and business success alike collapse; but his social fall is his moral rise, a contribution to society's ethical economy. Increasingly though, Howells's work, like Twain's, revealed a deep ambiguity in its treatment of commercial, corporate, technological America. Thus Lapham's 'virtue' is rooted in his pre-Civil War ethic of agrarian individualism and simplicity; his failure in the America of trusts and corporatism suggests what powerful pressures threatened Howells's world of domestic decency. Like Twain, then, Howells grew pessimistic, especially after the condemnation of the Haymarket Riot anarchists in 1886. In 1889 he moved from Boston, the old literary capital, to New York City, reflecting this in a new kind of novel, aptly called *A Hazard of New Fortunes* (1890), about New York as the modern technological city where social goodwill is collapsing, strife and strikes split the classes, and the form of the novel as he had used it is itself seen under threat. The task of writing about the new world is hence handed on to his character Kendricks, who claims that 'the great American novel, if true, must be incredible'. Howells saw his mode of social realism declining, supported the younger naturalists, and wrote of his despair to the third survivor of realism, Henry James.

James was the most cosmopolitan of the realists, and had moved to realism's fountainhead, in Europe. Earlier, James's expatriation had seemed to Howells an evasion of realism's task, an escape to Europe's 'romance'. In fact James's choice of milieu arose from his need for a dense social order that would set a realist art into motion; and his 'romance' was managed through a realist perception refined by contact with Flaubert, Turgenev, George Eliot. His classic requirement became 'solidity of specification', meaning not a reportorial but a registrative view of art. Art's task was not to record but to *make* life; reality was a constructed, not a recorded, thing. It was in the inherent tension of the novel between empiricism and idealism, realism and romance, naturalism's 'magnificent treadmill of the pigeon-holed and documented' and romance's 'balloon of experience', that the form best expressed itself. This was James's quest of the 1870s and 1880s; but by the beginning of the 1890s he too was beginning to feel under pressure, and he confronted Howells's pessimism with his own. 'I *have* felt, for a long time past,' he wrote in 1895, 'that I have fallen on evil days—every sign or symbol of being in the least *wanted*, anywhere by anyone, having so utterly failed.' Again, his crisis was partly personal, but it was also philosophical and aesthetic. However, for all his doubts, James responded to the aesthetic transformations of the 1890s, and made an extraordinary and innovative recovery. By the time of this letter he was already on a new path that would lead, with *The Spoils of Poynton* and *What Maisie Knew* in 1897, to the remarkable work of his late phase—work in which consciousness severs itself from the world's materiality, changing the entire grammar of fiction. By the century's turn, James was ready, in his essay 'The Future of Fiction', to suggest that the novel might reach a new level of self-realization. 'It has arrived, in truth, the novel, late at self-consciousness, but it has done its utmost ever since to make up for lost opportunities,' he noted, pointing to the new achievements that had grown in Europe and America during the nineteenth century's last decade.

3.

In America, these ferments are most visible in the work of the remarkable new generation of writers who began to emerge in the 1890s and took on strong character as a generation—partly because they shared aesthetic theories and preoccupations, partly because they shared the tutelage of Howells, partly because most had brief careers and early deaths. Often presented by the critics as strongly American, working, as Alfred Kazin put it, in his 1941 book of that title, 'on native grounds', they were in fact much influenced by European theories of naturalism. Above all there were the theories of Émile Zola, who in 1879 had set down his view of the naturalist novel in *Le Roman expérimental*. For Zola, the word 'experimental' had a scientific analogy. The novelist's task was to undertake a social or scientific study, recording facts, styles and systems of behaviour, living conditions, the workings of institutions, and deducing the underlying processes of environmental, genetic, and historical-evolutionary development. Naturalism was thus realism scientized, systematized, taken finally beyond realist principles of fidelity to common experience or of humanistic exploring of individual lives within the social and moral web to an experiment in the laws of social and biological existence.

In fact naturalism was, by the 1890s, beginning to decline in Europe—disturbed by new decadent, impressionist, aesthetic tendencies that seemed in tune with contemporary psychology. However in the United States, where technological systems seemed to prevail, evolutionary hopes were strong, the laws of social struggle were apparent, and social Darwinism was a popular creed, it acquired a special dominance. Another reason for the appeal of naturalism, with its scientific, often ironic world-view, was the fascination of the new American cityscape itself. For if the novelist was analogous to the sociologist, so was he to the journalist, the hard-boiled city-room reporter or the crusading investigator of social facts, the man who walked in the city, observed, explored, exposed. He was the man, and sometimes the woman, who had been there, in the place of experience— the ghetto, the stockyard, the apartment block, the battlefield, the social jungle. He was like the new photographer, with his hand-held camera, catching sudden vignettes of life. But he was also like the modern painter, preoccupied with shades and acts of perception, the blur and impression of fleeting modern urban reality, the strange angles of vision needed to take in the world of manifold contrasts. Indeed the analogy with painting drew the American naturalist novelists back towards the problems of form and subjectivity which also haunted the 1890s. The tense relation between art and life, impressionism and naturalism, became a dominant theme in the writing and criticism of the most impressive writers of the decade.

These young writers had been bred amid the transitions that ran so powerfully through nineteenth-century American society, making past accountings of experience seem incomplete. Hamlin Garland had been born on the economically depressed prairie, in what he called the 'middle border' area of Wisconsin, Iowa, South Dakota. He escaped by moving to Boston, and immersed himself in new social, political, and economic theories, turning to evolutionary thought to explain the bleak world he had left behind him; then he returned to Chicago and the West around 1893. Frank Norris was born in Chicago itself, where a new school of urban sociologists was exploring the hard world of immigrant conflict and social deprivation, and where a similar school of urban novelists would follow. He had bohemian leanings, went to Paris as an art student, and returned with Zola's novels to Berkeley, in California, another new centre of literary activity. It was a similar bohemian revolt that led Stephen Crane to break with the genteel morality of his religious background—he was born in New Jersey, the son of a Methodist minister—and moved to New York, to the 'mean streets' of the Bowery and the Tenderloin, aiming both to report the facts and refine his aesthetic sensibilities. For these writers, confronting a new American social experience, naturalism offered a view which questioned the conviction that man was a conscious and rational creature, that happiness is secured by virtuous behaviour, that the landscape of familiar experience offered all the moral pointers men needed. With this view, they could observe mass and mechanism, touch on unexplored areas of society, the life of working people, the problems of cities, the operations of social and genetic patterns. Their writing drew on the new 'brute fact' of American life; hence their insistence that literature derived from life rather than form. They turned to consciously modern settings—the shock city, the West, the ghettos, depressed homesteads, the skyscrapers, corporations and department stores—and period themes—the split between culture and materiality, idealism and underlying economic and sexual drives. Naturalism thus became a way of dealing with the fact of a modern America largely unexplored by genteel awareness. But it was also a formal obsession, part of the decade's aesthetic self-consciousness, not merely—as Zola himself emphasized—a reporting system, but an artistic movement.

A conflict between the passion to get at life and the pursuit of form can lead to a dualistic vision. Strikingly, for a generation ostensibly given over to 'life', most of these writers produced works of aesthetic speculation. Norris, in his essays in *The Responsibilities of the Novelist* (1903), urged that art should yield to life, 'the honest rough-and-tumble, Anglo-Saxon knock-about that for us means life'. He equally emphasized his 'naturalist' sources and stressed that naturalism was not a mode of report but of romance, requiring scale, exaggeration, and symbolic motifs. Hamlin Garland displayed a similar tension in the essays of his aptly titled *Crumbling Idols* (1894), where he defined his own tendency, 'veritism', as a reaction both against 'romance' and against Zola's sexual explicitness and lack of idealism. Veritism was a form of local realism, dealing with the nearby and the probable. But it also was a form of 'impressionism', a formal response 'based on the moment of experience, actively felt and immediately expressed'. Stephen Crane, a greater artist, though a weaker theorist, was obsessed with the same problems. Behind his stories and his one great novel, *The Red Badge of Courage* (1895), the naturalist pieties are evident. In the presentation copies of *Maggie: A Girl of the Streets* (1893), his first published fiction, printed at his own expense, he wrote that it tried to show 'that environment is a tremendous thing in the world and frequently shapes lives regardless'. His settings were the classic ones of naturalism: the big city, the battlefield, man exposed and adrift in a nature that is 'indifferent, flatly indifferent', as he puts it in his fine story 'The Open Boat' (1897). Crane wrote with persistent naturalist assumptions about the failure of religious and genteel explanations of life, and about the ironic status of the human agent. Yet that irony is also a *style*, a form of extreme artistic self-consciousness. He always stressed that the writer's essential property was his distinctive 'impression'—that key art-word of the period. Like all the better American writers influenced by naturalist thought, Crane in his work mixes an encounter with the 'real thing'—the place, the fact, the experience—with an insistence on the mode by which it is perceived and written about. Appropriately, his move to the garrets, tenements, and brothels of New York City was a move to both of the two cities dominating the times: the naturalist city of struggles, problems, and conflicts—which was also the decadent bohemian city of evanescence and artifice.

4.

For the modern reader it is surely Stephen Crane who best exemplifies the volatile mixture of American fiction in the 1890s. He aptly called his early writings—his initial 'city-sketches', collected in 1900, and his two key urban novellas, *Maggie: A Girl of the Streets: A Story of New York* and its companion piece, *George's Mother* (1896)—'experiments in misery': the misery is there, but so is the tone of formal experiment. *Maggie* and *George's Mother* are formal naturalism, and take their plots from Victorian melodrama, using methods and tones close to parody. *Maggie* is the story of an innocent—indeed over-innocent—girl from the tenements of Rum Alley who glimpses larger horizons beyond those among which she lives, becomes sexually attracted to a flashy young man who seems to offer them, and is ruined when he discards her. She then turns to prostitution, suffers moral condemnation from those around her, and kills herself. *George's Mother* is another apparently monitory fable, about a young man from the same tenement who rejects his mother's morality and temperance attitudes, turns to the exciting city, finds its saloons, sinks into alcoholism, and finally and shamefully fails to register the 'reality' of his mother's death as he concentrates on realities outside. The stories are conventional, but Crane deflates their sentimental potential with insistent irony—conventional lessons in morality occur inside the stories, and are part of the damage. As for the city itself, dominating both stories, it is duplicitous. It is the Darwinian jungle, where, in *Maggie*, the woman of 'brilliance and audacity' rules, snatching Maggie's lover from her and then discarding him for someone better, where traffic snarls on the streets and children fight animalistically for victory in tenement yards. It is also the place of dream, wealth, indulgence, the social theatre, where ever fresh roles are offered: George longs to 'comprehend it completely, that he might walk understandingly in its great marvels, its mightiest march of life, its sin'. Crane's naturalism is not unwavering. Inconsistent with her environment, Maggie is an innocent romantic who has 'blossomed in a mud-puddle' with none of the dirt of Rum Alley in her veins. She is however consistent with Crane's need for irony, his devotion to unexpected juxtapositions, his contrastive impressionism. Indeed his characters are impressionists of a sort, living by small acts of consciousness among contingent awarenesses. Over them is the larger condition: the city, dominant, gives rise to their competitive struggles, their fleeting mode of consciousness, their moral void. As George's mother dies in his presence, an 'endless roar, the eternal tramp of the marching city, came mingled with strange cries'. Beyond that is a larger condition still: that of Crane's distinctively toned prose. Concerned to disestablish the centrality of character, to tell the story obliquely, through scenes that pose contrasts and show the ironic displacement of mankind, he stylistically commands every situation.

The short story and the novella, dominant forms in the 1890s, yielded well to this mode of naturalistic impressionism. In *The Red Badge of Courage*, where Crane works at novel length, his problems evidently increase. Shifting from the city to another naturalist locale, the battlefield, he set the book in the American Civil War, which he had not known. As he explained, 'Of course I have never been in a battle . . . I wrote it intuitively.' But war was a key naturalist image of life; it was real and existential, a place where human delusions of heroism and power were tested, a field of struggle and competition. It involved the ironic nullification of the human self, the process of mortal reduction. Crane focuses the book on the battle itself. Political issues are absent, the characters have designations rather than names (The Tall Soldier, etc.), and individuals are swamped in the experiential texture. The central character, Henry Fleming, is named only once, and is otherwise called 'The Youth'. The book consists of his impressions over two days of fighting; events and objects become the correlatives of his mood. Henry becomes, in fact, the exemplary experiencer of war as embroilment in flux, movement, sensation, colour, fear and physical pain; the sequence of impressions itself nullifies his initial desire to perform a heroic role. In fact the technique itself overwhelms Henry's heroic self-image. His commanding consciousness dissolves; war's impact on him is that of sensation, producing a mechanical response. He encounters the brute fact of death, the indifference of nature. He is pushed to flee, then pushed back into battle again, acquiring—accidentally—his red badge, the initiatory wound, which is less a mark of heroism than entry into a modern world of exposure. The wound is a token of arbitrary and nihilistic reality, but also a sign of complicity with that reality. Henry ends the book 'a man', an initiate in experience.

The ending is troublesome to many readers (it was to Crane, who rewrote it several times) because its language suggests that there is a potential for heroism even in the hostile naturalistic world. Henry leaves the battlefield in tune with 'a world for him', and even indifferent nature seems to agree: 'Over the river a golden ray of sun came through the host of leaden rain clouds.' Given nature's performance in the book, this can be read as irony; rather it points to an ambiguity in Crane's impressionism. *The Red Badge* is very much about reality as immediate and hostile, assaulting the formal organization of consciousness, displacing its function into acts of perception, instinct, reaction, immersion, withdrawal. Crane marvellously realizes through Henry the visual instantaneousness of an exposed and naked world:

It seemed to the youth that he saw everything. Each blade of grass was bold and clear. He thought he was aware of every change in the thin, transparent vapour that floated idly by in sheets. The brown or gray trunks of the trees showed each roughness of their surfaces. And the men of the regiment, with their starting eyes and sweating faces, running madly, or falling, as if thrown headlong, to queer, heaped-up corpses—all were comprehended.

Impressionism moves towards abstraction, posing the scene, making the youth like a film-camera, his angle of vision always relative. *The Red Badge of Courage* has rightly been seen as the first modern war novel, prophetic in its vision and sensibility, vivid in its sense of war's horror and meaninglessness.

Crane's problem was whether this vivid impressionism could yield up a symbolist logic in experience; he always desired, he said, a 'hidden long logic' in his stories. It was not surprising that the book's double quality—its visionary naturalism, presenting consciousness in half-apprehending motion in a world of shifting, violent experience, and its symbolist aim of discovering a transcendent meaning or a revelation in the experience—should win it two different reputations. In the United States Crane was seen primarily as a naturalist. But when in 1897 he moved to England, he was befriended by Henry James and Joseph Conrad, who hailed him as 'a complete impressionist'. His work, said another admirer, H. G. Wells, was a 'new thing, in a new school', and he observed that 'In style, in method, in all that is distinctively *not* found in his books, he is sharply defined, the expression in art of certain enormous repudiations.' Crane displayed the technical complications of the effort to grasp and interpret the new. He was in fact quite close to what Conrad, James, and Ford Madox Ford were doing—creating the new novel of experimental modernism. But the book was also the exemplary story of adventure in war, as later American writers discovered. And Crane was always drawn to war's adventure, and the life of action that went with it. Like many writers in the decade, he became a war correspondent, covering the Spanish–American and Graeco–Turkish wars, risking his health and his life. Caught between two artistic possibilities, his work varied greatly in quality. But there was one great book, and he remains important to later readers because he walked the difficult edge of modern writing, trying to decipher the character of acts of consciousness, and processes of artistic perception, in a world from which most of the numinous external significances, the divine signatures of teleology, had been withdrawn.

Hamlin Garland's work shows similar tensions. It is significant that we remember him now not for the political novels like *A Spoil of Office* but for the short stories in the two volumes *Main-Travelled Roads: Six Mississippi Valley Stories* (1891; extended 1893) and *Prairie Folks* (1893). Garland's stories are indeed 'impressionist' lyric pieces, portraits of homesteaders and prairie people, trapped in primitive miseries and punitive economic conditions, left behind in America's shift from being a rural to an urban nation. The city shimmers on the edge of these pieces, a force both emancipating and corrupting, a new chance but a threat to the stubborn individuality of the landsmen. Often the focus is on the man who comes back, a version of Garland himself, returned from the city to survey the roots left behind. But though they deal with social issues the stories avoid overdirect commentary; they are presented through the impression and the tactics of contrast. Compositional artistry turns the circumstantial and deterministic into grounds for wistful hope and expectation—a theme hard to sustain at length, though Garland tries successfully in *Rose of Dutcher's Coolly* (1895). Later, passing beyond his 'veritism', he wrote sentimental Western romances; but the lyrical precision of the earlier stories remains his great achievement.

Crane and Garland both qualified and amended naturalism, treating it more as a world-view than a necessary form. But America had one powerful and positive exponent of Zolaesque naturalism in the 1890s: Frank Norris. The essays of his *The Responsibilities of the Novelist* set out the most coherent case for the relevance of naturalist method to contemporary American life and consciousness. They explain naturalism less as a form of social reportage, or an entirely deterministic world-view, than as a form of modern epic, a drama of the people which encompassed 'the vast, the monstrous, the tragic', reached into the unconscious parts of life ('the unplumbed depths of the human heart, and the mystery of sex'), and into the great evolutionary cycles and systems of history, nature, and community. Norris was no complex theoretician, but he laid down lore that helped establish the notion of the panoramic popular epic—the Great American Novel—which preoccupied so many of his successors. His two first ventures in naturalism came when, in 1894, he went from Berkeley to Lewis Gates's writing class at Harvard, where he worked on *McTeague: A Story of San Francisco*, published in 1899, and *Vandover and the Brute*. *Vandover*, left unfinished at his death, was lost in the San Francisco earthquake of 1906. It was recovered and completed by his brother, published in 1914, and is naturalism at its most literary, a *fin de siècle* tale about the artist and his double, a decadent fable about the degeneration of an artist into lycanthropy. Here is the '*bête humaine*' which so preoccupied the new thought; a much more fundamental and original treatment of it comes in *McTeague*, probably Norris's most powerful book.

Firmly based in San Francisco poor life, set in a world of deprivation, immigration, and urbanization, *McTeague* follows his own prescription that 'The novel of California must now be a novel of city life'. But it is also the story of a naturalist process, a movement towards degeneration. In it, an evolving chain of events, once set in motion, releases underlying forces, energies, and conflicts—especially those that come from the primitive, secreted desires of men and women, and their atavistic sources in the life of the race and the herd. The characters are shown as primitives. McTeague is a San Francisco dentist come from the mining camps, without a diploma. His qualification is strength, and he is massive, strong and sluggish, a dormant beast whose only pleasures are those of eating, smoking, sleeping, and playing his concertina. 'Mysterious instincts' attract him to one of his patients, Trina, a girl from a money-obsessed immigrant Swiss peasant background. Their courtship and marriage 'awaken' his animal sexuality and her avarice, the subconscious rhythms of their lives, and fate then reinforces their atavism. Trina wins, appropriately enough in a fatalistic novel, a lottery. McTeague, denounced by a jealous rival, Marcus, for practising without a diploma, is deprived of work, his strength turning back to brutality just as Trina's peasant carefulness turns to greed. Functionless, he steals his wife's money, runs away, then returns for the rest of her savings, and is now so debased that he kills her for them. With his canary, he flees back to the mining camps, where his strength is natural, and where his inner instincts lead him to gold. In Death Valley, Marcus, after the gold and the reward, finds him and handcuffs him. McTeague kills him, and the plot of fate and the plot of symbols coalesce. The novel closes with McTeague handcuffed to a corpse, his double, and 'stupidly looking around him, now at the dead horizon, now at the ground, now at the half-dead canary chittering feebly in its little gilt prison'.

It is a plot of clear naturalism, setting its hypotheses about atavistic instincts and desires to work, and pursuing them through an enlarging, expressionistic system in which fate, chance, and process conspire. 'Suddenly the animal stirred and woke,' Norris writes of the moment when McTeague is first tempted by the sight of Trina as she lies helpless under gas in his dental chair, 'the evil instincts that in him were so close to the surface leaped into life, clamoring and shouting.' If crude, this is powerful; Norris, in the language of naturalism, is striving to express the deep undercurrents of sexual energies and unconscious forces for which Freud would shortly provide a deeper explanation and a discourse. Norris is evidently after the psycho-social sum of his characters, in whom culture and nature, the aesthetic and the atavistic, habitually contend; in this sense they are the agents of forces which they do not control. This underlying subject pushes Norris towards a typological, symbolist, and mythic dimension. And the book's dominant symbol is gold itself, the California metal. When Trina presses coins against her body in bed, so substituting money for sexuality, one desire for another like it, or when McTeague hungers for a gold tooth that will advertise his dentistry parlour, they join a vocabulary of desire and participate in a symbolic system which links and structures the entire novel. *Vandover* and *McTeague* are American variants of pure naturalism, psychologically intense, socially alert, symbolically energetic.

After these early enterprises in bleak naturalism, Norris became a professional journalist and editor. He reported the Spanish–American War for *McClure's*, and turned for a while to more popular romance, novels in which love and a mild racism replaced his naturalist principles. Then, around the turn of the century, he ventured into a new naturalist stage—less bleakly despairing, more clearly reflecting progressive and muckraking sympathies. On the model of Zola's *Rougon-Macquart* cycle, he planned an epic trilogy which would be focused on the cultivation, marketing, and consumption of America's great crop, wheat—'straight naturalism with all the guts I can get into it'. A move away from the psychological naturalism of *McTeague* towards a sociological and evolutionary theme, and now concerned with underlying forces in life which are no longer guided by the *bête humaine* but by the outer force of nature, it was to cover the map of America and of Europe, the great global movements of life forces, biological and economic. Norris thus conceived not just one form of naturalism, but two. One was concentrated, despairing, filled with end-of-the-century unease about human victimization, the other was sprawling, an optimistic epic of American energies and resources, filled with progressive expectations and biological vitalism. In the event, only two volumes of the 'Wheat Trilogy' were written; before it was finished Norris died suddenly in 1902, from peritonitis. *The Octopus* appeared in 1901, *The Pit* posthumously in 1903, and the third volume, *The Wolf*, dealing with Europe, was never written.

None the less, we can clearly see the nature of the whole conception. Central to *The Octopus* is a figure of the writer, the poet Presley, who goes out to California to write a 'True Romance' about the Spanish-American past, but instead finds himself throwing bombs in defence of the farmers of the San Joaquin valley, a gigantic land space intruded on by the trusts and the railroads, who are bringing in industrial methods and weakening the farmers by cruel freight tariffs. This is the new True Romance, of modern forces and powers, and of the natural processes of the land—the seeding of the earth, the growing of the wheat crop, the large cyclical motions of the universe. Norris displays his reportorial skills and his indignation, but he also shows exploiters and exploited alike subject to this indurant process, which is ultimately transcendent and overarches the deaths, the greeds and selfishnesses of the human story. The wheat, 'that mighty world-force, that nourisher of nations, wrapped in Nirvanic calm, indifferent to the human swarms, moves onward in its appointed grooves,' displaying that 'all things, surely, inevitably, resistlessly work together for good'. While *The Octopus* deals with the natural landscape of this oceanic vitalism, *The Pit* turns to the railhead of it all, Chicago itself, where, around the wheat-trading 'pit' at the Board of Trade, another epic adventure, that of American business, is taking place. Like some of his naturalist successors, Norris here recognizes the figure of the businessman as the modern American hero, and he explores the warfare in the national existence between the material and the ideal, between economic energies and emotional and aesthetic ones, between commerce and culture, men and women. Again, however, the experiences of individual life—its heroisms, romances, failures, injustices, tragedies—are just aspects of larger cosmic cycles which may swamp the individual but nourish the race. Thus, apart from its political, muckraking side, Norris's work activates the American sense that great and noble powers work in the universe, powers that sometimes have a malign face but a grand indifference which finally works for human destiny.

Norris was a novelist of mixed attitudes and of mixed gifts, and his work varied uneasily between popular romance and theoretical naturalism. Yet he is a central figure in the late-nineteenth-century transformation of American fiction. Something of his importance can be seen in the transition of a metaphor. 'Nature was, then,' Presley thinks in *The Octopus*, 'a gigantic engine, a vast cyclopean power, huge, terrible, a leviathan with a heart of steel, knowing no compunction, no forgiveness, no tolerance; crushing out the human atom standing in its way, with nirvanic calm.' The world of nature, from which earlier American writers had drawn an image of extra-social freedom and transcendence, a life in myth and space, was itself now incorporated within the world of the machine that was once set against it. For Norris it is an ambiguous machine: it drives McTeague to his death, yet it nourishes the race. From this you might derive the optimistic biologism of a John Steinbeck, or the dark aggression in nature that lies behind Ernest Hemingway's world of war and slaughter. Norris's work, certainly, marked the end of an old liberal pastoral. Now nature too was a working process, just as naturalism was now a key part of American literary perception.

5.

The American fiction of the 1890s seems so important because in it a whole new body of themes and energies began to find expression, revealing and exploring much about American life that had until then remained unspoken. It was not only that the new writing gave a fresh account of the deep-seated processes—genetic, biological, sexual, social, and scientific—that lay beneath modernizing American life, or that it increasingly engaged with questions of consciousness and the unconscious. It also expanded the essential territory of American fiction, and here we see the beginnings of the city novel, the business novel, the immigrant novel, the Jewish-American novel, the black novel, the feminist novel. Abraham Cahan's *Yekl: A Tale of the New York Ghetto* (1896) and *The Imported Bridegroom* (1898) gave a voice to the vigorous, and often radical, Jewish immigrant culture developing in the great cities, a cultural and political source from which would spring many of the most important developments of the next decades. The Norwegian immigrant H. H. Boyesen wrote of the battles of wealth and urban poverty in *The Social Strugglers* (1893); Henry Harland, under the pen-name of Sidney Luska, wrote 'Jewish' novels like *As It Was Written* (1885) and *Mrs. Peixada* (1886) before he moved to London, joined bohemia, and edited *The Yellow Book*—the bible of aestheticism—in the 1890s. Black fiction in the 1890s took a rather more uncertain path, since it was largely directed at a white audience. But the dialect stories of Charles Chesnutt's *The Conjure Woman* (1899) and the fiction of Paul Laurence Dunbar—the poet who was also author of the novels *The Uncalled* (1898) and *The Sport of the Gods* (1901), about the northward flight of a victimized black family—show the beginnings of a tradition that would come to real fruition in the Harlem Renaissance of the 1920s. Women writers had played a large part in the development of nineteenth-century American fiction, not only in the field of the sentimental novel but in regional realism, as was evident in the excellent work of Sarah Orne Jewett. But it is now acknowledged that the most remarkable female writer of the 1890s was Kate Chopin, author of more than a hundred stories (some collected in *Bayou Folk*, 1894, and *A Night in Acadie*, 1897) and the novel *The Awakening* (1899). This story, about female consciousness struggling to break from the prison of gentility, concerns an intelligent, sensitive, well-to-do New Orleans wife, Edna Pontellier, who comes to sense the erotic needs and hidden forces that lie behind the polite fiction both of her marriage and her social life, and who moves through aesthetic and sexual awakening to final self-extinction.

The Awakening is in fact an apt title for many novels of the 1890s. Edna's hunger is as much for aesthetic sensation as for sexuality, and she expresses Chopin's own passion for art; that is why the book has aptly been described as 'the first aesthetically successful novel to have been written by an American woman'. There is a similar quest in Harold Frederic's *The Damnation of Theron Ware* (1896), the story of a minister trapped in the gentility and hypocrisy of small-town life who tries, also unsuccessfully, to break into a more aesthetic world, a world of greater experiental wholeness. The hunger for aesthetic experience was a mark of the European 1890s, a part of the new instinct towards consciousness, self-discovery, and the re-examination of religious, social, and gender conventions. It was also a way of questioning the onerous realism of genteel American life. Like Henry Harland, Frederic himself moved away from realism toward aestheticism, and from America to Europe. The remarkable Chicago author Henry Blake Fuller produced, in *The Cliff-Dwellers* (1893) and *With the Procession* (1895), two important novels of urban experience in the city where the great Exposition that celebrated the new American age was set. But he also travelled regularly to Europe, and wrote high-toned European romances of an aesthetico-decadent kind, *The Chevalier of the Pensieri Vani* (1890) and *The Châtelaine of La Trinité* (1892).

Lafcadio Hearn turned to Japan to capture the fleeting aesthetic moment in many stories, as well as in his Louisiana novel *Chita* (1889). If the 1890s looked to realism, they also looked to aestheticism and to romance, especially in its popular forms: the novels of Richard Harding Davis and Winston S. Churchill were enormous successes. The split between the two—materialism and aestheticism, realism and romance—could be said to mirror the split in American life between ideality and reality that George Santayana observed, the split that the philosophy of pragmatism attempted to heal. And it marked a spirit of transition in literary forms that was also evident in European writing, where the changes of the age and the pressures of new consciousness, new awakenings, were altering the form and structure of the novel.

By the end of the 1890s American fiction was beginning to reflect two things. One was the enormous variety and diversity of American life, and the speed of its modernizing change. The other was a mood of artistic ferment that expressed the spirit of a clearly transitory generation. The last decades of centuries generally display an awareness of change, and a mood both of closure and beginning. The American writers of the 1890s also seem transitory, and very much a generation, because many of them were to die young: Crane at 29, on a health trip to Germany in 1900; Harold Frederic, also by now an expatriate, at 42 in England in 1898; Frank Norris at 32 in 1902; Kate Chopin, a much criticized and disappointed writer, at 54 in 1904; Paul Laurence Dunbar, the black poet who had turned his talents to black fiction, in 1906. And, as the century turned, something of the spirit of ferment, of aesthetic, social and sexual radicalism, appeared to die too. In movements like Muckraking and in its general hunger for artistic and social experiment, it passed on a strong legacy, much of it not claimed again until the 1920s. The decade's fiction also pointed in two important directions for the future. One was to the growth of naturalism as a native American philosophy suited to the nation's evolution, as its experience moved towards city life, technological development, social progressivism and the world of the immigrant melting pot. The other was to a concern with aesthetic form and psychological consciousness, which looked beyond the material world into the flux of feeling and sensation and the potential of art. As the American novel moved into the new 'American century', these were the two main paths it would follow.

2
Modernity and Modernism: 1900–1912

The child born in 1900 would, then, be born into a new world which would not be a unity but a multiple. Adams tried to imagine it, and an education that would fit it. He found himself in a land where no one had ever penetrated before; where order was an accidental relation obnoxious to nature; artificial compulsion imposed on motion; against which every free energy of the universe revolted; and which, being merely occasional, resolved back into anarchy at last. He could not deny that the law of the new multiverse explained much that had been most obscure.

Henry Adams, *The Education of Henry Adams* (1907)

Henry James is a combination of two ways of writing and that makes him a general a general who does something. Listen to it.

Gertrude Stein, 'Henry James' (1933)

1.

IN 1900, as the twentieth century (which everyone said would be the American century) turned, Henry Adams attended yet another exhibition. This one was not in Chicago but Paris, and in the seven years between the two a new world had, Adams said, been born. In 1893 Roentgen had discovered X-rays; in 1898 the Curies had identified radium, 'that metaphysical bomb'; and the new automobile had now become 'a nightmare at a hundred kilometers an hour'. Thus the Paris Great Exposition of 1900 completed the process Chicago had begun; and there Adams found himself, he said, 'lying in the Gallery of Machines . . . , his historical neck broken by the sudden irruption of forces totally new'. What dominated the Gallery of Machines was an 'occult mechanism', the forty-foot dynamo, a machine designed to make more and more energy. 'Before the end', Adams reports, 'one began to pray to it; inherited instinct taught the natural expression of man before silent and infinite force.' Adams pursued this crucial symbol. For centuries people had worshipped the Virgin; now they would worship the Dynamo, and so depart the old universe for the modern multiverse. This would reshape all societies, but above all those with the power to multiply the most energy; that particularly meant the 'twenty-million-horse-power society', which was of course the United States. So, in the new century and its modern multiverse, the American must become either 'the child of new forces or the chance sport of nature'. Human relations would transform, not least sexual relations; Adams prophetically doubted whether the new American could 'run his machine and a woman too'. Adams's millennial vision of modern proliferation and change, which would dismiss old educations and values, drag the modern individual into a new 'supersensual universe', and the modern world toward the condition of entropy, was an extraordinary, a far-seeing, and for literature a deeply influential prophecy of the forces that were disturbing the western mind and the western social order itself, as the 'American century' came into being.

For some, like the young Gertrude Stein—just about to move to Paris herself for a lifetime of writing—the shift into the American century was laden with creative promise. As she would later explain, English literature had had five centuries and now there was enough of it, so American literature was 'the way to go'. For Stein the great transition was full of hope; for Adams it brought a mood closer to ironic despair. As for the American writing of the first twentieth-century decade, it hovered somewhere between Stein's sense of beginning again and Adams's sense of an ending—sometimes stimulated by the faith that a whole new evolutionary cycle was starting, with a special promise in it for Americans, and sometimes assuming, with naturalist pessimism, that an age of modern and mechanical determinism was in the process of formation, which would not expand but limit American lives. Thus it was entirely in tune with the mood of the times that, in the transitional year of 1900—as Senator Beveridge announced 'The twentieth century will be American...

The regeneration of the world, physical as well as moral, has begun...'—, a work by a new American writer should appear that seemed an instinctive response to Adams's vision of the age of the Dynamo. Its author had had no literary education; in fact he was the son of German Catholic immigrants who still spoke their native language at home in the American Midwest. Like a good many of his contemporaries and fellow-writers, he had broken with religious faith, and become a determinist, teaching himself on Tolstoy and Herbert Spencer, and reading in the new sociology, physiology, and psychology. He trained as a newspaper journalist and edited women's magazines; through the encouragement of a literary friend he was persuaded to try his hand at fiction.

He wrote the book haltingly, and so at odds with literary convention that its own publisher called it 'immoral' and tried to suppress it. It was a book about a modern individual trapped among Adams's 'supersensual forces', and drifting toward eventual entropy. Suitably to the age of the Dynamo, its first chapter was entitled 'The Magnet Attracting: A Waif Amid Forces', and begins:

> When Caroline Meeber boarded the afternoon train for Chicago her total outfit consisted of a small trunk, which was checked in the baggage car, a cheap imitation of alligator-skin satchel holding some minor details of the toilet, a small lunch in a paper box and a yellow leather snap purse, containing her ticket, a scrap of paper with her sister's address in Van Buren Street, and four dollars in money. It was in August, 1889. She was eighteen years of age, bright, timid and full of the illusions of ignorance and youth. Whatever touch of regret at parting characterized her thoughts it was certainly not for advantages now being given up. A gush of tears at her mother's farewell kiss, a touch in her throat when the cars clacked by the flour mill where her father worked by the day, a pathetic sigh as the familiar green environs of the village passed in review, and the threads which bound her so lightly to girlhood and home were irretrievably broken.[1]

The book was *Sister Carrie*, the author Theodore Dreiser, born in Terre Haute, Indiana; and the opening theme of the break

[1] References are to the Penguin American Library edition of *Sister Carrie* (1981), based on the restored Pennsylvania edition text. See the useful introduction by Alfred Kazin to the Penguin edition for the text's complicated history.

with the past and the entry of Carrie Meeber into a new world of goods and forces introduces one of the most powerful of twentieth-century American novels.

Sister Carrie outraged not only its publisher but most of its few early readers, and it was virtually neglected until it became a success in England, after which it was reissued in 1911. Its outrage lay in Dreiser's refusal to structure his fictional world, which is heavy and dense with the substance of things, the claims of the material, according to a moral perception. In his story of Carrie's ascent through the material world, in which she uses her own body as more material, chance usurps rational decision, instinct usurps moral guidance, and will and desire operate independently of convention. The story starts in the familiar universe of realistic things, but it soon steps beyond it. Another paragraph or two on, and Carrie is moving into a new force-field, as well as into a new fictional discourse:

When a girl leaves her home at eighteen, she does one of two things. Either she falls into saving hands and becomes better, or she rapidly assumes the cosmopolitan standard of virtue and becomes worse. Of an intermediate balance, under the circumstances, there is no possibility. The city has cunning wiles no less than the infinitely smaller and more human tempter. There are large forces which allure, with all the soulfulness of expression possible in the most cultured human. The gleam of a thousand lights is often as effective, to all moral intents and purposes, as the persuasive light in a wooing and fascinating eye. Half the undoing of the unsophisticated and natural mind is accomplished by forces wholly superhuman.

This passage begins in morality, but ends in naturalist theory, where the disposition of transhuman forces makes moral questions finally irrelevant. The transhuman is humanized and becomes sensual and enveloping; the human becomes increasingly material and mechanized. Carrie is no sooner on her train to Chicago than she meets her first human seducer, Drouet, the 'drummer' or commercial traveller, the 'smaller and more human tempter' who is really no more than one voice of the city. Dreiser immediately generalizes him, and makes him an emblem of the rootless, tempting city where moral order is sacrificed to larger expressionist forces. The novelist may imply a standard of morality, but he organizes his novel as a post-moral system. He talks of Carrie's 'undoing', but he sets her in a world so sensually to hand, so contemporary, alive, and restless, that her amoral viewpoint, which is her response to the force-field, seems inevitable.

One of the things that has often been noticed about *Sister Carrie*, and variously read as the book's strength or weakness, is that it moves on to create a world in which there are no real human attachments. Some displacement of the person is characteristic of naturalism, and makes the tendency a post-liberal one; it depends on a new economy of relations between person and process. But what is noticeable in Dreiser is precisely that the force he removes from people he relocates in things. The city and the machine, goods and property, have romantic powers, and indeed the capacity to make choices for human beings. The city tempts, like a 'magnet', says Dreiser, but also like a lover, who is merely a human magnet. Carrie may start out as the 'waif' caught amid forces 'wholly superhuman', but she soon becomes a most effective user of them; as a result, her apparent 'downfall' is actually her energetic ascent. By the end of the first chapter, she is being assimilated by the 'great city', Chicago itself, with its massive mobile detail, its commercial 'power and fact', its tempting wealth and degrading poverty. And while Carrie enters at the bottom, an untrained job-hunter, an object (' "We're not exactly in need of anybody," he went on vaguely, looking her over as one would a package'), she finishes, one city further on, at the top, the actress-dancer in a world of decadent love, the bearer of its roles and masks. A 'little soldier of fortune', she not only adapts to but becomes an urban process, a moving principle of amoral energy.

In *Sister Carrie*, naturalism turns towards expressionism, and finds the literary means to display not only the ironies but the energies of American urban culture, or post-culture. Crane had used naturalism as a mode of aesthetic perception and a tactic of irony. Norris had seen it as a neo-philosophy generating the plots of modern romance. Dreiser takes up a position of personal engagement; he is literally a part of the naturalist world. He delights in the struggle, moves emotionally along with Carrie,

shares many of her wants, and looks with her at the alluring
material possibilities of the great dream theatre of city life. His
characters, too, generally understand that they are *within* a
naturalist world, and respond to its laws of energy; they know
their own shortage of self. At the same time Dreiser stands
outside, as naturalist commentator, generalizing, explaining
human action in neo-scientific terms, moving from detailed
specifics ('her total outfit consisted of') to the large generalities
('Half the undoing of the . . . natural mind is accomplished by
forces wholly superhuman'). He sees much more than Carrie,
and distances her, but he takes each scene of her life as a self-
justifying event, and shares her sense of living in an exciting post-
moral world. The result is that *Sister Carrie* is founded on an
unmasked economy of want, a sexual economics in which the self
is an object, objects have selves, and the body is a none too
intimate instrument in social success.

Carrie's essential psychology is given us on her first seduction,
after she loses her job at the shoe factory, and Drouet reappears
and offers her money. Into her morning-after reflections, Dreiser
enters with Spencerian behaviourist views. Morals are social
products, and if the voice of conscience ('only an average little
conscience, a thing which represented the world, her past environment, habit, convention, in a confused way') complains,
other, stronger voices speak in her. There is the 'voice of want',
desiring not just money but those things in the material world
that makes it more than material ('Fine clothes to her were a
vast persuasion; they spoke tenderly and Jesuitically for themselves. . . . The voice of the so-called inanimate'). Dreiser
speaks Jesuitically too, creating a version of experience in which
desire metabolically wins. So Carrie soon drops Drouet for
Hurstwood, his social superior, a saloon manager, 'genteel',
'respected', 'an interesting character after his kind', following
desire's higher economics. In turn Hurstwood leaves his failing
marriage and steals from his employers to win Carrie's energy. In
front of his employer's safe, his mind functions as a machine, a
'clock', wavering between two commanding instincts, one towards
convention, the other towards desire; as he holds the money,
uncertain, the safe door snaps shut. By symbolic transposition,

machinery becomes his mind, his mind becomes a machine. The two then flee to New York, a 'newer world', and follow out their appropriate spirals of motion: Carrie's upward, Hurstwood's downward. (Dreiser supports all this with semi-scientific psychological theories.) At last Carrie becomes the actress Carrie Madenda, her onstage face 'representative of all desire'. We see her at the last in her rocking chair, in perpetual but entropic motion—the material girl, the tainted modern star, her economic wants satisfied, yet needing (like the author himself) something more, a realm of art and culture beyond the material. Meanwhile Hurstwood sinks into the realms of naturalist disaster, becoming a strike-breaker, a Bowery bum, finally a nameless suicide who ends in a pauper's grave. Dreiser emphasizes the ironic contrast, but he typically shares Carrie's final lack of concern—for, by the end of the novel, the laws of inevitability have become paramount.

The novel (now available in its full, unedited version) always brought mixed critical reactions. 'It is not intended as a piece of literary craftsmanship,' Dreiser said of it, 'but as a picture of conditions done as simply and effectively as the English language will permit.' Yet the book does have strong literary pretensions, and pretentiousness—one reason why the original text was edited. The author's local stylistic gestures can make us uneasy; but Dreiser's power lies in style in a larger sense—his capacity to create fictionally a vigorous world that is represented mechanically and causally, yet overflows with vital energy. Material life becomes abundant with hieroglyphics; individuals in it toss on a 'thoughtless sea', moving either with or against force, in a total metaphoric flow encompassing success and failure, consciousness and the expressive voice of things. In these terms, *Sister Carrie* is the strongest of Dreiser's books. *Jennie Gerhardt* (1911) tells a similar story, but with more caution and more Christianity. His 'trilogy of desire', *The Financier* (1912), *The Titan* (1914), and *The Stoic* (1947, posthumous), about the financier Cowperwood, who struggles upward from poverty to sexual and economic success, is an ambiguous portrait of capitalism, with some progressive and increasingly Marxist doubts. These are counterbalanced by a deep admiration for Cowperwood's Nietzschean energies. *The*

'*Genius*' (1915) is about an energetic and sexually active artist, and is in part a portrait of the novelist himself.

But Dreiser did write one other great novel, *An American Tragedy* (1925), when he revived his naturalism to explore a decade when the American dream now seemed tainted with the materialism he so well understood. In this book he sees from the standpoint of the victim alone; now the kinetic energies he had earlier seen as a part of American life work only for its destruction. The book is highly documented, based on an actual murder case, and it critically analyses a social process—Clyde Griffiths's evolution from bitter poverty to social promotion, and then finally to the electric chair. The naturalist crux is at the centre of the story: if man is the product of circumstances and determinants, in what sense may he be guilty of the crime, murder, for which Clyde is charged? Clyde is incompetent in his ambitions and divided in his will, torn between his pregnant mill-girl mistress and the rich girl he wants to marry so that he can win his place in the American sun. But he is a product of American expectation and of the pressure towards success and social ascent. Dreiser makes the novel turn on a naturalist irony. Clyde wants to be rid of his mistress; he takes her out on a photographic expedition in a boat on the lake; his inward conflict between murder and kindness makes him make a move towards her; the boat rocks, the (symbolic) camera strikes her, and she drowns. Clyde is charged with murder, and much of the book is given over to the complex legal arguments in the courtroom. Dreiser takes the fundamental naturalist questions—How do motive and intent arise in a world where mind merges with matter? How do we relate desire to act? How does the clock or camera of the mind function?—and applies them to a compassionate concern with injustice. *An American Tragedy*, powerful as it is, thus becomes a simpler book than *Sister Carrie*: a fiction of social protest and a challenge to the American dream, rather than a work of cosmic irony or denuded modernity. It marks an essential direction in which American naturalism moved, though, by the 1920s, it already seems dated—in fascinating contrast to that other tragedy of the American dream, F. Scott Fitzgerald's *The Great Gatsby*, which came out in the same year.

2.

In fact, the period between *Sister Carrie* and *An American Tragedy* saw naturalism become a staple mode of American fiction. *Sister Carrie* may have been attacked and neglected, and Dreiser put off novel-writing for a decade. But over the immediately following years other writers, like Upton Sinclair and Jack London, turned naturalism into the great American adventure story, populist and popular. Both were writers of extraordinary abundance, entrepreneurs of fiction. Upton Sinclair, when he died, left more than eight tons of papers to Indiana University; Jack London made over a million dollars from writing, and produced more than fifty books—novels, stories, and socialist propaganda—between 1900, when he began to write, and 1916, when he committed suicide. Fed by the rise of progressivism and the growth of muckraking journalism, naturalism turned—as Dreiser himself was to turn—towards social protest and political exposé. It voiced popular indignations, challenged the trusts, explored the shame of the cities, and found in all this a romance of liberation which consorted with the mood of these progressive and adventurous times.

Upton Sinclair wrote several romances before he turned to the radical naturalism of *The Jungle* (1906), still his most famous and most successful novel. A book that interestingly compares with *Sister Carrie*, it too is set in the underside of Chicago, in its workplaces, bars, and immigrant ghettos. It too begins with the allure of the city—this time for two young immigrants, Jurgis and Ona, who have come from the Lithuanian forest and from feudal European injustice to America, 'a place of which lovers and young people dreamed'. But in the classic naturalist set-piece scene of the immigrant wedding with which the book opens the seeds of disillusion are already present; a 'subtle poison' is in the air as the great city, greed, and capitalist competition break up the old European folk solidarities and leave individuals exposed. Jurgis, seeking to make a life for himself from his honesty, strength, and independence, soon becomes a victim of the competitive American system. As a foreign labourer he is exploited to depress the wages of others; he moves from being the virtuous worker to becoming the scab and the bum, like Dreiser's Hurstwood. Hurstwood, though, fails from within, from a want of energy; Jurgis fails from without, through the corruptions of the system itself. He can therefore be rescued by rescuing himself, by learning the facts of the oppressive process and discovering the philosophy of socialism.

So the book ends not on victimization but in hope. The old community may have gone, but can be replaced by working-class solidarity. In fact at the close utopia seems at hand, as we see Jurgis thinking about a 'great potato-digging machine', as the pain of his destroyed family is healed by the responsive glances of a beautiful girl entrant to the party, while the socialist vote mounts in the election. *The Jungle* starts out a much more subtle novel than it finishes, but its switch from an artistic to a propaganda function served its purpose. As a result of the book, Roosevelt initiated an enquiry into the food laws, and reforms were made in the meat-packing industry; Jack London called the novel 'the *Uncle Tom's Cabin* of wage slavery'. Sinclair went on to write numerous novels of indignant social documentation, heavily researched, often about money (*The Metropolis*, 1908) or business processes (*King Coal*, 1917; *Oil!*, 1927), culminating in the 11-volume *World's End* sequence, started in 1940, which takes its radical hero Lanny Budd melodramatically through the international political landscape of the western world. Sinclair's work was often coarse, but he made it apparent that populist naturalism in the novel could become the discourse of record and reform, as well as the basis of prodigious publication, and a massive commercial adventure in writing.

That was a lesson equally evident in the career of Jack London, the great writer-hero of the pre-war years. London's life itself became a popular adventure, recorded in his writings. Illegitimate, he grew up in San Francisco, and was a cannery worker, sealer, hobo, and gold prospector in the Klondike before he turned to writing, which proved the greatest opportunist adventure of them all. Like Sinclair, he was filled with evolutionary, libertarian, and political ideas, culled from Darwin, Haeckel, Frazer, Nietzsche, and Shaw, ideas which he deployed with a popular touch and a sense of adventurous melodrama. But where Sinclair wrote of cities and social problems, London wrote mostly of the outdoors, of travel, violence, adventure. His writing was popular with children as well as adult readers, and as an adventure novelist he is still read widely today. The politics were deeply and instinctively felt, however, and his social and socialist ideas abundant, though it would be hard to call them other than confused. He adopted a scientific world-view towards 'this chemical ferment called Life', but it was a mixture of myths of democracy and myths of strength and superiority, particularly including his own. It came naturally to him to see life—whether outdoors or in the mills and factories—as a battle of wills, forces, and energies, mirroring the struggle in nature itself. Social protest exists in his work, but its central issue is survival, the evolutionary instinct, the law of the tribe and pack, and the justified rights of the winner.

That work poured out in a variety of forms. He wrote the boys' adventure story, so popular in an era of imperialism and adventurism (*White Fang*, 1906); the political fable of the future (*The Iron Heel*, 1907); the sea-story (*The Sea Wolf*, 1904); the novel of racial characteristics and superiorities (*A Daughter of the Snows*, 1902); the autobiographical novel of his own idealism (*Martin Eden*, 1909). London's better work is a blend of sharp political curiosity and awareness, self-taught ideas transmitted in popular form to others, heroic self-dramatization, strong life-hunger, and apocalyptic despairs alleviated by an adventurous sense of romance. Two books of 1903 suggest the mixed funds he could draw on. *The People of the Abyss* is reportage, derived from his experience in the East End of London, where he spent several months as a tramp, penetrating the unknown jungle on society's doorstep. As he exposes its horrors politically, he himself stalks through this jungle less as reformer than as Nietzschean superman, commanding the life around. The fictional *The Call of the Wild* shifts the jungle back into nature. The story of Buck, the 'aristocratic' dog forced to encounter 'the reign of primitive law' when he is stolen, taken off to the Yukon, and put into a dog team among savage beasts 'who know no law but the law of club and fang', it is about the recovery of old instincts. Buck becomes leader of this primal animal community, knows 'blood longing', and finally becomes a killer, 'surviving triumphantly in a hostile environment where only the strong survived'. It was heady lore for adventurous Rooseveltian times, part of the new century's attempt to recover the vitalism and primitivism that civilization and gentility had silenced. The intricate connection between the two books, both concerned with the collectivity of experience and the laws of struggle, with groups, packs, tribes, and classes, is not hard to see. Tribes need leaders, evolution needs individuation; in all of this we find life's true adventure.

There were, however, novelists of the new century for whom naturalism was less an ebullient mode of literary action than a philosophy for a post-religious age, a form of metaphysical pessimism and fatalism. One such was Ellen Glasgow, a fine writer who emerged from that historically battered and pained region, the South. She came from, and was the troubled historian of, a Virginia where the traces of feudalism and chivalric romanticism had outlasted the Civil War. In fact the 'expiring gesture of chivalry' is the theme of her early fiction—*The Battle-Ground* (1902), *The Deliverance* (1904). At first her treatment is sentimental, though she recognizes the need for a historical stoicism rather than false creeds of nostalgia, traditionalism, and gentility. As the satire grew sharper, and the unreality of the prevailing mores more apparent, in novels like *Virginia* (1913), a bitter naturalist sense of cosmic indifference grew in her work. The very titles of her late books—*Barren Ground* (1925), *Vein of Iron* (1935)—suggest the bleak and deprived space in which human beings attempt to find purpose, to erect culture, sustain institutions, hold ideals and illusions. Modern feminists have sometimes found the ultimate stoicism of her strong and intelligent heroines hard to take, but this seems to miss the ironic force of her vision. Ellen Glasgow is very much a novelist of culture and social mores, but in her books comedy of manners moves steadily towards a deeply tragic sense of life. Institutions contest with harsh nature, history displaces individual lives, ritual and code are built over void. Her novels were—as she said in the preface to *The Sheltered Life* (1938)—'the prolonged study of a world that, as the sardonic insight of Henry Adams perceived, no "sensitive and timid natures could regard without a shudder" '. Yet, dark in vision, they are also formally very exact, the work of a writer of enormous culture and intelligence penetrating to the void over which that culture is built.

3.

Thus in many forms naturalism developed, in the American fiction between 1900 and the First World War, into a familiar and inclusive usage, capable of expressing attitudes as various as political radicalism and a deep sense of human irony. Yet, as Philip Rahv once observed, naturalism came along to make its inventory of a material and process-ridden world at the point when it was just beginning to dissolve.[2] It was a form of positivism, and positivism was under challenge from the new sciences, particularly psychology; a form of realism, when realism was under challenge by new arts exploring the inward and the aesthetic. Science, as Adams saw, was growing increasingly relativistic, looking into uncertainty and chaos, assuming that reality was not objectively given but subjectively apprehended through consciousness. In America, this view was shared by pragmatism, of which William James, teaching philosophy and psychology at Harvard, was an originator. In *Principles of Psychology* (1890), he explored the gap between mind and action, noting that reality was not immediately apprehensible, but required to be approached provisionally, through the empirical, or pragmatic, assumption that order is 'gradually won and always in the making'. Hence attention must fall on to the mechanisms of consciousness themselves. So, where science had once seen an objective observer, where Crane saw a picture-taking shutter connecting inner and outer experience, and Dreiser a clock of thought, James offered a more fluid and, in the event, crucial metaphor: 'A "river" or a "stream" are the metaphors by which it [consciousness] is most naturally described.'

That metaphor was readily transmuted into literature, and particularly a new kind of literature that was just beginning to

[2] Philip Rahv, 'Notes on the Decline of Naturalism', in *Documents of Modern Literary Realism*, ed. G. J. Becker (Princeton U.P., 1963), 591–8.

emerge. In this William James himself had some part. He undoubtedly influenced his brother Henry, as well as one of his own most famous pupils, Gertrude Stein. In 1897, Henry James returned, with *The Spoils of Poynton* and *What Maisie Knew*, to the novel. *What Maisie Knew*, which, said one contemporary critic, added 'a whole new concept of reality to the art of fiction', particularly marks the change in his later work, which clearly points it towards modernism. *Maisie* is a novel of consciousness under test; its theme is the process by which the mind—that of the child Maisie, the 'light vessel of consciousness' on whose perception the book is centred—responds to or rejects impressions, experience. James explains this in his preface: he has, he says, given Maisie a vivacity of intelligence, 'perceptions easily and most infinitely quickened', so that she can 'know' the promiscuous adult world in which she grows up. He takes up his own narrative position beside and with the little girl's understanding, at the same time substantiating round it the adult social complexities she must make sense of. It was a pragmatist method, requiring the depiction of a process of apprehension both in character and author, and deriving, as William James said, from both a mental and a moral process. If reality is not to be known except by being taken in, consciousness must become the crucial question. So, in Henry James's late work, it does.

In 1900, the year of Adams's multiverse, James put aside a book, *The Sense of the Past*, he had started to write, and sketched a different scenario. He wanted, he said, to give 'the picture of a certain momentous and interesting period, of some six months or so, in the history of a man no longer in the prime of life, yet still able to live with sufficient intensity to be a source of what might be called excitement to himself, not less than to the reader of the novel.' This is the sketched-out plot of *The Ambassadors*, not finally to appear until 1903; a book started after it, *The Wings of the Dove*, appeared in 1902. These two books and their immediate successor, *The Golden Bowl* (1904), represent the centre of James's late phase, which coincides with the artistic ferments of the new century. They return to the international theme he had earlier discarded, and its motion from innocence to experience. But now the problem is not to learn from experience but to know what experience *is*—how it is redeemed from life's contingency and order, given form by the perceiver, perceptual shape by the novelist. The apprehensive and the compositional process become analogues. James, in *The Ambassadors*, 'sticks close' to his centre of consciousness, Strether, and the changing coloration of his consciousness as he grasps the 'inner' story, that of Chad Newsome. By starting the novel with Strether's arrival in Europe, and keeping all the material as an aspect of his consciousness, within the 'discriminated occasion' of his awareness, James holds the whole book within an apprehensive mode of vision.

This is in striking contrast to the method of *Sister Carrie*. Both books start with a discarding of the past, and an arrival in a new place, where a new force-field grasps the characters. But where Carrie in Chicago is immediately engulfed, almost sexually, by the process of reality, Strether in Europe can never know reality directly and outright. He works with impressions, potential, powerful, but neither determining his conduct nor forming an implacable reality 'out there'. Where Carrie is the waif amid forces, Strether is the 'enquirer', and the important process lies not outside but within the self, from the very first words forward. The essential concern is with the way the 'reservoir' of Strether's mind is filled with the forceful 'current' of new impressions, and this is displayed at its most complex when he sees the two lovers boating on the river, as in, exactly, an impressionist painting. Now, as James says in his preface, he 'at all events *sees*; so that the business of my tale and the march of my action, not to say the precious moral of everything, is just my demonstration of this process of vision'.

Related and yet different concerns run through *The Wings of the Dove* and *The Golden Bowl*. In *The Wings of the Dove* James sacrifices his intimate identification with a parallel consciousness, Strether's, to a more oblique angle of attack. The method is one of complex interaction between his own textual position and a 'modern' character who is moved through a harsh world of things, which refracts and interacts with her. The book begins (the contrast with *Sister Carrie* is again sharp):

She waited, Kate Croy, for her father to come in, but he kept her unconscionably, and there were moments at which she showed herself, in the glass over the mantel, a face positively pale with the irritation that had brought her to the point of going away without sight of him. It was at this point, however, that she remained; changing her place, moving from the shabby sofa to the armchair upholstered in a glazed cloth that gave at once—she had tried it—the sense of the slippery and the sticky.

The sympathetic character gone, person and context can be related and located only by a very oblique grammar ('She waited, Kate Croy . . .'). Here and in *The Golden Bowl*, the work is aesthetically and morally obsessed with consciousness; but it is concerned to reflect the harsh material surface of modern life, forcing the novelist into distancing manœuvres. Indeed the bowl itself, the symbolic flawed object which stands in the shop as Prince Amerigo and Charlotte acknowledge that they have sacrificed love to material need, concentrates just this. *The Golden Bowl* is a novel of hardened form, of aestheticism grown ironic. The characters may *live* as consciousnesses, but they are positioned as objects, indeed *objets d'art*, vessels of being with cash value. Maggie Verver tells Amerigo in her love speech that he is 'a rarity, an object of beauty, an object of price'. Charlotte's body is seen by the Prince as like 'some long, loose silk purse'. And the book is dominated by the collector Adam Verver, whose spirit is likened to 'a strange workshop of fortune . . . one with the perfection of machinery'. In this novel and *The Sacred Fount* (1901), written a little earlier, James moves most surely into the modern force-field, and responds—as indeed Dreiser does—by finding a new relation between consciousness and material substance. By the end of *The Golden Bowl*, the material and weighty world of things has won, a physical world beyond feeling or consciousness that must claim its due while sustaining its unreality.

One effect of the complexity of James's late method is that he left his public, as well as his literary successors, with two ways of reading his work. To some, his essential contribution was to the extension of realism and the development of the social and moral novel, which he helped to turn into a negotiable American form. To others the significant element was his contribution to modernism, his translation of realism into something quite other and quite new. 'Can you see that any day was no part of his life,' Gertrude Stein wrote in her portrait of James; or, as she put it in another place, 'the form was always the form of the contemporary English one, but the disembodied way of disconnecting something from anything and anything from something was the American one.' The curve of James's career in fact echoes a fundamental development from nineteenth-century to new twentieth-century practices in fiction. In the event, both his contributions—to the social novel of manners and morals, and to experimental modernism—were profitably to feed American writing.

In the line of the social novel, the great inheritor was undoubtedly Edith Wharton. When Percy Lubbock once defined Wharton herself as 'a novel of [James's], no doubt in his earlier manner', we can see at once what he means. Wharton's fiction shares much with that earlier manner. A product of the New York patriciate, born the rich, polite, and anxious Edith Jones, she grew up to a world in which social codes and customs were intensely real, the conflict of the classes significant, the rise of new wealth, commercialism, and corrupt politics after the American Civil War a serious anxiety. At the same time her books, her very act of writing, arose from the imprisonments of an unhappy society marriage and the imprisonment of women within social and puritanical conventions. Like a Jamesian heroine she fled to Europe to become, like James, an expatriate; their withdrawals were shaped in part by a sense of decline and debasement in the America they knew. They wrote of similar milieux, similar international themes, similar feelings of dislocation towards their native land, similar agonies about the gap between cultural and aesthetic desire and material fact, similar visions of the new American woman. But both were uneasy about the connection others saw between them. She complained saying in a letter of 1904 that 'the continued cry that I am an echo of Mr James (whose books of the last ten years I can't read, much as I delight in the man) . . . makes me feel rather hopeless'. She wrote, after all, from one generation later, from a different gender, from a much starker sense of the direction of historical change, from a different social standpoint, and with no particular appreciation of the later Jamesian complexities.

Yet both worried about the relation of society and consciousness, and were caught between two different models of that relation. Both shared a 'traditional' view that society is composed of people becoming more aware of their own, and others', true nature through sensitivity and introspection, and that personality is concrete and genuine behind outward appearance, and a more 'realist' or 'naturalist' view that people are shaped and perhaps even created by their social conditioning and status. Hence a sense of ironic contradiction inhabits the work of both writers. As with Ellen Glasgow's novels, Edith Wharton's are battlefields in which two perceptions of the self, one voluntarist, devoted to morals and culture, the other determinist, concerned with individuals as victims of society and process, contend. Her books are about values, but they are also about their economic derivation. In one of her best books, *The House of Mirth* (1905), the heroine, Lily Bart, is seen in the light of both visions, with consequent irony. Lily is the 'highly specialized product' of a civilization that needs specimens of beauty to exhibit, 'a rare flower grown for exhibition' in high society; but her moral scruples afford her no basis for survival in a system based on sexual exploitation and economic energy. Lily attempts gradually to bridge the two by behaving not as a social product but as a moral agent. But this threatens her position and sets her on a downward spiral, and she comes to suspect that morality has no social support, is merely 'a perpetual adjustment, a play of party politics, in which every concession had its recognized equivalent'. This might be said to be the naturalist or determinist crisis. However Edith Wharton does not finally support this view, respecting also the ideal of cultured society for which in this novel Seldon speaks, a 'republic of the spirit'. The outcome is irony, and the result tragedy, for there is no real class to enshrine morality, especially for women, who are not at all in control of their economic destiny. In Wharton's world, morals and culture have place, but not power. So the moralist may desire one world, and the naturalist perceive another. Hence

Wharton's writing is filled with a distinctive sense of waste, founded on emotional renunciations, sometimes stoical self-confinement, and a sense of universal inhospitality.

Her books explore this in various ways. *Ethan Frome* (1911) moves towards naturalism in its story of the loveless imprisonment of an unhappily married farmer who attempts suicide with his mistress, fails, and then must live out the rest of his life with his wife and the injured lover. *The Custom of the Country* (1913), probably her best book, is the story of Undine Spragg, a frankly erotic heroine with 'the instinct of sex', a Carrie Meeber looked down on from above in her social ascent, grasping for 'something beyond', 'a more delicate kind of pleasure'. As the title suggests, the book is a social satire, an exploration of an America where cultural décor and material desires mesh strangely. The custom of the country in question is the increasingly popular American sport of divorce, which enables Undine's erotic and social mobility. Undine is a decoration who knows her 'trading capacity', her sexual rate of exchange. In fact sexual economics provide Wharton's most powerful image of the modern entrepreneurial woman, operating on the fringe of the utilitarian economic process to win her way. Like Carrie, Undine ends up with everything, and nothing. On her fourth marriage, to a European aristocrat, she now possesses nearly all the elements: American energy and money, European rank and culture. But one small thing is missing: 'She had learned that there was something she could never get, something that neither beauty nor influence nor millions could ever buy for her. She could never be an Ambassador's wife [because she is divorced]; and as she advanced to welcome her first guests she said to herself that it was the one part she was really made for.'

It is a book of extraordinary economic unpeeling, its irony made partly from Wharton's position of European and cosmopolitanized patrician detachment, but above all from the intense satirical delight she takes in 'the chaos of indiscriminate appetites which make up [New York's] modern tendencies'. Her broader perspective on the subject is seen in the great novel of her maturity, *The Age of Innocence* (1920), a backward glance into the past. Here she departs the modern scene to look at the New

York of her own youth, extinct by then, and already dying in the 1870s, when the novel is set. Established patrician society, the world of the old Four Hundred, is already being displaced by the robber-baron wealth of the Gilded Age, the 'new people' New York is beginning to dread but also to be drawn to. The old rich begin to marry their children to the new, the world of politics is becoming corrupt, and most forms of decent human action seem denied. The cultured, intelligent, and responsible are caught up in a Henry Adams-like crisis of sterility, unable to find any form of significant action. Wharton sees this from the inside and the outside, both sympathetically and critically, for this is a world where even innocence is an artificial product, and the older wealth lives by a provincialized, puritanized, protective version of European culture, which it uses mainly for self-justification, appurtenance, and decoration. However it also possesses a moral dignity and honesty absent from the new rich who are now displacing and undermining it.

By now Wharton was one of America's finest social satirists and observers of the evolving American order; with the book she became the first woman writer to win the Pulitzer Prize. But like her earlier books, this is a novel of renunciation. Newland Archer, the sensitive, cultured, and unhappily married hero, cannot find a use for his intelligence in this rapidly changing American world. His drama comes when he falls in love with the Europeanized, mocking Countess Olenska, who returns to the United States and challenges the prevailing rules and mores. Their relationship is finally defeated, and this is the basic paradigm of the story. Archer elects to stand by the old order, and loses his chance for the freedom Ellen Olenska represents. Unlike his Jamesian namesake Isabel Archer in *The Portrait of A Lady*, he is destroyed not by his pursuit of freedom but by his refusal to take it; and like her he ends the book in a state of silent renunciation, standing in Paris, looking up at the window of the Countess. He feels around him the city's richness, 'the incessant stir of ideas, curiosities, images and association thrown up by an intensely social race in a setting of immemorial manners', and knows he has lost the flower of life. Wharton's books owe much to the social and moral tradition of early James, but they also deal, in a spirit of stoic naturalism, with those who attempt to sustain culture and intelligence in a rapidly changing history that is moving into the age of indiscriminate modern appetites. If there is a notable tradition of female social satire in modern American fiction, through to Mary McCarthy and Alison Lurie, Wharton is perhaps its essential source.

4.

'The others all stayed where they were, it was where they had come but Henry James was on his way,' wrote Gertrude Stein in her essay 'What Is English Literature', where she explained that Henry James was a true American novelist, and not of endings but beginnings. Stein was referring to the late experimental spirit in James, to which she owed as much as Wharton did to his earlier fiction. Stein too was a Europeanized cosmopolitan, but of a very different kind from Wharton. Born in Allegheny, Pennsylvania, to a wealthy Jewish immigrant family of aesthetic tastes, she spent part of her childhood in Vienna and Paris, and knew herself to be a new woman from the start. Back in the United States in the 1890s, she seized all the new opportunities afforded for female emancipation, going to study at the Harvard Annex (now Radcliffe). Here she worked with the new philosophers of pragmatism: George Santayana, Josiah Royce, above all William James. Pragmatism was an attempt to resolve precisely that late nineteenth-century crisis of American thought that saw intellect and culture as divorced from action, and sought new theories of mind to solve the problem from which, in effect, Newland Archer suffered. James looked to new theories of consciousness, proposed not a solid and objective but a pluralistic universe, and turned attention toward the psychology of awareness—the means by which we find emotion, generate action, and create reality from within.

It was a portrait of consciousness that deeply attracted Stein: 'I went to college and there for a little while I was tremendously occupied with finding out what was inside myself to make me what I was,' she said later. She shared William James's behaviourist and naturalist orientation: 'I was interested in biology and

I was interested in psychology and philosophy and history, that was all natural enough, I came out of the nineteenth century and you had to be interested in evolution and biology,' she was to explain. But if she came from the nineteenth century she did not intend to stay there: 'I was there to kill what was not dead, the nineteenth century which was so sure of evolution and prayers.' She worked on experiments in automatic writing, became something of a pre-Freudian psychologist (Freud never had much impact on her work) and unsuccessfully tried medical studies at Johns Hopkins. Then her brother Leo, an art historian and Harvard aesthete, encouraged her to look from behavioural science to aesthetics. She began to write, experimenting with artistic form and the behavioural act of writing itself, which she felt revealed the underlying principles of mental action. She started a book, soon set aside and published posthumously as *Things As They Are* (1950), dealing from experience with a three-cornered lesbian relationship, which owed something to William James in its thought, and his brother Henry in technique, for it used the method she called 'disembodiment', or abstraction. Now she and Leo moved to Paris, where she went looking, she said, for 'gloire'. But where Edith Wharton found her natural or social home on Right Bank patrician Paris, Gertrude and Leo chose Left Bank, bohemian, atelier Paris, setting up a salon that would become a centre of artistic modernism.

For their arrival, in 1903, coincided with a period of radical developments in art in which they gradually became central figures. The Steins were collecting, and became involved with the Post-Impressionists, notably Cézanne, then with the Fauves and the movement that was to become Cubism. Meanwhile, Gertrude had begun a translation of a work of late-realist naturalism, Flaubert's *Trois Contes*, which developed into a reconstruction, with an American setting. Appearing as *Three Lives* in 1909, its three linked stories, 'The Good Anna', 'Melanctha', and 'The Gentle Lena', are psycho-portraits of three servant girls in Bridgepoint, presumably Baltimore. They draw on some of Flaubert's naturalist assumptions, but aim to render the consciousness of the girls rather than tell their stories, to create complex studies of simple persons. In what is generally recognized as the most interesting story, about the mulatto girl Melanctha, Stein concentrates on the rhythms of the girl's thought-speech, with a distinctive intonation. Loose sentencing and repetition are emphasized; present participles and verb-nouns dominate the telling, creating rhythm and rhyme. Here for the first time the texture becomes distinctively Steinian. 'Sometimes when they had been strong in their loving, and Jeff would have inside him some strange feeling, and Melanctha felt it in him as it would soon be coming, she would lose herself in this bad feeling that made her head act as if she never knew what it was they were doing.'

This is naturalism in process of decomposition. Causality and pattern diminish, consciousness dominates, the aim is a neo-scientific study of the rhythms of mind. As Stein explained in her later lectures and essays ('Composition as Explanation', 'Portraits and Repetition', 'Poetry and Grammar'), this method represented the breakthrough to a modern mode of composition. Its post-causal present tense she called 'the synchronic present', explaining: 'there was a continuous recurring and beginning there was a marked direction in the direction of being in the present although naturally I had been accustomed to the past present and future and why, because the composition around me was a prolonged present.' The repetition or recurring was memoryless, and based on a new grammar in which, as in painting, the noun or realistic object is depleted ('A noun is the name of anything, why after a thing is named write about it'), and verbal and adverbal forms predominate. It was a literary version of the method of abstraction, post-naturalist, post-impressionist, moving onward from Flaubert and Cézanne. And, just as Cézanne was engaged both in creating and de-creating his paintings, in order to convey both the inner energy of subject and the perceptual art of their creation, so in prose Gertrude Stein moved towards a verbal version of estrangement and abstraction.

These were the methods Stein tried to take further, to novel length, in her next major project, *The Making of Americans*. This ambitious work was largely written over the key Cubist years of 1906–8, though not published until the 1920s, and not printed in full until the 1950s. *The Making of Americans: The*

Hersland Family (1925) merges two interconnected enterprises. One is the composition of a cubist novel, the other the composition of a novel about Americans, a Great American Novel which would be the epic of the sensibility of a nation. Stein actually saw Americans as natural cubists—products, that is, of the new composition, newly positioned in history and time. Hence the title is doubly apt: the book is about the making of the nation through immigrations and settlement ('The old people in a new world, the new people made out of the old, that is the story I mean to tell') and the fictional or compositional problem of creating their story out of words and tropes. The underlying task—that of creating a national epic of foundation, which covers three generations of a German-American family, the Herslands (the implication of the name is clear; they were based on the Steins)—is familiar, the compositional mode new. It is a tale less of individual characters or discriminated events than of rhythmic repetitions and variations, an implied timeless history of mankind, distilled through Americans because they especially possessed the sense 'of the space of a time that is filled with moving'. And 'the space of a time' is exactly the subject of the novel, and the nature of its form. Diverging from realism and story sequence, operating less as narrative than as a spatial disposition of words, it is indeed parallel to Cubism.

Never short of confidence (she once observed that there were three twentieth-century geniuses, Picasso, Whitehead, and herself), Gertrude Stein was very happy to explain the importance of the project: 'A thing you all know is that in the three novels written in this generation that are the important things written in this generation, there is, in none of them a story. There is none in Proust in *The Making of Americans* or in *Ulysses*.' The comparison is to a point justified. *À la recherche du temps perdu*, *Ulysses*, and her novel are all classics of the Revolution of the Word, endeavours to build a new continuum of experience based on consciousness. But where Proust draws on involuntary memory, and Joyce on myth and archetype, Stein, finding memory too much engaged with causality and chronicity, and myth not sufficiently subjective, emphasizes compositional rhythm itself. All three books display the need to violate old narrative logics. Joyce finds an element of historical crisis in this need, and Proust a sense of loss, but for Stein it is a matter of experimental joy. Prose repetition was the heart of the method, as she emphasized in her supporting essay, 'The Making of *The Making of Americans*' (1935).[3] Here she stressed the book's relation to her work at Harvard, where she had studied the fundamental tropes of speech repetition ('I was sure that in a kind of a way the enigma of the universe could in this way be solved'). It was a way to reach the 'bottom nature' of mankind, for language rhythm mimes the deep structures of consciousness, the way every person shows aspects of every other. So a novel can move from anyone to everyone, through 'all the kind of repeating there is in them'. As Stein said: 'I had to find out inside everyone what was in them that was intrinsically exciting and I had to find out not by what they said not by what they did not by how much or how little they resembled any other one but I had to find out by the intensity of the movement that was inside them.' Stein's method, though, raises serious problems of concentration. The book contains hundreds of pages of repetition systems, making it one of those books it is better to have read than to read. This challenged the relevance of the novel form itself to the modern task, and became part of a modernist argument for the Death of the Novel.

The Making of Americans is a crucial work of American innovation, a high modernist novel we are now coming to understand better. But it is important that to find her 'intensity' Stein felt the need to turn away from the novel, the form that encouraged 'remembering' and narrative. *The Making of Americans* virtually disproves itself. And Stein now sought the short form, the brief piece that might offer the verbal equivalent to the concentration and instantaneousness of a painting: to the collage, the Cubist figure painting, or still life. From 1908 on her work is best understood as a form of prose painting. Many of the paintings are portraits, 'portraits of anybody and anything . . . That started me composing anything into one thing.' They took as subjects fellow artists like Picasso or Matisse,

[3] In Gertrude Stein, *Lectures in America* (1935; reissued London, Virago, 1988).

writers like Apollinaire, patrons and friends. From 1911, like painters themselves, she turned more towards still life and collage, as in her next book, *Tender Buttons* (1914), where narrative gives way to verbal montage. Mixing cubist concentration with surrealist associationism, the pieces start by naming an object or subject, then develop systems of verbal, mental, or rhythmic association, ranging from rhymes or puns to very personal connections. Feelings of synaesthesia are drawn on to create a sensuous, rhythmed prose. The hard is softened, or the soft made hard, as in the book's title itself. This book marks the high point of Gertrude Stein's importance as an innovator; it also established her influence in America at the time of the Armory Show.

But after this her own work itself began to soften, towards the indulgences of *The Autobiography of Alice B. Toklas* (1933), witty and fascinating, but a work of veneration of Gertrude Stein written, of course, by Gertrude Stein. By this time, Stein's place in modern experiment had become accepted by many younger American writers, to whom she became guru and arbiter during the expatriate, avant-garde Twenties. She became a central translator of the experiments of painting into fiction, and of the experiments of Europe into America—the place she always regarded as experiment's natural home. Her work was an amalgam of European-influenced forms and American experiences, and she rightly saw that the thought of William James, and the writing of Henry James, had already pointed in the direction of such a modern and modernist cosmopolitanism. Her own writing is often read as the very antithesis of naturalism; what it rather shows is that there was a far greater connection between naturalism and modernism than is sometimes supposed. But, like Ezra Pound in poetry, Stein marks an essential stage in the modernization of American fiction. And if the best work of the crucial next two generations of novelists displays a thinning of the naturalist surface, a questioning of many of the traditional premises of narrative, a changed economy of work and stance, a more emphatic commitment to exploring the process of writing, above all a sense of the world—especially the American world—as a 'new composition', then all this truly owes a very great deal to the explorations and the influence of Gertrude Stein.

3
Artists and Philistines: 1912–1920

[O]ur artists have been of two extremes: those who gained an almost unbelievable purity of expression by the very violence of their self-isolation, and those who, plunging into the American maelstrom, were submerged in it, lost their vision altogether, and gave forth a gross chronicle and a blind cult of the American Fact.

Waldo Frank, 'Emerging Greatness' (1916)

One's first strong impression is of the bustle and hopefulness that filled the early years from 1911–1916. . . . Everywhere new institutions were being founded—magazines, clubs, little theatres, art or free-love or single tax colonies, experimental schools, picture galleries. Everywhere was a sense of secret companionship and immense potentialities for change.

Malcolm Cowley, *Exile's Return* (1934)

1.

IN 1913, Americans were disturbed and affected by an exhibition that was very different in kind and spirit from those grand expositions of modern technological and cultural marvels which had so troubled the mind and education of Henry Adams. In this year, under the sponsorship of the Association of American Painters and Sculptors, a remarkable exhibition of paintings was put on display in New York City, and then moved on to Chicago and Boston. This Armory Show brought the American public face to face, for the first time, with the experimental movements in painting that had been developing in Europe in the century's first decade, since Impressionism: movements like Fauvism, Cubism, and Expressionism, painters like Van Gogh, Cézanne, Picasso, Brancusi, Duchamp. Their works were set alongside another tradition of the modern, the work of American painters of the naturalist 'Ashcan school'. The two strands of modern art seemed in contention. The new naturalism, strong in America, was factual, reportorial, socially aware; the new Post-Impressionism from Europe represented a challenge to realism, an anarchic vitalism, an image of the modern as displacement in perception, a breaking up of forms. The impact of the Armory Show was very like that of its London counterpart, the show organized by Roger Fry at the Grafton Galleries in 1910. Much of the response was ribald. Art students in Chicago burned a copy of Matisse's *Blue Nude*; Marcel Duchamp's *Nude Descending a Staircase* provoked widespread parody; but some were impressed and changed into Moderns. Among the 30,000 Americans who saw the 'sensational' show, there were those ready to affirm naturalism as the true American impulse, aligned with the nation's rising progressive principles; and others sensed that the new European forms were a genuine expression of contemporary experience, and touched on the deeper complexities and possibilities of American life.

The Armory Show made such an impact because it arrived in the United States at a remarkable modern turning point. This was an era still excited by progressivism and radicalism. In the election for Presidency which brought the reforming Woodrow Wilson to office in 1912, electors had the choice of three candidates running on versions of the Progressive ticket, and the Socialist Eugene V. Debs amazingly polled a million votes in the land of gold and capitalism. This new radical spectrum reached across from progressive liberalism to left-wing radicalism, and the urgent voices of Big Bill Heywood, John Reed, and the anarchist Emma Goldman suggested that the United States might shortly come into a revolutionary age. The new experimental art movements that were now springing up joined with the political groups in seeking a radical emotion, a great emancipation, a modernizing new start. All this was fed by great demographic and social change, and expressed the mood of a generation that more than ever felt consciously in transit from an older to a new America—moving from small town to big city, from a 'puritan' consciousness to new artistic and social liberation, from white Anglo-Saxon culture to a melting-pot age. There were movements for sexual reform and liberation, encouraged

both by feminist argument and the growing influence of Sigmund
Freud. If it was a progressive, it was also a bohemian, age.
Young people moved to the bohemian artistic ghettos of the big
cities. New political and artistic groups were springing up everywhere, little magazines were flourishing. In 1911 the politically
radical magazine *The Masses* (later *The Liberator*, suppressed for
its pacifism after America entered the war), a mixture of social-
ism, anarchism, and feminism, began in New York's Greenwich
Village, shortly followed by *The New Republic*, an organ of
Europeanized liberalism that offered itself as Wilson's wartime
conscience. In 1912 the literary avant-garde made its strike in
Chicago with one of the first of the new 'little magazines',
Poetry (Chicago), shortly to be followed by *The Little Review*.
Many of the new feelings and changes had come out of the 1890s.
Now they reflected an age which saw around it a new landscape
and cityscape, a new separation from the past, and a new hunger
for radical expression and action.

In *A Preface to Politics* (1914), Walter Lippmann sought to
define the new mood. It was one where 'the goal of action in its
final analysis is aesthetic and not moral—a quality of feeling
instead of conformity to rule'. Older progressivism had drawn
intellectually on scientific positivism and naturalism. Now a new
spirit of thought, emphasizing intuition, feeling, life-force, and
creative evolution, took strength from the ideas of Bergson, Sorel,
Nietzsche, Freud, Wells, and Shaw. In 1909 Freud had lectured
in America, and his ideas of the unconscious, of repressed
forces, of sexual revolution spread as far as the popular press
(Mabel Dodge serialized an account of her psychoanalysis in
the Hearst papers). Henri Bergson's romantic ideas of creative
evolution and intuition acquired influence, their acceptance
being, said the liberal magazine *The Nation*, 'the expression of a
revolt from the dreary materialistic determinism of the closing
years of the last century'. A new romanticism thus seemed to
underlie the modern movement, though many criticized it. The
young expatriate T. S. Eliot sought a new 'classicism', the 'New
Humanist' Irving Babbitt, read it as a force 'allied with all that
is violent and extreme in contemporary life from syndicalism to
"futurist" painting'. The new tendencies sought their revolt not

just in politics but in art and in consciousness itself, and this produced an alliance between political radicals and the artistic avant-garde. When progressive radicalism grew disillusioned, by the entry into world war, by doubts surrounding the Bolshevik revolution in 1917, by the Versailles peace talks of 1919, when its political energies were sapped by the Red Scare of the same year, and when the America of the 1920s turned to a rampant new commercialism and social conservatism, it was in the arts rather than politics that radical challenge continued. Progressivism weakened, but the experimental avant-garde enlarged, generating a modernist art which not only experimented with new forms, but also challenged the age's materialism, the nostalgic return to old American values, the revival of Puritanism.

The message of vitalism, abstraction, and modernism was not lost on the generation of 1913. 'Looking back on it now,' Mabel Dodge (Luhan) wrote in her autobiography *Movers and Shakers* (4 vols., 1933–7), 'it seems as though everywhere, in that year of 1913, barriers went down and people reached each other who had never been in touch before; there were all sorts of new ways to communicate as well as new communications. The new spirit was abroad and swept us all together.' Moreover the new infusion from Europe, which the Armory Show represented, was helped by the fact that Americans had been involved in it already—expatriates like Ezra Pound and Gertrude Stein, who now became important transatlantic missionaries and mediators. When Harriet Monroe started *Poetry (Chicago)*, her 'foreign correspondent' was Ezra Pound, who introduced not only expatriate American poets like T. S. Eliot, 'H.D.', and Robert Frost, but the newest French tendencies. *Poetry* became a magazine in contention, divided between Pound's cosmopolitan modernism and 'Imagisme' and Harriet Monroe's American progressivism, which promoted the presence of many significant new Midwestern poets, like Carl Sandburg and Vachel Lindsay. It was a version of the same contention apparent in the Armory Show, where Matisse and Duchamp appeared beside the native naturalists. 'Mr Lindsay did not go to France for *The Congo* or *General William Booth Enters Into Heaven*,' Monroe declared in a strong attack on Pound. 'He is revealing himself in relation to direct experience, and he is not adapting to his work a twilight zone which is quite foreign to him, as it is, generally speaking, to the temperament of the nation.' In the event, the lessons of modernism were adapted, and with remarkable speed. Amy Lowell was soon crossing the Atlantic to wrest the Imagist movement in poetry from Pound, to bring it back to America. Gertrude Stein came to be seen and valued as both the literary and the American wing of the Armory Show. Or as Mabel Dodge, who having 'sat' for one of Gertrude Stein's prose poems had good reason to promote her, put it: 'Gertrude Stein was born at the Armory Show.'

But the main reason for this adaptation was the emergence in America of a new generation of writers who responded to and in varying degrees were influenced by the rising modernist spirit. At first it was the poets who were most notable: Robert Frost, William Carlos Williams, Wallace Stevens, Marianne Moore, Edgar Lee Masters, Vachel Lindsay, Carl Sandburg. New experimental theatre groups, like the Provincetown Players, also emerged; Eugene O'Neill and Susan Glaspell emerged out of this. Social criticism intensified, in the work of Randolph Bourne, H. L. Mencken, Walter Lippmann, and Van Wyck Brooks, who saw these ferments as 'America's coming of age'. Fiction was somewhat slower to respond to the new experimental spirit, and the modern movement did not really fully flower in the novel until after the First World War and into the 1920s, which would prove one of the great ages of the American novel. But by 1912 the advance signs were already there, above all in the work of a group of writers who—like many of the poets—came chiefly from the Midwest or West, and who—like many of the contemporary painters—possessed a strong quality of native feeling even while they were responding to the mood of Europeanized formal exploration that would reshape the American fiction of the following generation.

2.

It was in 1912 that Willa Cather—the daughter of a Virginia family that moved out to the pioneer West of Nebraska in 1883, when she was nine—decided to become a full-time novelist. Educated at the University of Nebraska, she became a teacher, later a journalist, and worked for a time in New York City as editor on the muckraking magazine *McClure's*, which had printed the work of many of the naturalists. Cather had published a volume of poems in 1903, a collection of stories, *The Troll Garden*, in 1905, and in 1912 her first novel *Alexandra's Bridge* appeared. But, advised by her friend Sarah Orne Jewett to write from closer knowledge of her own background, she began to produce the pioneer novels for which she is best known, beginning with *O Pioneers!* (1913), a book about Norwegian settlers who come to the Nebraska plains to struggle with the land. The book, she said, was 'written entirely for myself; a story about some Scandinavians and Bohemians who had been neighbors of ours in Nebraska when I was eight or nine years old', and it is most remarkable for its use of lyric rather than narrative conventions, and for its portrait of the strong and self-reliant heroine, Alexandra, who inherits the task of imposing form on the formless land. The books that follow—*The Song of the Lark* (1915), *My Ántonia* (1918) and *One of Ours* (1922)—explore the life of men and, especially, women against the land and landscape of Nebraska, Colorado, and the Midwest with an ever-increasing sense of the theme's complexity. In *The Song of the Lark* the heroine is an opera singer who has to break free of the 'self-satisfied provincial world of utter ignorance,' but in *My Ántonia* the attempt to break free leads the heroine toward a deeper understanding of and engagement with the world she had attempted to escape.

Cather may appear to be a very regional novelist. She was also a highly formal and literary writer who wrote out of a deep sense of culture, and is one of the finest American women writers of the century. Her collection of essays *Not Under Forty* (1936) expresses her debt to a substantial tradition of fiction, particularly to Flaubert, Henry James, Edith Wharton, and Jewett. Here she explores both the socio-moral tradition of the European novel and the task of the writer dealing with regional and pioneer material. Her pioneers are never primitives, and they are not represented naturalistically, as in some of her predecessors. She held that the task of the novel was not documentation but suggestion and selection ('The highest processes of art are all processes of simplification. The novelist must learn to write and then he must unlearn it; just as the modern painter learns to draw and then learns when utterly to disregard his accomplishment'). She also indicated her devotion to the 'timeless' qualities of the novel—just as, in her fiction, it is clear that the protagonists are looking for what is eternal and lasting, what is cultural, as well as natural both in the land and in the great achievements of human habitation. Her next novels—*A Lost Lady* (1923) and *The Professor's House* (1925)—showed a growing delicacy of theme, and an increasingly symbolist way of writing; they were also concerned with the threat brought by modern life to the traditional and developed standards that had come to the American lands through pioneer and Indian life. Her characters constitute a kind of prairie aristocracy, and her strongest heroines are usually those who are essentially and morally committed to life—a commitment she was able to render with high intensity and a strong sense of symbolism. Thus *The Professor's House*, the story of the aptly named Tom Outland, deals with the complex metaphoric relationship of modern housebuilding and the deeper culture and half-lost world of Indian cliff-dwellers in the mesa settlements of the Southwest.

Over the 1920s Cather's interest in the religious history of the continent increased, and she began exploring the Indian history of the Southwest, coming to the view that 'the story of the Catholic Church in that country was the most interesting of all its stories.' This led to the most interesting of all *her* stories, *Death Comes for the Archbishop* (1927), which goes back to the experience of the nineteenth-century French missionaries who came to New Mexico to revive the faith of the Indians through the building of a great cathedral. *Shadow on the Rock* (1931) was similarly about spiritual pioneering in Quebec. There would be a further collection of stories, *Obscure Destinies* (1932), and two late novels, *Lucy Gayheart* (1932) and *Sapphira and the Slave Girl* (1940). Cather's work was an enduring celebration of life, but it was also a celebration of the artist who perceives it. It marks the growing preoccupation with aesthetics and form which was so to change American fiction and draw it away from naturalist documentation—a tendency that happened as much in regional as in national or expatriate fiction. This was one reason why Cather, along with Ellen Glasgow, was able to represent for her successors, particularly though not always women, a serious and formally exact practice of fiction. Those successors include Katherine Anne Porter, who also wrote of the Southwest and Mexico, and whose stories in *Flowering Judas* (1930) and *Pale Horse, Pale Rider* (1939) are both powerful records of regional life, seen usually through a female protagonist (often 'Miranda'), and works of great formal precision; Jean Stafford, author of *The Mountain Lion* (1947), set in Colorado, and the stories of *Children Are Bored on Sunday* (1953); and the remarkable Southern writer Eudora Welty, author of *The Robber Bridegroom* (1942), and the fine stories of four decades gathered up in *The Collected Stories of Eudora Welty* in 1980. Welty celebrates Cather's work in her essay collection *The Eye of the Story* (1979), noting its purity of artistic commitment. As she observes, though in Cather's novels men and women fall in love, and individuals matter, 'love of art—which is love accomplished without help or need of help from another—is what is deepest and realest in her work.'

3.

If Cather was one expression of the great change of American culture in 1912–13, then Sherwood Anderson was undoubtedly another. Indeed he was to become virtually its embodiment, for he dramatized his own revolt—a revolt out of commerce and into art—to coincide almost exactly with it. He too was born in the Midwest, in a small Ohio town one generation on from its first settlement, so that pioneer memories here too were strong. Like Cather, he was to retain a lasting suspicion of the processes of modernization and mechanization that were changing the American spirit. Like her, he was born in the 1870s, which made them both of the same generation as Crane, Norris, Dreiser, and Stein. But he came to writing late, and famously. Having worked as labourer, soldier, farm-hand, advertising man, and paint-salesman, he walked out (as he often explained, especially in his memoir *A Storyteller's Story*, (1924)) on wife, family, and the paint factory he by then owned in Elyria, Ohio, to head for Chicago and enter its newly opening world of bohemianism and artistic experiment. Anderson exaggerated the story; he was already writing before the break, the break was actually a breakdown, the marriage continued for some while longer, and so did his work in advertising in Chicago. But, as he perceived, his story had ultimate symbolic truth. He was enacting the period's own shift from the confining country to the emancipating city, from puritanical repression to bohemian creativity, from material obsessions to organic values.

For art was now protest, and protest became, indeed, the essential theme in and motive of his fiction, which was to be everywhere imbued with his desire to find and release psychic energies that might discover new forms of art and new attitudes towards experience. His work, like Cather's, was to be an expression of fundamental and creative force, a painful personal motion towards the discovery of the spirit through art. This was to be a persisting theme of the Twenties, as, revolting against what seemed to be the limited and traditional conventions of American life, it turned to art as a way of rediscovery. Anderson's central subject was always to be that unfolding awareness of possibility, allied to an attack on the materialist limitations that stifled it in 'puritan' American culture. At first he attempted to do this by developing the methods of the naturalists who went before him. His first novel, *Windy McPherson's Son* (1916), dramatizes, for the first but not the only time, the story of his own move from small town to big city, and his escape from commercial servitude. It expresses his anger at the cultureless and sterile void that modern mechanical America was becoming; this generates the psychological frustration of his hero and the distorted desires that shape him. *Marching Men* (1917) tells the opposite story, of the man who moves up the ladder of material success and social advancement, which proves meaningless. This book looks to a progressive political solution in the collective energies of the marching proletariat. But neither naturalism nor politics quite fitted Anderson's needs and hopes as a writer, and his concern was chiefly with individual and artistic renewal. This meant that, like others of his contemporaries, he soon felt the need to move beyond naturalism and into new forms and experimental techniques. His friend and fellow novelist Waldo Frank saw the point when he reviewed *Marching Men*. Under the headline 'Emerging Greatness,' he sensed that the naturalistic impulse was an irrelevance, and that Anderson was seeking to push its 'elemental movement' towards 'form and direction, the force that causes it being borne into the air'.

It was through his new formal preoccupations that Anderson became one of the most important and influential writers of his generation. Of fundamental significance to him was reading Gertrude Stein's *Three Lives*; he had mocked it at first, then came to feel that it 'contained some of the best work done by an American'. The Armory Show visited Chicago, and Anderson read Stein's *Tender Buttons*; here he found, he said, a bareness of composition and a sense of the priority that form had over content which he realized was vital 'for the artist who happens to work with words as his material'. The result was that 'I became a little conscious where before I had been unconscious,' and the new spirit of aestheticism he saw growing alike in American writing and painting began to penetrate his work. While working on the early novels, he had been publishing a number of different short stories with a common setting—a small Ohio town very like the one from which he had come. Now he began linking them together, rather in the manner of the key short-story cycle of the time, Joyce's *Dubliners* (1914). Joyce had called his stories tales of a paralyzed city; Anderson's are stories of a paralyzed American small town, unable to satisfy the desires of its citizens. Joyce used naturalist methods and materials, but pressed them towards symbolic form and towards what he called 'epiphany', at once a crystallization of the characters' experience and an aesthetic disclosure of symbolic form. Anderson's stories also moved towards symbolist revelation. When *Winesburg, Ohio* appeared in 1919, at the very beginning of the Twenties, it had enormous impact, especially on younger writers, because it dealt with an essential theme—the breaking free of the limitations of American small town life and values—in an essential manner—a psychological and inward awareness of human need—with what was to become an essential technique—the method of prose symbolism.

Thus the twenty-six stories in this small volume are a cycle not simply because the stories of the various separate characters together make up the typical life of one small American town (which we see only indirectly) nor indeed because what they all share in common is a very modern loneliness. The fundamental link in the book is an artistic one: the stories explore two kinds of creativity driving towards experience and disclosure—that of the characters at the centre of each separate story, that of the author himself, seeking a formal deliverance from his writing. Like *Dubliners*, *Winesburg* can be read naturalistically, as an account of individuals trapped by social confinement and paralysis, narrow human experience, and the puritanical burdens and guilts of American small-town life. So, in the story 'Godliness', Jesse Bentley, driven by puritan religious zeal into increasing the potential of his land, becomes a dour, selfish figure, a product of 'the most materialistic age in the history of the world', who discovers that his own nostalgic desire for individualism is curiously meshed with the coarse new commercialism. Jesse becomes malformed by the forces within him and the forces that surround him, grows narrow and distorted in changing history. This expresses Anderson's essential theme in the volume—the ways in which external and internal limitations on freedom produce psychic distortion, a containment of human creativity, a clutching at a single narrowed truth.

In this way, Anderson's characters, in different fashions, become what he liked to call 'grotesques'. His original title for the collection was to have been *The Book of the Grotesque*. He retained it for the first and prefatory story, a small credo for the volume, depicting a writer like himself who recognizes that individuals become grotesque when they seize one truth from the many, make it their own, and 'try to live . . . life by it'. In fact Anderson's use of the term is perplexing, because he meant two things by it. On the one hand, the grotesque was his subject. Like his friend Edgar Lee Masters, whose poem cycle *Spoon River Anthology* (1916) was also an influence on him, Anderson wanted to portray a gallery of damaged small-town figures, caught in moments of distortion and loneliness, the conditions of their distortion, the moments of their self-discovery. But he also wanted to make the grotesque his *method*, a modern technique of writing. As he said, 'in *Winesburg* I made my own form.' The grotesque was his modernist means for depicting an estranged world, to distil its nature and concentrate on the forms by which distortion might disclose underlying creativity. The stories are modern experiments, avoiding traditional plotting and self-explaining methods of causality. Anderson declared that there were 'no plot stories ever lived in any life I knew about'. His aim, he said, was to give the feel of 'a story grasped whole as one would pick up an apple in the orchard', and what he was seeking, was 'a new looseness', to show 'lives flowing past each other, the whole, however, to leave a definite impression'. One essential way to perceive modernism is to see it as an art that insists on its internal frame, on the active presence of the medium used, on the 'foregrounding' of the artistic activity, so that the achievement of the story's form becomes part of the story. This was how Anderson's work now developed, in an endeavour to render the intuitive, the unspoken, and the unconscious as essential realms of experience, manifest both *within* the story and in the *making* of the story.

Anderson's stories were thus both psychological and aesthetic—one reason why they are readily open to Freudian readings. Anderson claimed he knew Freud only at second hand, but he wrote at a time when Freudianism was being widely assimilated in America. The stories of *Winesburg* certainly have an intense psychological content, a serious concern with sexual repression and with the intimate relation of sexuality to creativity. They are also, however, concerned with the possibilities of creative recovery, above all through the creative act of the stories themselves. In 'Hands', Wing Biddlebaum's nervously moving hands may indicate suppressed homosexuality, but they also are an image of the hunger for expression, and call for an artistic elucidation. The restless activity of these hands, 'like unto the beatings of the wings of an imprisoned bird, had given [Wing] his name. Some obscure poet of the town had thought of it.' The 'obscure poet' is linked with the task of discovering 'many strange, beautiful qualities in obscure men'; but such imprisoned motion calls for elaborate tactics of artistic surrogation. Winesburg is full of quiet poets and potential writers, above all the young reporter, George Willard, a classic period portrait of the artist as a young man. He is the one who will make the journey out, to whatever success or failure. And he becomes the partial but not complete confidant of the silent, imprisoned citizens, whose desires can only be expressed obliquely, wordlessly, in corners, in the dark, creating the beginnings of the appropriate images which can then be transfigured, not by Willard but by the author beyond him, into oblique but revealing form. Wing is thus a typical citizen of a town that is alive with half-hidden creativity, one of many 'twisted apples' transmitting incomplete messages of need, messages like the always crumpled notes, the 'paper pills', of Doc Reefy. And, hungering for an artist to speak for them, these characters call by implication for an art of a new kind that can manifest, newly signify, their unfinished utterance.

That notion of unspoken depths beneath the surfaces unifies *Winesburg*, and indicates the nature of its task. Its characters are repositories of the untold, trapped in voyeuristic pain; but direct utterance cannot reveal the truth, for the truths are too many. Ray Pearson, married to a nagging wife in 'The Untold Lie', wants to utter his truth, to warn a friend not to marry, but finally accepts the value of silence: ' "It's just as well. Whatever I told him would have been a lie," he said softly, and then his form also disappeared into the darkness of the fields.' Like his form itself, speech is illusory, and statement will not serve to give the *meaning* of a statement, or make a story. Anderson must find a symbolic form which self-consciously enquires into the capacity of language and art to reach towards revelation. Completeness may not come in life itself, and George Willard cannot amend the lives of others or greatly help himself; but it may come in form, in artistic coherence. Like Ray Pearson, Wing Biddlebaum retreats into darkness at the end of 'Hands'. He is now the town victim, but beyond the damaged life remains the transcendent power of the image that has dominated his story. The tale ends as it began with Wing's hands, which 'flashing in and out of the light, might have been mistaken for the fingers of the devotee going swiftly through decade after decade of his rosary'. The social plot limits; the verbal plot, always there in these storyless stories, reveals. George Willard, the potential artist, the one character who can leave the tight puritanical world of Winesburg to follow his 'dreams', points a way. Yet even he remains within the stories, and his understandings are never more than limited. He links the separate stories by being in them; but it is only the work itself, made coherent through its own poetic existence, that can achieve timeless completion—a modernist and symbolist faith.

Winesburg was Anderson's one outright triumph, though remarkable volumes of short stories—*The Triumph of the Egg* (1922), *Horses and Men* (1923), and *Death in the Woods* (1933)—followed it. His aim to take the modernist methods he had developed in short fiction into the novel, exploring 'the new American life, . . . the whirl and roar of modern machines', proved rather less successful. His novels of the 1920s were an assault on the deadliness of material American life, an attack on modern commercialism and industrialism, which were eroding the organic centres of American life and generating sexual aridity. They also attempted to relate social issues to aesthetic redemptions. *Poor White* (1920) is a powerful story about a poor young man, Hugh McVey, from the Mississippi Valley, who is drawn from this Twainian landscape by a New England woman who encourages in him a puritanic industriousness. Moving to Ohio, he invents machines to supplant painful toil, to find that they also suppress creativity; men and machines alike become grotesque. The fable is explicit: 'It was time for art and beauty to awake in the land,' Anderson writes; 'Instead, the giant, Industry, awoke.' What is missing can, it seems, be replaced only by the aesthetic sense, and by poetic style and technique. His work moved towards experimental rhetoric, and his next two novels—*Many Marriages* (1923), about modern sexual aridity, and *Dark Laughter* (1925), about the paralysis of the white industrial mind, undercut by the dark laughter of the black servants—are comparable with 'poetic' avant-garde works like E. E. Cummings's *The Enormous Room* (1922), or William

Carlos Williams's *The Great American Novel* (1923), with its cry of 'Break the word . . . If I make a word I make myself into a word.' Anderson's books both deal with the period theme of mind severed from body, rational thought from vital flux, of contemporary emptiness and sterility, through methods of impression, monologue, rhythmic poetic flow. 'There is an idea of a new novel form floating in me, something looser, more real, more true,' he said of *Many Marriages*, 'I want to go after that.' In *Dark Laughter*, the debt to Joyce, Stein, and the experimental text is plain. Yet Anderson's lyric discourse seemed never to become more than discourse. For the next generation of experimental writers, he was to be an important precursor, but not an entire success.

By now he had moved to the bohemia of New Orleans, and met and helped William Faulkner, whose early work was influenced by him. Faulkner also saw the problem: 'He worked so hard at this [exactitude] that it finally became just style,' he said; 'an end instead of a means: so that he presently came to believe that, provided he kept the style pure and intact and unchanged and inviolate, what the style contained would have to be first rate.' Faulkner parodied him briefly, as did Hemingway, whom he also helped, at length in *The Torrents of Spring* (1926). The doubts were understandable, yet Anderson's role in opening up the fiction of the Twenties to modernist possibilities was crucial. As Waldo Frank said, he led the way out of the naturalistic devotion to 'the blind cult of the American fact', and brought home a recognition that works of art are aesthetic objects with their own value and values. Faulkner, who praised as well as parodied, was helped to his own sense of regionalism, his own challenge to industrialism, his own sense of dark laughter. Hemingway mocked, yet that portrait of the young artist adrift in a world of general pain that starts in George Willard becomes, in his Nick Adams, a figure pushed to new pressure when violence becomes commonplace and the landscape loses all reassurance. Stein praised him: 'really except Sherwood there was no one in America who could write a clear and passionate sentence,' she said. For Anderson art was the antithesis to puritanism, and puritanism was increasingly the American mode of mind and

being. If many writers of the next generation found the space
between style and life, and between the bohemian present and
the rooted organic past (the next troubled passage for American
prose), they learned much of the way from Anderson's example.

4.

Sherwood Anderson and Sinclair Lewis are often compared, and
it is not hard to see why. Not only did they share similar Midwest populist origins; the main subject of both was American
small-town life, its power in American culture, and the Twenties
revolt against it. That revolt led them both towards the city and
the idea of the transcendence of art. Both developed beyond
naturalism, but in two different directions. Anderson's primary
quest was towards form: Lewis was always drawn towards the
cult of the American fact, though he was to turn naturalism into a
mechanism of modern social satire. Born in 1885 in Sauk Centre,
Minnesota (which would become 'Gopher Prairie' in *Main Street*,
the book that established his reputation), Lewis left his small-
town background for an Eastern education, initially at Oberlin
College, then at Yale. In the East he was socially unhappy, but
here he rejected his fundamentalist religious background to
become an atheistic socialist. He then moved in pre-war progressive circles, working with Upton Sinclair on his Helicon Hall
settlement project, then in a communitarian experiment in California, through which he met Jack London, to whom he began
selling plots. Back in New York in 1910, Lewis moved on the
fringes of radical circles, met Emma Goldman, read Shaw and
Wells, and moved from hack writing to larger literary ambitions.
H. G. Wells clearly influenced his earlier novels. *Our Mr Wrenn*
(1914) is about the preoccupying theme of the times, the little
ordinary man trapped in dull routines but hungering for an
adventurous release, a land of romance beyond the real. However it was when the war ended, and America turned away from
progressivism towards commercialism and 'normalcy', that Lewis
found the subject that made him a major writer.

That subject, as for Anderson, was the small town and the
Midwest he had left behind. That world, for Lewis, was the

heartland of the prevalent mood of ruralism, isolationism, and national nostalgia, of the uneasy politics of Red Scare, and rise of Prohibition. He observed an America that had 'gone through the revolutionary change from rustic colony to world-empire without having in the least altered the bucolic and puritanic simplicity of Uncle Sam', and he turned a critical eye back on his own origins. He wrote of 'Gopher Prairie', the typical American small town, whose Main Street is 'the continuation of Main Streets everywhere', and of 'Zenith', the Midwestern commercial city of Middle America. This was the America where the composing of an advertisement was considered an act of artistic creation, and the Ford car standing outside the Main Street garage stood for 'poetry and tragedy, love and heroism'. Lewis was never fully to know what the higher culture he desired for America was, but he knew that what obstructed it was 'the village virus', the small-town celebration of 'dullness made God'. He did know this small-town material, and seized on it in an excited mixture of love and hate, celebration and satire. His two key books, *Main Street* (1920) and *Babbitt* (1922), were remarkably toned—lingering, even loving satires that none the less gave the intellectual unease and despair of the Twenties one essential mythology. As H. L. Mencken, who shared Lewis's mixture of disappointed radicalism and obsession with the follies of what he called the American 'booboisie', put it, they were the work of 'the one real anatomist of American Kultur'.

Lewis's success came from his full, intimate knowledge of the world he wrote about. He populated it, amassed its detail, reproduced its material décor, its institutions, its operative sociology, so that the reader could take from his books about the imaginary Western state of Winnemac both a loving recreation and an angle of critical distance. His technique is neo-documentary or sociological: Lewis works like a researcher in displaying the institutions and rites, the goods and chattels, the ideologies and sexual mores. Sociology was one of the main exploratory instruments of the Twenties, one of the ways of encompassing the deep sense of change that came in the decade. So *Main Street* fascinatingly compares with Robert and Helen Lynd's study, *Middletown* (1929), which anatomized a middle-American,

middle-way American town. Lewis had the sociologist's capacity
to identify, document, and recognize the weight and function of
contemporary American kitsch, to penetrate an entire cultural
process and iconography. The approach let him show Main
Street not just as a place but a state of mind, Babbitt not just as
an individual but as a fundamental American type, an instance
of 'Babbittry'. At the same time Lewis possessed a novelist's
satirical distance, a tone that mocks and deflates, if not quite
totally. His satire, never quite poised, reveals him as a materialist
with romantic longings, a man with one foot still firmly in the
world he satirizes. His books have the power often possessed by
middle art, that of re-creating without entirely interpreting a
fundamental cultural situation.

So *Main Street* assaults 'the contentment of the quiet dead',
and fundamentalism, strict moralism, self-justifying commercialism. That deadness comes alive in Lewis's hands as a kind of
dreaming innocence from 'good little people, comfortable, indus-
trious, credulous', and above all limited, accepting, even being
excited by, the fundamental change that Lewis observes—the
change from an old pioneer world to a new world of business and
commerce, from American idealism to a bland, patriotic materialism. We see all this through the eyes of Carole Kennicott, a
modern American girl with 'a quality of suspended freedom',
whose marriage to the doctor in Gopher Prairie ties her to the
town. She rebels, in *bovaryste* fashion, against 'dullness made
God', and hopes either to restore this 'smug in-between town,
which had changed "Money Musk" for phonographs grinding
out ragtime' to simplicity, or to bring it into touch with modern
artistic culture. Carole's romanticism is itself unsophisticated,
and her sentimentalism ('I just love common workmen') is
based on the dreaming illusions shared in some fashion by
nearly all Lewis's characters. He clearly half admires Carole,
maybe more than the modern reader might; but he does see her
faults, recognizes her patronizing ways, and displays her inevitable defeat, since her desires are in part romantically absurd.
She does escape briefly, to the big city of Washington; but he
has her come back to Gopher Prairie and lapse into 'the humdrum
inevitable tragedy of the struggle against inertia'. By now,

though, Gopher Prairie has changed; perhaps the essential story of *Main Street* lies in the town's transformation from the world of the buggy to the world of the Ford and the Buick, from market village to modern commerce. The book ends as Gopher Prairie attempts to meet the Twenties by trying to become a centre for industry and state institutions, employing a booster, Mr Blausser, a man of Punch, Pep, and Go, a sharp satirical personification of a self-vaunting new America (the America of Bruce Barton, who wrote a life of Jesus as the most successful businessman of all time) which hides empty materialism under proud and optimistic rhetoric.

That new America, the America whose business is business, led Lewis forward to his next book, *Babbitt*. Surely his best novel, *Babbitt* is set firmly in the world of the early Twenties, in the bustling commercial, stoutly Republican, Midwestern city of Zenith, where beneath the modern skyline of office buildings— 'austere towers of steel and cement and limestone, sturdy as cliffs and delicate as silver rods'—the spirit of small-time business and suburbanism rules supreme. Zenith is the small town grown big, and in it all-American mores still flourish, in perfect confidence that they represent the very best the booming nation stands for. The loving touch with which Lewis constructs his very modern cityscape suggests something of the tone of the novel; again he sees both dullness and a kind of splendour in this changing mid-American world. But what we need is the ideal American innocent best able to enjoy it, and Lewis wonderfully creates him in George Follansbee Babbitt, the 46-year-old realtor and Prominent Citizen who is Lewis's Mr Pooter, as well as an earlier version of John Updike's 'Rabbit' Angstrom, the small man who floats confidently in the American mainstream. Babbitt is a boyish *naïf*, obsessed by his goods and possessions, setting sail in his brave and dangerous automobile towards the pirate world of his office. Henpecked, intimidated, and vaguely unsatisfied by his family life, he none the less sees himself as the all-American male, 'a God-fearing, hustling, two-fisted Regular Guy, who belongs to some church with pep and piety in it, who belongs to the Boosters or the Rotarians or the Kiwanis'. He is the joiner, the man who attaches himself to every church, business club, lodge, and community institution that will give him confidence, success, amusement, identity, and prestige ('Nothing gave Babbitt more purification and publicity than his labors for the Sunday School'). Lewis creates him with the greatest satirical pleasure, for he provides his author with perfect access to all the typical commercial activities, business groupings, mercantile fantasies, and male dreams that perfectly suit Lewis's mixture of sociology and social irony.

Babbitt thus becomes the ideal example of the Middle American male of the Twenties, and indeed since. He loves the touch, feel, and substance of material American reality. Mechanical devices are 'symbols of truth and beauty', and give him 'a delightful feeling of being technical and initiated'. He sees himself as both the beneficiary and the missionary of the commercialism and prosperity that is bringing new bustle and growth to the nation; as long as these things remain real for him his loyalty and faith persist, despite the fact that he feels he has never really done anything he wants to. At the same time Lewis, again in the manner of Wells, gives him the little man's boyish innocence that finally pushes him toward the moment of rebellion. Lewis called the book a GAN about a TBM—that is, a Great American Novel about a Tired Business Man—and Babbitt finally does grow tired of worshipping at the shrine of the new 'religion of business' then sweeping America. In his mild and romantic way, he comes to question the class-conscious, anti-intellectual, often racist opinions he learns from the newspapers, and the endless pressure towards success. He begins to rage against 'mechanical business', 'mechanical religion', and even 'mechanical golf'. His fantasy of escape, like Carole Kennicott's, finally gets nowhere. He dreams of finding his way back into a more 'natural' American past, but his frontier fantasies are finally defeated by attacking mosquitoes. Babbitt returns to the fold, determined never again to stray away from the Clan of Good Fellows, though he does hand a warning on to his son not to yield to the pressures of conformity. He ends the book as that familiar Twenties figure, the small anti-hero, beaten in the sex war and the mechanical war, eternally caught between conformity and restless longing.

Like all Lewis's work, *Babbitt* has its elements of sentimentality, but it does strike a remarkable balance between naturalism and satire, and still stands up as a classic presentation of Middle American values. Alas, Lewis was never able again to repeat the triumph of *Main Street* and *Babbitt*. In *Arrowsmith* (1925) he endeavoured to create a positive and reforming American hero, in the figure of a crusading doctor who is surrounded by corruption and misunderstanding. *Elmer Gantry* (1927) more successfully portrays a fundamentalist and revivalist religious charlatan of a kind popular in the Middle American culture in the Twenties and since, and has considerable satirical and moral power. With *Dodsworth* (1929) he returned again to 'Zenith', this time trying, much more naturalistically, to depict a character who displays some of the strengths and virtues of Midwestern simplicity. But his romantic fight with materialism and American provincialism had lost something of its bite, and with the loss of satirical energy his novels began to appear more commonplace. By 1930, when he won the Nobel Prize for Literature, the embodiment of the new spirit of American fiction and of American critical self-awareness, his powers were already in decline, and a whole new generation of American novelists had emerged to challenge him.

There are some writers whose gift it is to record and document the spirit of their times, and others who have the power to create a new and radical form of writing. Lewis made his impact not with the radical methods of his novels, nor with the stylish immediacy of his characters, as Fitzgerald would. His novels are modern because of their exact social attention, their awareness of the shaping processes of American experience, above all the shift from older frontier values to modern commercial prosperity in the American heartland; they catch at a significant moment the social, emotional, and political processes that were bringing a different, modern spirit into American life. His best tone was always a mixture of observation and distrust. He was the satirical realist who was none the less drawn towards popular romanticism, the hard critic of American mores who still believed in some ideal and innocent promise. But for the younger writers who began to appear as his success came, it was Sherwood Anderson and not Sinclair Lewis who seemed to offer the better guide to fiction's future. Anderson himself noted the difference between the two of them, observing that Lewis had 'an amazing attention to the details of lives', but no instinct for the inward forces that were driving them, or the forms needed to express these. This is true, and for most of the newer writers it was not Lewis's solid, detailed, firmly amassed social world but Anderson's attempts to adventure into form and consciousness that seemed the way to the novel of American modernity.

4

Art-style and Life-style: The 1920s

The uncertainties of 1919 were over—there seemed little doubt about what was going to happen—America was going on the greatest, gaudiest spree in history and there was going to be plenty to tell about it. The whole golden boom was in the air—its splendid generosities, its outrageous corruptions and the tortuous death struggle of the old America in Prohibition. All the stories that came into my head had a touch of disaster in them.

F. Scott Fitzgerald, 'Early Success' (1937)

Whole departments of [the puritan's] psychic life must be repressed. Categories of desire must be inhibited. Reaches of consciousness must be lopped off. Old, half-forgotten intuitions must be called out from the buried depths of his mind, and made the governors of his life.

Waldo Frank, *Our America* (1919)

1.

'As I figure it:', Henry Adams noted in an apocalyptic equation as the twentieth century turned, '—1830 : 1860 :: 1890 : x, and x always comes out, not 1920, but infinity.' Adams was constructing one of his laws of proliferating modern energy, but he might equally well have been offering a prophecy of the sense of acceleration, change, and uncertainty that affected most Americans in the 1920s, the decade when, according to the sociologists Robert and Helen Lynd, in *Middletown* (1929), Americans were 'probably living in one of the eras of the greatest rapidity of change in the history of modern institutions'. One reason for this sense of change and dislocation was undoubtedly American involvement in the First World War, the first major foreign conflict in which the United States had participated. When President Woodrow Wilson declared war on Germany in 1917 and sent American troops to Europe, to 'make the world safe for democracy', this was an unprecedented act of international involvement which both cosmopolitanized the nation and destroyed much of its progressive confidence. For Europeans the consequences of the First World War were clear. The shattering of the nineteenth-century European order, six million dead, political and economic chaos spreading across the centre of the continent, the emergence in Russia of the first twentieth-century revolutionary state, all this left behind a sense of general despair and a growing conviction about the decline of an entire era of civilization. In the United States, its soil untouched and its economy stimulated by wartime production, the effects were different. The United States emerged as an economic beneficiary, a creditor rather than a debtor nation, a land of technological leadership, a major world power. It also emerged anxious about international affairs, fearful of foreign entanglements, disturbed by the Versailles settlement and potential American involvement in the League of Nations. When Wilson, enfeebled by his reforming efforts in post-war Europe, died, and President Harding took office in 1920, it seemed that America was determined to turn back on itself, concentrating on economic growth, technological development, and commercial expansion—the logical development of the basic American virtues of individualism, self-advancement, and the pursuit of abundance for all. As President Calvin Coolidge (Harding's successor in 1924) was to say, the business of America was, surely, business.

But as America came out of a brief post-war depression and the Twenties economy boomed, producing consumer goods and new household technologies—radios, telephones, refrigerators, family cars (along with the great new highways to go with them)—and new mass entertainments—the movies, the sports events, the music of jazz—it was obvious that cultural and economic change was everywhere. If the Twenties was an era of Red Scare and Prohibition, of declining progressivism and of conservative politics, an era when many longed for the old simplicities and for 'normalcy', it was also an era of radical changes in mores and life-styles. The new wealth did what progressivism could not: it shifted the USA from a production- to a consumption-centred economy, redistributed income, and split the past from the present, the country from the city, giving American culture a gloss, a bustle, a metropolitan vigour and a high-rise technological face that spread its messages and images right across the nation. With changing patterns of wealth and with new generational values came a new kind of Americanness: the age of Prohibition and puritanism, of Babbitts and H. L. Mencken's 'booboisie', was also the age of psychoanalysis, black jazz, flappers, filmstars, petting, speakeasies, and metropolitanism. Americans could look about with a new confidence at their historical position, while at the same time they came to realize that they had for the first time taken the leading role in a larger world history where modernization, influenced by American styles and practices, was changing values and patterns of culture everywhere.

Thus the sense of cultural disorientation and modern disorder that affected so many Europeans had its impact on American minds too. For many young Americans, the end of the First World War marked the beginning of a new era—the Twenties—quite as clearly as a decade later the Great Crash of 1929 would mark its end. This is particularly evident in the novel of the Twenties; it has been pointed out that it was the experience of the war that made the writers of the Twenties into a distinctive generation. That was partly because the European battlefields became, for the moment, very literary battlefields, and a fair number of the new generation of writers and would-be writers, seeking the opportunity for experience beyond their generally Midwestern origins, found attendance at the war's 'reality' a literary necessity. So, as a new generation began to dominate American fiction in the early 1920s, it was shaped by the work of several writers who had experienced military service or became pacifist observers of the European turmoil. John Dos Passos, Ernest Hemingway, E. E. Cummings (poet as well as novelist, author of *The Enormous Room*, 1922), and Edmund Wilson (critic and novelist, author of *I Thought of Daisy*, 1929), were ambulance drivers, and Hemingway was famously wounded on the Italian front, turning his wound into the key metaphor of life in the damaged, sterilizing, lost-generation post-war age. Others almost went: F. Scott Fitzgerald had just completed his officer training and was about to embark for France when the

Armistice was signed, so that his European service finally took different form—he followed the expatriate drift to Paris that also Europeanized many American writers during the 1920s. William Faulkner trained with the Royal Canadian Air Force, encouraged the notion that he had actually served in France (he had not), and wrote, like many of his contemporaries, tales in which the myth of the returning veteran, burned with an experience and historical knowledge denied to his innocent contemporaries at home, was dominant.

For all these writers, war was Europe, and Europe was, famously, 'experience'. Most of them began to write on its battlefields or in its shadow, and create the story of a generation severed from the last one by the very knowledge of war. Amory Blaine, in Fitzgerald's first novel *This Side of Paradise* (1920), considers he belongs to a new generation dedicated more than the last to the fear of poverty and the worship of success; grown up to find all gods dead, all wars fought, all faiths in man shaken—including the faiths of pre-war progressivism. John Dos Passos's first novel, *One Man's Initiation—1917* (1920), tells the story of the innocent hero growing to maturity amid the chaos and violence of collapsing European culture. Indeed 'culture', as a body of established artistic values, codes, and mores, was one of the casualties of the European collapse; if 'experience' came from Europe, it no longer meant the established arts or immemorial manners, but horror, extremity, and historical exposure. Old sentimental attitudes, old codes of moral value, old attitudes to honour and patriotism had collapsed during the war, demanding a new kind of writing, less romantic and sentimental, more specific and closer to the cruelties of experience. Language itself was scarred and needed to be reconstructed, while those who had been to the war felt themselves cut off from those who had remained at home: in the story 'A Soldier's Home,' Hemingway's Krebs comes back from the war to the Midwest to find older values and modes of speech no longer of use to him. There was an apocalyptic new history, in which the individual needed a new initiation—new perceptions and modes of speech, new kinds of existential self-awareness—to survive. Or, as Thomas Wolfe put it in the title of one of his novels, *You Can't Go Home Again*.

So one key form of the Twenties was the war novel: Dos Passos's two works of growing disillusion, *One Man's Initiation* and *Three Soldiers* (1921), stories of the self trying to understand its new human situation, which he would follow a decade later by the vast historical and social assessment of *U.S.A.*, where the great turning point for the nation is, exactly, the First World War; E. E. Cummings's experimental *The Enormous Room* (1922), the story of his confinement in a French prison camp after he declared, as Dos Passos had, his pacifist views; realistic battlefield novels like Thomas Boyd's *Through the Wheat* (1925); novels about the 'separate peace' favoured by the disenchanted modern hero deprived of past sentimental feeling, above all Hemingway's classic *A Farewell to Arms* (1929). These were mostly books in which the fact of war enforced a new style, a new generational attitude, a new set of relations between man, nature, machine, culture, and history. From the war novel was born the *post-war* novel, the novel that, permeated by awareness of war and the historical crisis it had brought, made it the commanding metaphor, the image for a world that had been severed from its past and radically modernized. Thus Fitzgerald explained the genesis of *This Side of Paradise* by saying 'I was certain that all the young people were going to be killed in the war, and I wanted to put on paper a record of the strange life they had lived in their time,' and he was sure that the book had become the great post-war success it was 'simply for telling people that I felt as they did, that something had to be done with all the nervous energy stored up and unexpended in the war'. Hemingway's *The Sun Also Rises* (1926) is—just like D. H. Lawrence's *Lady Chatterley's Lover* (1928)—a book about a post-war generation, lost and castrated not just by the physical wound that debilitates the hero but by the sense of crisis that affects the behaviour and sexuality of the expatriates who surround him in post-war Paris and Spain. Images of waste, decline, and sterility, of downward historical curve, dominate in Twenties writing not only in Europe but in America, and not only in the famous dismay of Ezra Pound's poem *Hugh Selwyn Mauberley* (1920) or T. S. Eliot's *The Waste Land* (1922), but in the 'Valley of Ashes' sequence of Fitzgerald's *The Great Gatsby* (1925), the circling emptiness and futility that runs through the American community in Paris in *The Sun Also Rises*, the image of the wasted, wounded soldier that intrudes into the bohemian world of Faulkner's *Soldier's Pay* (1926). But where in Europe the modernist writers of the Twenties struggled to understand the war in the light of the collapse of an entire era of culture, American writers largely strove to understand it as a symbolic form of the modernizing exposure that had become a universal feature of the age of speed, mass technology, the city, and the machine.

2.

Perhaps the dominant tone of American fiction in the 1920s was its mood of flamboyant decadence, an air of transitional sensibility expressed as a desperate hunger for new style. Hemingway decorated *The Sun Also Rises* with the famous tag 'You are all a lost generation', saying he got it from Gertrude Stein (she in turn ascribed it to a petrol attendant in Spain). The important word here is perhaps less 'lost' than 'generation', for one of the great marks of the Twenties was its strong generational sense. In an age that seemed to have withdrawn from politics and ideology, the form in which the Twenties consumed themselves was through 'style', drawing on a general youthful excitement with the fast-changing experiment of modern life. This was the era when bright, brittle, and half-cynical works like Anita Loos's *Gentlemen Prefer Blondes* (1925) were all the rage, and *New Yorker* wit and smartness or Mencken-like mockery prevailed. Decadent texts abounded; James Branch Cabell (*Jurgen*, 1919) and Carl Van Vechten (*Nigger Heaven*, 1925; *Parties*, 1930) were just two of the writers who captured the spirit of the times as one of anxious hunger for new style. Floyd Dell in *Moon-Calf* (1920) told the story of Midwestern youthful revolt, and carried it forward into one of its key locations in *Love in Greenwich Village* (1926). Fitzgerald's Amory Blaine is a classic decadent hero, the golden boy of the time 'hallowed by the haze of his own youth', and the expatriated characters of *The Sun Also Rises* are all more period stylists, Bright Young Things of an age marked by changed youthful manners and mores. In most decadent writing, the rules of gender transform and sexual relations grow ambiguous; so they do in Hemingway, with his boy–girl heroines, in Fitzgerald, the supposed fictional inventor of the 'flapper', and in Faulkner, where sterile sexual relations and incest are characteristics of a dislocated historical condition, brought about not only by the First World War but by the collapse of social and dynastic order in the Old South. In these novels history is persistently consumed as fashion, the music, the hair-dos, the note of the season have to be captured, for time races and it is important to grasp small moments of arrest. As Lionel Trilling once said, *The Great Gatsby* is one of the great novels of the Twenties precisely because of its sense of the power and pleasure with which we consume the evanescent instant of fashion: 'it grasps a moment in history as a great moral fact.'

This strong sense of decadence came not just from the impact of the First World War but from the nature and pace of post-war American development. The compromises of Woodrow Wilson's Versailles Treaty, rejection by the US Senate of the proposed League of Nations, the Red Scare, Prohibition, the return to what President Harding called 'normalcy', a state of commercial energy coupled with political inertia—all this helped intensify that sense of ideological vacuum, purposelessness, and cultural sterility coupled with the endless vigorous excitement of social and technological change which characterized the American Twenties. In *U.S.A.*, the vast three-volume novel in which Dos Passos sought to capture the American history of the first quarter of the century, he made 1919 the fulcrum—the year of anti-Bolshevik feeling and defeat for progressive expectations that opened the way to cynicism, flaunted capitalism, pure materialism, isolationism, and intolerance. The paradox was that the Twenties was a conservative decade which none the less set in train some of the most decisive changes of modern American history, changes in personal psychology, moral expectation, national dream and illusion. As credit ran free and personal spending boomed, as the middle class expanded and new highways and mass production homogenized the nation, modernity moved at an ever-accelerating pace. While some looked nostalgically back to the rural past, others turned to the excitements of the high-rise city, and this mixture of American nostalgia and hunger for change and innovation seemed exemplified in all the crises and dramas of the period—the Scopes 'Monkey' trial, the Sacco and Vanzetti case, Lindbergh's solo flight across the Atlantic, the revival of the Ku Klux Klan.

But if the American fiction of the Twenties was touched by a sense of crisis and conflict, it was by no means a fiction of despair. Indeed it was lit with the new excitements of American life: the vogue for jazz, the wonder of the automobile, the rise of the movie, the vigour of the city, which Dos Passos captured in *Manhattan Transfer* (1925), or the drama of its mean streets, caught by Dashiell Hammett in *The Maltese Falcon* (1930). Black culture found a sudden power of expression in the work of the Harlem Renaissance, of which a fine example is Jean Toomer's prose and poetry novel *Cane* (1923). It was a fiction deeply touched with a note of aesthetic dissent from the materialism and puritanism of contemporary American life, one reason why many of the writers of the decade sooner or later found their way either to the bohemia of Greenwich Village, or better still to Paris, the centre of post-war modernism, where it was possible to find bohemia and the bottle at the cheapest rates of exchange. Some of them were motivated by progressivist disappointment and irritation with the social order of the times. In 1922 Harold Stearns collected an anthology of protest essays, *Civilization in the United States*, which expressed the dismay of many, and concluded that there was so little civilization left in the United States that the best thing was to get out and go to Paris. Others went for the small presses, the little magazines, the atelier instruction in the arts of the Modern, where one could learn to write in the spirit of European modernism under the tutelage of Gertrude Stein and Ezra Pound, James Joyce and Ford Madox Ford. For this, above all, was a revolt against puritanism and into art, the revolt Sherwood Anderson had promoted. Yet what these writers often wrote of was the small town world they had left behind, and, drawing on the modernist lore of cultural collapse, on the techniques of stream-of-consciousness and modern irrealism, they groped towards a new mythology that expressed both the depressions and discontinuities, and the vivid and modernizing excitements, of a contemporary America that had begun to fascinate Europeans and penetrate the spirit of new European culture.

In Paris, Gertrude Stein said, it was possible for writers to find themselves 'all alone with English and myself', and equally to discover that the modernist arts were art-forms entirely in tune with the new 'space–time continuum' of American life. Many of the post-naturalist or neo-symbolist methods developed in European modernist fiction—the rapid cutting, the spatial forms, the mechanization of human figures, the sense of psychic damage, the troubled, vivid, and half-abstract urban cityscapes—became appropriate means for depicting contemporary American experience, ideal aesthetic tactics for expressing the conflict of generations, the tempo of change, the dislocations of consciousness, the fragility of sensibility, the self-consciousness of modernity. The American 1920s saw an outburst of experimental fiction which in one way linked the new American novel with the great adventures of modernism which dominated the European Twenties—yet in another provided the ideal means for responding to all that was speeded and accelerated about contemporary American existence. Dos Passos attempted to portray Manhattan as the great modernist city through the expressionist techniques of *Manhattan Transfer*; likewise, in works like *The Sound and the Fury* (1929), William Faulkner applied new, Joycean experiments with consciousness to the disordered regional spirits of the American South. Urban writers like Carl Van Vechten, Floyd Dell and Joseph Hergesheimer took up modernist techniques. So did the black novelists and story-writers of the Harlem Renaissance, like Jean Toomer. A key ambition, teased by William Carlos Williams in his *The Great American Novel* (1923), was to use methods of modernist discontinuity to create the great American epic. That was the ambition of Stein's *The Making of Americans* (1925), and two other books published the same year, Theodore Dreiser's *An American Tragedy*, a naturalist exposure of the American dream, and Fitzgerald's *The Great Gatsby*, a symbolist tragedy on the same topic. The aim of making the great American epic guides Thomas Wolfe's grandiose autobiographical fictions, the much more complex aesthetic and social ambitions of Faulkner's Yoknapatawpha saga, and Dos Passos's attempt to use epical fragmentation for expressing the damaged coherence of twentieth century America in his vast sequence *U.S.A.*.

These inclusive reportorial and aesthetic ambitions are one thing that distinguishes much of the Twenties American experiment from their European equivalents. The European modernist works of the Twenties are in almost every case works of despair or extreme disorder, displaying a deep sense of psychic, cultural, and historical extremity, especially after the publication of Oswald Spengler's *The Decline of the West* in English in 1922. American fiction reflects a considerable unease, but not far away is an optimistic excitement and a national confidence. Even so this was the decade when a younger generation, of remarkable quality, was ready to assimilate into their fiction the great formal experiments that had been upturning the European fiction of the last two decades, and it marks the departure from the age of naturalism to one of complex formal innovation and aesthetic curiosity, paralleling what had happened in American poetry a decade earlier. They undertook this task in their own way, and with a strong American conviction. Their works contain many of the Spenglerian dreads and apocalyptic anxieties of similar works in Europe; they also return to American myths, and express the conflicts of Twenties American culture. Stimulated to aesthetic experiment by the predominantly apolitical temper of the times, they also attempt to grasp at the spirit of American culture as hope and possibility, and display the typical American desire for a new coherence and wholeness. Such was their achievement that during the Twenties the American novel moved from being at the beginning of the decade a provincial relation of the European novel to taking, by the end of it, a major role in the modern experiment. As Malcolm Cowley observed, in a book of this title, it was a great 'second flowering', comparable in force to the great American naissance of the 1840s and 1850s, when Poe, Hawthorne, Melville, Emerson, Thoreau, and Whitman gave the United States its first great literature (and most of these writers were revived during the Twenties, to become the great antecedents). Thus the wave of youthful new novelists who appeared in America after 1918 gave American fiction what it had long lacked, a radical excitement, an originating power, an international reputation. In the Twenties, 'something subtle seemed to pass to America, the style of man,' noted Fitzgerald. So, to a considerable degree, did the style of the novel.

3.

No writer set out more determinedly to capture in fiction the tone, the hope, the possibility, and the touch of despair of the Twenties than Francis Scott Key Fitzgerald. For a long time he appeared to his critics a mere popularizer and chronicler, so obviously immersed in the themes, fashions, and styles of his times that he never achieved the literary power to consider and criticize. Certainly the writer who made a fortune for performing the Twenties in public, who was so readily allured by the wonder of the rich and the dream of success, was more than most novelists an author who lived and worked through immersion in his own public world. For this he finally paid a high cost, to his famous marriage to Zelda Sayre, to his psychic life, to his writing and his reputation. It often seemed that the glittering style of his books, encrusted with beautiful women and wealthy heroes, was no more than a version of the glittering popular name he sought for himself, that his preoccupation with the all-inclusive hero, the man who embodies all the hopes and dreams of those around him, was an expression of the self he sought to be. And Fitzgerald undoubtedly threw himself exotically into the pleasures and the pitfalls of his own gaudy time; he was, more than most, an essentially social novelist. It was he who made sure that the Twenties was known as 'the Jazz Age', that the new goods and chattels, the new expressions and sexual styles, made their way into fiction. His famous essay 'The Crack-Up' sums up this singular identification. The historical development of America in the 1920s, moving from glittering excitement to danger, was his own psychic curve; the Great Crash was the exact analogue of his own psychic crack up; the political reassessment of the Thirties was the match for his own endeavour to put his spiritual house in order. Such identifications were so potent exactly because Fitzgerald always chose to live them as such, making his literary experimentation part of the period's social and sexual experimentation, making the style of his life an essential component of the style of his art. This made his work itself appear innocent, his writing seem short of formal skill. It has taken time for us to see that there was much more, and that the innocent performer of the Twenties became, in his mature work, one of the finest of modern American novelists.

Fitzgerald was born in Saint Paul, Minnesota, in September, 1896, and saw himself as a child of the new century. A Midwesterner of Maryland stock, he went back East as soon as he could in quest of the life of the East Coast patriciate from which he felt himself to be descended. It takes a true provincial to see the charm and glow of status and wealth, and Fitzgerald, the aspiring young man from Summit Avenue, St Paul, was always drawn by the golden glow in the East. When he went to Princeton in 1913 he entered a world that was all promise, wealth, and dream, that parvenu dream would be the most fabulous of the stories he had to tell. The other key story was the story of a generation. When, in 1917, he was working on the novel he then called *The Romantic Egoist* and would be published as *This Side of Paradise*, he wrote grandly to his friend Edmund Wilson, 'I really believe that no one else could have written so searchingly the story of the youth of our generation . . .'. *This Side of Paradise* came out in 1920, exactly as the Twenties started, and became an immediate bestseller, rivalling in the lists a work by another Minnesotan, Sinclair Lewis's *Main Street*. But where Lewis satirized the American vanities of the Twenties, Fitzgerald offered an entirely different, quite unsatirical view of the world of post-war modernity. Heavily influenced by Compton Mackenzie's now little-read *Sinister Street*, it followed the period vogue for young man's novels; its young hero, Amory Blaine, is the exemplary post-war dandy, socially and sexually ambitious, who makes his own life the subject of a social and aesthetic experiment, conducted through the pursuit of religion, love, and money. Amory is indeed a 'romantic egoist', drawn on the one hand by a narcissistic investment in his own youth and beauty, and on the other by all the dreamy and fragile promises society and immersion in experience can offer him. Above all there is

Princeton's 'glittering caste-system' and the beautiful and wealthy woman who embodies all he desires but stands just beyond his reach. Style becomes a desperate expenditure of the self, and beauty and money turn into transposed versions of each other. Far more energetic than good, the book none the less lays down, if in unresolved form, many of the themes that would subsequently dominate his fiction: the temptation, danger, and damnation of self-love, an awareness of the alluring fragility of all experience, and a compulsive neo-religious idealism that, invested back into American society, somehow attempts to make it shine with a transcendental glory—the themes he would eventually bring into perfect focus in *The Great Gatsby*.

With characteristic honesty Fitzgerald was later to identify the book as 'one of the funniest books since *Dorian Gray* in its utter speciousness', but it was a work that signalled to a generation its presence as a generation, and its remarkable unexpected success threw Fitzgerald into a role he coveted—the style-setter for the times, the filter and promoter of its public moods and sexual fashions. It also enabled him to marry his remote woman, Zelda Sayre, and together the two of them went on to perform the Twenties as an exotic dance of romance and decadent cynicism, as they chased the excitements, spent the wealth, drank the champagne, travelled, enjoyed the playboy delights, and equally consumed the underlying moral and economic fragility. Zelda (eventually a novelist herself) was the new woman, the flapper displaying the boyish toughness, sexual ambiguity, and moral vagueness of a time of changing sexual roles. Scott was equally the new man, capturing style in all its topicality and writing for 'my own personal public—that is, the countless flappers and college kids who think I am a sort of oracle'. Their expensive transatlantic life forced Fitzgerald to write against the clock, in several senses, and he found problems in distancing himself from his own stories or finding time to develop his talent. The titles of his next books of stories—*Flappers and Philosophers* (1920), *Tales from the Jazz Age* (1922)—show his obsession with capturing the period themes. At the same time he was capable of giving his stories a serious treatment and, as he noted, the stories all 'had a touch of disaster in them; the lovely young creatures in my novels went to ruin, the diamond mountains of my short stories blew up, my millionaires were as beautiful and damned as Thomas Hardy's peasants.' That touch of disaster is very clear in his next novel, *The Beautiful and Damned* (1922), a story about a degenerating hero and a degenerating marriage, which mixes social lyricism with a tale of decadent decline. Gloria and Anthony Patch want to make their marriage into a 'live, lovely, glamorous performance', based on the American premiss that 'something is going to happen'. But false dreams, moral carelessness, and the pressure of time soon take their toll: 'I don't want to live without my pretty face,' cries Gloria. Hastily written and heavily autobiographical, the book—though perfectly successful—lacks a confident tone, and there was little about it to suggest that his next work would be one of the greatest American novels, the book T. S. Eliot would identify as 'the first step the American novel has taken since Henry James.'

But by now Fitzgerald was growing increasingly conscious of having squandered his talents, and as he began his next book he determined to show himself the conscious artist he believed he could be. That book consequently displays a new seriousness, sometimes explained by the critics as showing for the first time he could stand back and survey his own experience. Yet if anything Fitzgerald's sense of his immersion in his times had increased; just like his character Dick Diver in *Tender Is the Night* (1934), who feels compelled to risk his own sanity and intelligence in order to understand and redeem the crisis consciousness of others, he saw it as the writer's task to be a 'performing self', as it has been called, an active agent taking risks with his life and entering all the places where the times are most fully enacted. Both his personal and fictional styles were modes of involvement; but now, in his better work, he began increasingly to understand the compelling forces behind this psychic overextension. With *The Great Gatsby* (1925), one of the most notable of American twentieth-century novels, this mixture of involvement and understanding reaches an extraordinary balance. The book is a classic of formal control (Fitzgerald had learned it in part from Conrad); it is also a book that seeks exactly to enter its own time and place while reaching beyond it—just as its central character, Jay Gatsby, aims to do. It is the story of a gross, materialistic, careless society of coarse wealth spread on top of a sterile world; on to it is cast an extraordinary illusion, that of the ex-Jay Gatz, the self-created Gatsby. A man whose poor past and corrupt economic supports are hidden in his own glow, Gatsby likewise decorates his entire world through his love for Daisy Buchanan. Society is decadent in one way, Gatsby in another: he is a dandy of desire, a desire that has been redirected from its human or material object into a fantasy, a dream of retaining a past moment in an endless instant of contemplation. His aim, in effect, is to transfigure money into love—a symbolist dream, an assault on reality, the system, the clock of time itself. The clock still ticks, and Fitzgerald hears it; Gatsby is a corrupt dreamer, Daisy a corrupt object of love, married to a violent, damaging husband, surrounded by 'carelessness' and social indifference, her voice full of money. But he grants the grandeur of the invented self and the gaudy worth of its passions: 'The most grotesque and fantastic conceits haunted [Gatsby] in his bed at night. A universe of ineffable gaudiness spun itself out in his brain while the clock ticked on the wash-stand and the moon soaked with wet light his tangled clothes upon the floor.' Gatsby embodies the symbolic aim of the book itself, a figure floating on the American dream while beneath him a confusing record of economic and social facts unravels.

Gatsby is a coarse Platonist, devoted to the pursuit of a 'vast, vulgar and meretricious beauty', but his dream sustains its force, partly because the book allows him to invest naturalist fact with his personal intention, and recognizes symbolist desires, and partly because it is mediated through a narrator, Nick Carraway, who consciously stills the voice of judgement. Carraway's peculiar tolerance comes because he is himself involved in a fantastic life in which he is something of a parvenu, but also because he is the instrument of Fitzgerald's oblique method of interpreting the tale. *Gatsby* is a novel of modern dream-life; and its means call for something more than naturalism or direct moral assessment. It is itself a semi-symbolist text, set in the surreal world of the modern city, New York and its environs, its startling detail thrown up in instants and images—in the shifting fashions in clothes and music, the décor of hotel rooms, the movements of traffic, the ash heaps and the hearses that catch Carraway's eye on his mobile, hyperactive way through the populous landscape. As narrator, Carraway becomes a voice of what Fitzgerald called 'selective delicacy', filtering impression and sensation in an order appropriate to his growing understanding of Gatsby's nature, distributing about him a landscape of generative images, so that Gatsby, who might be thought of as a corrupt product of this world, is gradually distinguished from it, set against it, finally made a victim of its carelessness. The novel's theme is the suffusion of the material with the ideal, of raw stuff becoming enchanted object. This is so not just because of Gatsby's peculiar powers and qualities, but because it is the basis of the mode of writing itself, as it invests Gatsby's actions, parties, and clothes with a distinctive, symbolic glow.

Two alternative worlds, one of careless wealth and the other of ashen poverty, are set in contrast in the novel—watched over by the absent god, the sightless eyes of Dr Eckleberg. But the real contrast is between the contingency of both these worlds and Gatsby's search for a transfiguring vision, for a world beyond the clock of historical time, for a life meaningless unless invested with meaning. Fitzgerald's aim is surreal, the making bright of certain evanescent things so that they have the quality of dream. But at the novel's end that dream is withdrawn, and another surreality, the nightmare of an unmitigated mass of material objects, takes its place. Gatsby's death is the product of carelessness and chance. Nick imagines it:

I have an idea that Gatsby didn't himself believe that it [the phone call from Daisy] would come, and perhaps he no longer cared. If that was true he must have felt that he had lost the old warm world, paid a high price for living so long with a single dream. He must have looked up at an unfamiliar sky through frightening leaves and shivered as he found what a grotesque thing a rose is and how raw the sunlight was upon scarcely created grass. A new world, material without being real, where poor ghosts, breathing dreams like air, drifted fortuitously about . . . like the ashen. fantastic figure gliding toward him through the amorphous trees.

On the one hand there is the world of time arrested, the past held suspended, of love and dream; on the other there is a modern world of dislocated, rootless, and grotesque images. From the mixture Fitzgerald distils two essential components of modernist writing. The book made him the extraordinary historian of those two interlocking worlds—the world of modern history invested with a timeless myth, where the clock is tilted back like the clock on Gatsby's mantelpiece as he kisses Daisy, and the world of history disinvested, reduced to fragments without manifest order, a modern waste land. This tension and ambiguity persist into the famous ending, where Fitzgerald both recreates 'the American dream', the dream of an innocent, pastoral America created by man's capacity for wonder, and also sees it as a nostalgic desire for that which time itself defeats. As Gatsby is an artistic surrogate, chasing with his 'creative passion' a symbol that is both transcendent and corrupted, *The Great Gatsby* is a symbolist tragedy—about the struggle of the symbolic imagination to exist in lowered historical time, and about that symbol's inherent ambiguity, its wonder and its meretriciousness.

Gatsby is probably Fitzgerald's best, certainly his most finished, book: a realization of his talents in the Twenties, a sign of his power to enter a world both gaudy and destructive and distil a meaning from it. He had succeeded not just in internalizing the times—the spirit of a 'whole race going hedonistic, deciding on pleasure'—but in realizing them as form. But, as Twenties unease grew, Fitzgerald internalized that too, sensing the economic cost to be charged, the moral interest due. Though it was a formal success, *Gatsby* was not a financial one. Fitzgerald now had to undertake the production of countless popular magazine short stories to maintain his life-style, delaying his next novel, which was in any case going through many drafts. Behind the public façade, the marriage to Zelda was now strained, as each fought for self-preservation and survival. The Crash of 1929 destroyed the symbolic base of their existence, and by 1930 what was latent in the inner politics of that marriage—Zelda's schizophrenia, Scott's alcoholism—was evident. 'No ground under our feet', he noted in his ledger, as the life-style they had both promoted began to tear to pieces. He now began to read Spengler, Henry Adams, Freud, and Marx, and sensed the need for a

'Great Change'. He grew aware of the historical displacement of the rich, looked towards the roots of his own wealth, began to grant the reality of the historical process and to probe the sexual disorder of the times.

All this went into the plan for his next novel, *Tender Is the Night*, a troubled and troublesome book of which we have two versions. Fitzgerald described it as follows: 'Show a man who is a natural idealist, a spoiled priest, giving in for various causes to the ideas of the haute Burgeoise [*sic*], and in his rise to the top of the social world losing his idealism, his talent and turning to drink and dissipation. Background is one in which the liesure [*sic*] class is at their truly most brilliant & glamorous.'[1] The background is the expatriate, socialite French Riviera where Americans gather, art and wealth converge, the great gaudy spree goes on past its season, and a post-war generation attempts to reconstruct an existence after the war has shelled the old society to death. But cause is divorced from effect, and on the map of modern disturbed geography amusement lies next to *Angst*, the French Riviera close to the Swiss psychiatric clinics in which the price is paid. *Tender Is the Night* is a novel of psychic disorientation, seen not only as itself, but in relation to the processes of history—thus, says Fitzgerald, 'At that moment, the Divers [his central couple] represented externally the exact furthermost evolution of a class.' The book is set in a world of chance, violence, and unexplained deaths, with echoes of the war sounding constantly in the background. The method is panoramic and expository, but historical scope is related to an inner violence and despair—above all to the insanity of Nicole Diver and the way this implicates her husband, the psychiatrist Dick Diver, the modern saviour who seeks to heal the pains and bear the burdens of these rich disintegrating psyches in a disintegrating, sexually confused, and perverse world. Like Gatsby, Dick attempts to unify the chaos and give a meaning to the disorder.

[1] Fitzgerald's 'General Plan' for the book, reprinted as Appendix B in Arthur Mizener, *The Far Side of Paradise* (1951; rev. edn., 1965). A revised edition of *Tender Is the Night*, edited by Malcolm Cowley and incorporating some of Fitzgerald's own ideas for the book's rearrangement, appeared in 1951. The complicated history of the text is analysed in Matthew J. Bruccoli, *The Composition of 'Tender Is the Night'* (1963).

Like Gatsby, he is an idealized hero, a man with a 'fine glowing surface' who distils bright moments of transcendence, making life into a successful and ever-moving party. Diver is the master stylist—'there was a pleasingness about him that simply had to be used'—and much of the early part of the novel is about his powers of unification, his capacity to make the world fall into place for others. His powers are more than psychiatric, they are sacral. He blesses the world he enters, and is indeed its 'spoiled priest'.

But to do this Diver must indeed dive into this collapsing historical world, must risk his initial integrity—'He knew . . . that the price of his intactness was incompleteness'—and his illusions—'they were the illusions of a nation, the lies of generations of frontier mothers who had to croon falsely that there were no wolves outside the cabin door'—in the chaotic, war-shattered life of his times. Marrying Nicole, one of his patients, wealthy and corrupt, he assimilates her mixture of amusement and pain. His humanism becomes tarnished, his disintegration slowly begins. A redemptive figure at the start, at the end he is broken by drink, violence, and emotional strain. No longer able to perform the symbolic trick—once done with elegant ease—of lifting a man on his back while surfing, he fades from the significant history of the book in its last pages. Like Fitzgerald, he becomes the implicated man, and the implication draws him into the heart of the disaster, the psychic overextension, that is now Fitzgerald's essential theme. The book's awareness is psychological, social, and economic all at once; what we see is a top surface, a world of individuals propelled by underlying processes into expressive action which reveals what those processes imply. *Tender Is the Night* differs from *Gatsby* in having two methods of presentation. One is spatial–symbolic, a method appropriate to the priestly artist-figure at the book's centre who is seeking to hold on to romantic integrity and wholeness amid destructive time. The other is historical–evolutionary, the story of that time as system, a developing history with which Fitzgerald was not attentively concerned. Process and symbol struggle to give the novel an oblique chronology, and Fitzgerald was never sure of its true order of construction. In fact he began to amend it even after publication, which is why the contemporary reader now has the original and a reconstructed text to choose between.

The novel's incompleteness has a certain appropriateness; for incompleteness and exposure were now a main concern. In the notable essays of 1936 and 1937, 'The Crack-Up' and 'Early Success', he looked at the disintegration of his earlier style in life and art, playing his thirties against his twenties, the Thirties against the Twenties, distilling his concern with exterior and inward dissolution. By now the alcoholism was serious, Zelda was in a mental hospital, and Fitzgerald turned towards Hollywood for a job as screenwriter. His last novel—*The Last Tycoon* (1941)—set there, is yet more incomplete; the book was left unfinished at his early death in 1940. But evidently it was to tell a story similar to that of *Tender Is the Night*, the story of another master stylist and integrative man, destroyed by disintegrative forces in the external world and in his own emotional life. But where *Tender Is the Night* had been expository and extended, *The Last Tycoon* would reach back towards some of the methods of *Gatsby*: surrealistic concentration on scene, and use of the first-person narrator, so that the action is seen through Cecilia Brady, the rich Bennington College junior with an ironic view of Hollywood but in love with Monroe Stahr, the 'last tycoon'. Again there would be a bonding of image and age, consciousness and economics. Hollywood, the setting, is the great dream-factory of American illusions—Nathanael West was also displaying its surrealist significance in *The Day of the Locust* (1939). Stahr, the last of the great producers, living among these distorted and manufactured images, attempting to retain command, is a man who 'had just managed to climb out of a thousand years of Jewry into the late eighteenth century', and who cherishes 'the parvenu's passionate loyalty to an imaginary past'. He is at the end of his period of possible existence: unionization, modern complexity, contemporary disintegration threaten him, and he is the now-failing hero: 'There was no world so but had its heroes, and Stahr was the hero. . . . The old loyalties were trembling now, and there were clay feet everywhere; but still he was their man, the last of the princes.'

Like *The Day of the Locust*, *The Last Tycoon* is a classic novel of cultural images caught at a point of extreme distortion. History too has become distorted in the modern dream-factory world. Stahr is compared to past American Presidents, the princes who must relate their inner lives to public needs and fantasies. But Andrew Jackson's home is closed, and a man dies on its steps, while Abraham Lincoln appears in the commissary, 'his kindly face fixed on a forty-cent dinner, including dessert, his shawl wrapped around him as if to protect himself from the erratic air-cooling.' An absurdist, half-finished landscape of plasticized dreams and desires surrounds Stahr, and is part of him, outward history and inward psychic world. Apocalyptic disturbances overtake him; at the beginning of the book is a grotesque scene where an earthquake sends a flood sweeping through the studio lot, carrying a floating head of Siva on which two 'survivors' ride. From the head descends a woman who bears the face of Stahr's dead wife—a woman he now pursues through a sequence of transitory, fragmented scenes, as one might decadently pursue both survival and death itself. The book is made of such concentrated images, and predicts Stahr's downfall—tragedy set in waning history. The tragedy was in a sense Fitzgerald's own. A writer who had always struggled with the problem of unifying form and time, art and process, hoping to find a romantic and a moral value, he had watched the old dream of wealth and wonder redeemed pushed to extremity. Moreover his career was declining, his sensitivities were raw, and he had intimations of his own coming death. *The Last Tycoon* as we have it, unfinished, ends with a work note he had written to himself: 'ACTION IS CHARACTER'—a fair epitaph for a writer who had struggled through living to generate an experimental form for modern experience.

4.

It was a phrase that, if in a different way, equally well fitted Fitzgerald's friend and rival throughout the Twenties, Ernest Hemingway. As his fellow expatriate in Paris, Fitzgerald had helped Hemingway with the end of *The Sun Also Rises* and encouraged his publication. By the Thirties, Hemingway, disliking

'The Crack-Up' essay and Fitzgerald's frank exposure of weakness, was emphasizing the distance between them. Like Fitzgerald, Hemingway was a writer firmly engaged in his time— he called his first real book *In Our Time* (1925)—and felt bonded to his own generation, those who had to cope with the unreasonable wound of war. Like Fitzgerald, he saw the task as relating a life-style to an art-style; the writer was a performing self who assimilated and distanced areas of self so that they provided an economy of form. But where for Fitzgerald this had meant taking open risks with himself and with experience, and where, in the event, this would prove true for Hemingway as well, the important issue for Hemingway was, exactly, economy— a reined self-expenditure, a stylistic and bodily toughness, a controlled use of words. Technique, in life and writing, was precision—the precision that, Hemingway came to feel, Fitzgerald lacked. Hemingway's fictional construct was always to be a clean, well-lighted place, a world of the hard, well-registered minimum. Fitzgerald loosely amassed material, and wasted it and himself; Hemingway's was always to be a world where romantic feelings and pains were hidden causes, never quite stated, a specified, exact, exclusive world, with its own type of terrain, its *paysage moralisé*, its own geography of sanctified places, special drinks, guns, and rods, its own distinctive ways of speech. Over that terrain, moving with the same toughened and selected economy, as its appropriate tenant, passes the specified Hemingway hero. He crosses the dangerous troubled estate with a certain air of ease and comfort which cloaks but does not fully conceal what lies behind: the tension, the insomnia, the wounds, the pain, the modern nightmare.

It was this capacity to produce a style of pure limitation that made Hemingway seem to readers and critics an experimenter both with modern experience and modern form. His hard objectivist technique was, as critics have pointed out, analogous to modernist poetic doctrines of 'impersonality' and the 'objective correlative'; at the same time it is conditioned by personal experience. Hemingway was born in 1899 in Oak Park, Illinois, and grew up in a family divided, with a powerful, genteel, evangelical, and repressive mother, and a weaker, finally a suicidal, father. Male roles and functions were driven from the house and into a world of nature both initiatory and meaninglessly cruel—the world of the Michigan woods, where the family spent their summers, and which Hemingway would evoke in many of his stories. In 1917 Hemingway went to work as a journalist in the *Kansas City Star* newsroom; he then extended his encounter with 'reality' when he joined the American Field Service as an ambulanceman and served on the Italian front, where he was wounded in 1918. The episode became the key existential encounter and he sought, in a sense, to repeat it thereafter in stylized situations of sporting danger, as bullfighter, boxer, big-game hunter, fisherman. Returning home to an America that now seemed bland and sterilized, he worked as a journalist and returned in 1921 to Paris as a special correspondent, with letters from Sherwood Anderson introducing him to several of the expatriate gurus. Though he later played down the episode, he sat with profit at Gertrude Stein's feet and assimilated much of her modernist lore. Bohemian decadence was not, on the face of it, Hemingway's style. He preferred to model himself on the journalists, the soldiers of fortune, the sportsmen, those who functioned through skill, professional competence, above all in the presence of a centralized event, a 'real thing' that must be confronted under rituals of formal control. 'Begin over again—and concentrate,' Stein told Hemingway, when she looked at his early writings. Concentration then became his fiction's aim, and it was to make him into a major modern stylist, whose minimalist methods have affected writers ever since. As he explained later in the memoir *A Moveable Feast* (1964), he learned to instruct himself in the making of a new prose style that looked less like an aesthetic mannerism than an elimination of all loose references. 'All you have to do', he tells us he told himself, 'is to write one true sentence. Write the truest sentence that you know.' What Hemingway meant by this is best seen in the kinds of sentence he learned to write: attempts to merge the act of writing with the act of being by setting limits against false verbal action or false impressions of experience. In this modernist realism, language marks the point of intersection between the existential self and an outward and knowable event, which is purged of false association and concentrated down to a linguistic essence. Modern language theorists might dispute his account, but for Hemingway language in effect contains what is authentic in the self, and becomes the hard firm intermediary between consciousness and object or event, showing the struggle of that encounter with a taut and economic authenticity.

Hemingway's extraordinary new linguistic economy, so greatly to affect modern writing, was first displayed within the tight frame of the short story, where some of his best work is to be found. He published two short volumes—*Three Stories and Ten Poems* (1923) and *in our time* (1924)—with an expatriate press in Paris. An enlarged *In Our Time* appeared in the USA in 1925, establishing him as a writer. Containing fifteen stories and many untitled vignettes, it presents in seven of these stories the character of Nick Adams, clearly the author's surrogate; he was to appear again in the later story volumes *Men Without Women* (1927) and *Winner Take Nothing* (1933). The central theme of these autobiographical stories is initiation. Some deal with Nick growing up in a Midwestern family with a genteel mother and a defeated doctor father, discovering the pains of first acquaintance with death and violence, and the natural life of the Michigan woods. Others deal with Nick's participation in the violence of the First World War, the battlefield being seen as a place of naturalistic horror, in which the corpses of the dead appear worth no more than the dead animals of the Chicago stockyards back home. In both worlds nature consumes its own creations. This produces a spirit of stoicism, through which one learns to depend only on those things one cannot lose. Desire rashly expended, emotion released too far, produces a tragic outcome. Words themselves, being potentially a form of sentimental emotion, must be contained to convey the precise nature of an event without decoration or romanticization. Here is the Hemingwayesque style: adjectives cut down to a considered few, metaphors and even causal connectives cut away, objects functioning as subdued symbols, often of loss or sterility, to produce an ironic realism or materialism in which a small number of details live starkly, carefully juxtaposed one to another. In an age when much modernist writing was moving toward the exploration of consciousness, Hemingway's mode of writing could appear notably unpsychological. It does not go inside, but projects action outward; this is why the terrain is so exactly mapped, and place, season and detail are crucial. But this outward world is effective precisely because it is a total metaphor for an inward and psychic condition, as the reader fills the empty spaces and the area of implied pain and hysteria.

Hemingway's pursuit of this hard, clean, well-lighted modern style does much to explain his parody of his original mentor Sherwood Anderson in the volume *The Torrents of Spring* (1926), one of his lesser books. It also explains the theme and spirit of his remarkable first novel, *The Sun Also Rises* (1926), published in England as *Fiesta*. This is a book explicitly about the making of modern styles in life and emotion, a novel about the war-damaged Twenties which are seen both as a historical condition and a time of fashion, doubly a new era of style. In one sense it is Hemingway's most obviously fashionable novel, set in the expatriate Paris and Spain of the bohemian Twenties, among American and European artists and cosmopolites, and their various attachments, drinking and sporting companions, and general hangers-on. Later Hemingway heroes would largely have to content themselves with war, big game hunting or deep-sea fishing, but in this most social of his novels there are similar codes and rituals of behaviour. The novel remains one of Hemingway's best because it gives a clear social and historical location for his vision, just as did those Nick Adams stories about life in Italian hospitals after he has been wounded in war. Jake Barnes, a writer and this book's first person narrator, has also received a genital war wound, and his enforced sexlessness explains his contained stoicism and his need to search for a new manner of living: 'I did not care what it was all about. All I wanted to know was how to live in it. Maybe if you found out how to live in it you learned from that what it was all about.' The process of 'learning to live in it' and then learning 'what it was all about' is the collective endeavour of nearly all the characters. The book is indeed a complete Baedeker of post-war social, moral, and historical knowledge, a compendium for learning the correct codes and knowing the right places, the right drinks to drink in

them, above all the right tone of voice and the right sensibility—
an initiate's guide to place, time, and feeling.

What Fitzgerald and Hemingway shared together was essentially the decadent or modernist belief that history does express
itself in fashion, or the instant of style. Style is a condition, and
the achievement of *The Sun Also Rises* is its convincing presentation of just what that condition is. By acquiring a style of life
and speech, we indeed begin to learn what 'it'—that historical
condition—is all about. The novel is a portrait of a modern
elect, the 'herd' of initiates who in one way or another seek the
territorial, social, emotional, and sexual maps appropriate to
their troubled selves, in a world where style and cynicism have
replaced traditional religion, idealism, and sexual morality. A
hard new romanticism prevails, the romanticism of stoic and
managed pain, shaped from the need to show strength and
exactitude, and select the right occasions of pleasure, joy, and
physical satisfaction amid the corrupting illusions of modern
experience. In the clean, tight performance of Romero's grace-
ful bullfighting in Spain, or in the momentary natural joy of the
fishing trip, these moments of exactness come, providing small
essences in the chaos of contemporary existence. *The Sun Also
Rises* opens with two epigraphs. One is the famous phrase
Hemingway claimed he had got from Gertrude Stein: 'You are
all a lost generation.' The other is a passage from Ecclesiastes,
about the endurance of the earth and the recurrence of life
beyond each single generation. Hemingway intended them to
be read together, to indicate that beyond the ephemeral and the
fashionable there is the natural and the eternal.

None the less the book does turn firmly on the idea of the
coming of a distinct new generation of those who function in a
new nature and a new history, transfigured and tested by war and
its aftermath. Expectations reduced, they bear certain kinds of
psychic trauma and certain kinds of knowledge unknown to their
predecessors—or, for that matter, to their more innocent contemporaries. Barnes's friend, or acquaintance, Robert Cohn uses
the wrong language, reads the wrong books (W. H. Hudson),
likes the wrong countries, for the wrong reasons, and feels the
wrong feelings. The most resonant symbol of the new experience

is the wound, whether actual or symbolic. This almost intolerable intrusion of violence into the self points to the modern exposure, the threat of death and annihilation, the vacancy of present history, the need for physical reality, which most of the major characters feel. It is the wound that leads on into a world of trauma, sleeplessness, loss, consciousness of *nada*, the void in the universe. It also creates common consciousness in those who—like, above all, Jake Barnes and Lady Brett Ashley, the British aristocrat man–woman whose nymphomania is the counterpart to Jake's enforced sterility—share the insight of the modern, mixing romantic desire with a sense of its displacement. Beyond nothingness and sterility there are glimpses of renewal. Jake's wound is in fact an ambiguous symbol, affording him strange protection against sexual disorder and the new, androgynous world of sexual relations. In this world decadent indirections are necessary; Jake's impotence, Brett's nymphomania, are complex interlocking images of sterility turned to heroism. The book's final image, of the policeman's upraised baton, suggests the entire condition of its world; direct emotion is obstructed but redeployed indirectly, either as a wasteful using up of experience or as a contained lonely purity. The need is to find the clean line; Jake's impotence keeps him within a world of tight male comradeship, of men without women, the things one cannot lose. Though it is 'pretty to think' that things might be otherwise, prettiness is not to be had. But contained survival *is* possible in the right places, beyond the social world, in the primitive pastoral life glimpsed in Spain and on the fishing trip. Indurant nature, the abiding earth with its muted hostility, can be encountered, if finesse and craft are present, in a ritual, managed expenditure of self.

Much of Hemingway's later fiction concentrates on versions of that encounter, with nature and the separate self. *A Farewell to Arms* (1929), his next novel, confronts the war directly, seeing it chiefly as a grotesque manifestation of nature. Set on the Italian front, amid disease, slaughter, and retreat, the book's careful topography enfolds and limits the bleak, nihilistic events, the records of corpses and of the empty movements of military men. Mountains, lakes, and rain are both context and condition;

metonyms in Hemingway's disconnected prose, they become metaphors, like the rain that washes over the deaths that haunt the book. Lieutenant Frederic Henry, the narrator, is the flat recorder, another modern stylist cut off from the discourse of the past: 'I was always embarrassed by the words sacred, glorious and sacrifice and the expression in vain. Abstract words such as glory, honor, courage, or hallow were obscene beside the concrete names of villages, the numbers of roads, the names of rivers, the numbers of regiments and the dates.' Yet the feeling suppressed by Henry's controlled method of nominalization leaks out as tragic symbolism. Similarly his controlled response to the horrors of war is put at risk when he falls in love with Catherine Barkley, a British nurse, and, making his 'separate peace' by deserting from the Italian army, he hopes to make it a peace for two. The feeling suppressed in *The Sun Also Rises* is released, and the two attempt to construct a collective solitude from love: 'We could be alone when we were together, alone against the others.' But the images of threatened death in the rain accumulate; nature and war alike battle against any such attempts at sentiment or domestication. The ironic landscape generates a tragic outcome. Catherine dies in childbirth, sacrificed to the inexorable process of pain: 'That was what you did. You died.' Naturalism now reveals itself as a lasting tragedy for the human individual within the indifferent landscape:

Once in camp I put a log on top of the fire and it was full of ants. As it commenced to burn, the ants swarmed out and went first toward the center where the fire was, then turned back and ran toward the end. When there were enough on the end they fell off into the fire. Some got out, the bodies burnt and flattened, and went off not knowing where they were going. But most of them went toward the fire and then backward toward the end and warmed on the cool end and finally fell off into the fire. I remember thinking at the time that it was the end of the world and a splendid chance to be a messiah. . . . But I did not do anything.

Indifferent or mutely hostile nature generates its own controlled reaction: as the book ends Lieutenant Henry, returned to a condition of stoic isolation covering tragic pain, walks back to his hotel in the overwhelming rain.

In Hemingway's novels and stories of the Twenties verbal and emotional economy thus unite to form an existential, central modern style, a complex formal attenuation comparable to period tendencies in painting. His next book, the reportage study *Death in the Afternoon* (1932) is mainly about Spanish bullfighting, but again it is about the style-making process and the exactitude it required. Hemingway here still reflects: 'the real thing, the sequence of motion and fact which made the emotion and which would be as valid in a year or in ten years or, with luck and if you stated it purely enough, always, was beyond me and I was working very hard to try to get it.' But at the same time both *Death in the Afternoon* and *Green Hills of Africa* (1935), also a work of reportage, involve considerable personal display. By now the style, which depends exactly on the rhythm of expression and containment, was beginning to harden into mannerism, and Hemingway himself to harden into a tough-guy hero performing as publicly in his own way as Fitzgerald did in his. His theme increasingly became male self-testing, but there was another change; like so many American writers in the Thirties, Hemingway was moving away from the ethic of solitude into a communal or social ethic. *To Have and Have Not* (1937) is the story of Harry Morgan, a liquor smuggler who has shipped contraband from Cuba to Florida during Prohibition, and then during the Depression tries to secure his survival as an independent entrepreneur by increasing acts of corruption. The book deals with economic carelessness and injustice. The buccaneer Harry, who says 'I don't know who made the laws but I know there ain't no law that you got to go hungry', shows courage and tough male skill in the decadent and collapsing world. But as he dies he offers the new Hemingway lesson: ' "No matter how a man alone ain't got no bloody chance." ' It is the reverse lesson from the Twenties novels; what is more, it seems superimposed on an uneasy, lesser book.

For Whom the Bell Tolls (1940), with its Donnean principle that 'No man is an Ilande,' also embodies Hemingway's new sense of social engagement. About the Spanish Civil War, it involves its growingly committed hero, Robert Jordan, in a Republican sabotage operation behind the Fascist lines, and in a love affair with the Spanish girl Maria, raped by the Falangists who have murdered her father. Jordan begins as the old provisional Hemingway hero ('if he were going to form judgments he would form them afterwards'). But he acquires a belief in the value of sacrifice, that once absurd abstraction; and love—once the main area of risk and betrayal—here becomes a complex mystical union, not only with the other ('one and one is one') but with nature and the earth itself. Like the dying Harry Morgan, Jordan, having accomplished his mission, lying wounded and waiting at the book's end for death amid a nature that has now become tolerant and receptive, finds he has learned a lesson from life: 'I wish there was some way to pass on what I've learned, though. Christ, I was learning fast there at the end.' As Jordan moves from an existential to a transcendental world, so Hemingway moves from an existentialist to a transcendentalist mode of fiction, in which the old tragic naturalism and nihilism yield to a new humanism. The tense modern self at last finds a mode of satisfyingly heroic action, and becomes not stoic victim but active agent. The novel is as notable a record as any we have of the crucial Spanish conflict, but in encompassing this change Hemingway's tight prose was already losing something of its precision. The result is a striking release of much that, it would seem, Hemingway's previous style and perception had striven to contain: his work now turned towards a ripe modern romanticism.

Life indeed now seemed to conspire to let that romanticism grow; he increasingly conducted himself as his own best hero. After having been a war correspondent in Spain and running a decoy ship off Cuba hunting German submarines, he became a correspondent in Europe in the Second World War, flew missions with the RAF, formed an irregular army in France, and liberated the Ritz in Paris ahead of the French army. His wound became the most famous since Philoctetes', his sleepless nights the most famous since Lady Macbeth's. He became an image of modern endurance, an heroic stylist even to himself; at the same time the underlying unease was increasing. *Across the River and Into the Trees* (1950), appearing after a ten-year interval, is the story of such a legendary man, Colonel Robert Cantwell, as much a version of the later Hemingway as hero as were his previous heroes of his earlier self. He is heroic but also wounded and damaged, as Hemingway now was. He feels an instinctive comradeship for 'those who had fought or been mutilated'; his terrain is that of sport, war, and élite society, of Venice, gun emplacements, and shooting platforms. He is a universal insider and a deeply ritualized man, a man of ultimate codes. Human experience is brought to a sequence of personal acts and graces, from fishing to eating to love-making, and these rituals must have the same precision of style as Hemingway earlier gave to language. Indeed the complex idea of an exclusive language points to a social Elect, and now Cantwell is the leader of one. What justifies his election is his wound and what he makes of it; and a main theme of the book is his return to, and his ordering of, the place where it happened. In one sense this is a summative book, the realization of Hemingway's principles of a lifetime. But, though it starts brilliantly, it acquires a curious absurdity, becoming a pastiche or parody of the earlier and more tentative Hemingway style. Cantwell reaches 'accurately and well for the champagne bucket', he 'stands straight and kisses true', and in peacetime restaurants has a table in the corner to keep his flank covered. In this hardened form, the Hemingway code and the Hemingway sentence become clichés—much as Anderson's codes and sentences had when Hemingway parodied them some twenty years before.

But it is of course the purity of its limitation that links Hemingway's work so deeply with modern experience and style. The linguistic economy becomes a purified universe and a purified morality, a distinctive world brought down to a given terrain, a given version of history, a given use of the self in all things. That self, made authentic by one's risk-taking human performance, is a romantic derivative of the quest to know truly, and is forged outside society from fragile inward resources, which then acquire the capacity for truthful discovery. As in decadence, the morality of right sensations becomes central. Yet acts of authentic violence can become just violence, physical self-celebration a losing cause as age takes away what strength and endurance have given, and the underlying desperation therefore increases again. And now what in Hemingway's life had seemed secure and morally justified was indeed being taken away, as, after a series of major accidents, his battered body began to lose the strength for the key male rituals he had celebrated: drinking, hunting, fighting, making love. His next book, *The Old Man and the Sea* (1952), with its essential message of endurance, its assertion that a man may be destroyed but not defeated if he secures his own humanity, responds to this. It is a naturalistic novel with a humanistic outcome, a tale of ritual encounter between the old Cuban fisherman and the forces of erosion itself, as he battles first with a giant marlin, which he tames and catches, then with the predatory sharks that reduce the prize to a skeleton he nevertheless brings home to port. The mode is simple and epical, a method of symbolic allegory with powerful Christian allusions; its lesson seems far away from Hemingway's early note of nihilism, but was implicit in it. Its myth of heroism, humility, and the moral virtues of endurance undoubtedly helped Hemingway to win, in 1954, the Nobel Prize for Literature.

Yet the novel had its dark underside, made apparent when some of the other sea stories with which it was to have been linked appeared—posthumously and not fully completed—as *Islands in the Stream* (1970). The three tales of the book are about Thomas Hudson, a painter living in Cuba, whose personal life mirrors Hemingway's own. Hudson is a broken stoic, who keeps passing beyond the limits of his own control, as he loses his dependence on strength, sexuality, comradeship, and fatherhood. The stories are about wear and tear, and the familiar tragic dimension is now extended into a realm of total loss, of extreme pain and sexual regret and deprivation, after two wrecked marriages. The stoic spirit is pushed to its limits; the Hemingway hero, the hero of experience and expertise, is now plagued by the conflict between the remains of romantic hope and a rising despair. Physically weakened and thus deprived of many of the essential 'realities' of the to-the-hilt physical living both his human performance and his writing had celebrated, Hemingway now grew fearful of himself and doubtful of the motives of others. When the writing that ultimately justified all the action no longer came, the shadow of nothingness that had underlain even his most optimistic and humanistic novels from the 1930s to the 1950s became everything. Life-style and art-style were together collapsing, coming to the end of a complex heroic enterprise. On 2 July 1961, he drew that, his largest story, to a tragic conclusion, killing himself with a shotgun, as his father had many years before.

5.

Hemingway's vision of a world that had been brought by war to the end of its innocence, requiring new styles alike of life and art, was shared by many of his generation. The First World War seemed a turning-point for many Americans, if for various reasons: as a failed moral crusade, as an entry into European corruption, as a capitalist plot to protect investment and stave off western revolution. It was in the last guise that John Dos Passos saw this war, and the surprise is that he should have gone to it at all. The illegitimate son of a self-made lawyer of Portuguese stock, he was a lonely, weak, withdrawn child who once noted of himself: 'was ever creature more dependent on literature for life and stimulus.' Moreover, by 1916, when he left Harvard, he had been moving towards radical, anarchist, and pacifist principles, under the influence of Emma Goldman. Yet the war attracted him as an essential reality, and he went to France and Spain to be nearer to it, trying to persuade his father to let him join the ambulance corps. And this, on his father's death, he did, explaining meanwhile to his friends that he had not 'gone militarist' but 'merely wanted to see a little of the war personally' and face 'the senseless agony of destruction'. In letters, diaries, poems, and a novel he began to write collaboratively with Robert Hillyer, he condemned 'the mountain of lies', the 'merry parade that is stifling in brutishness all the fair things of the world'. But though war was 'suicidal madness', it was also the ultimate experience, calling for immersion and expression: 'I want to be able to express, later—all of this—all the tragedy and hideous excitement of it. I have seen so little I must experience more of it, & more. The gray crooked fingers of the dead, the dark look of dirty mangled bodies . . .'.

Dos Passos now began on a stylistic quest that took him

through various forms and manners of the novel, as he tried to establish the right tones and the right historiography for the experience he felt he must render. The initial report comes, quickly, in *One Man's Initiation: 1917*, first published in England in 1919. Like Barbusse's *Le Feu*, it is an immediate, confused book, a subjective response, as the title suggests. It is centred on one individual and sensitive soldier, Martin Howe, who has origins very like Dos Passos's own, and who sees the war primarily as a violation of his cultural values and his sense of form. Dos Passos is clearly guilty about this aestheticism, which seems like a mode of withdrawal. Larger historical issues lie behind the book—the mountain of lies issued by the government, the brutal effects of the army machine, the potential of the rising revolutionary fervour which Dos Passos sees in the army and to which he came to attach a cleansing hope—but these are present only impressionistically; the true concern is with Howe's own uneasy personal awarenesses and his aesthetic pain. That Dos Passos wanted to take a less personal, a broader, a more historical and explanatory view is evident in his second war novel, *Three Soldiers*, the very title of which suggests a wider span, and the sense of war as a collective experience.

Three Soldiers has an elaborate structure, a design intended to display war as a massive machine, crushing individualism—a machine that spreads outward into general life. The three soldiers are Andrews, a sensitive composer who begins to assimilate mechanical military rhythms, until he revolts romantically against regimentation; Chrisfield, the farm boy from Indiana, unthinkingly brave and instinctive, pushed towards the murder of those who now organize and limit his manhood; Fuselli, the city clerk who hopes for the great adventure and ascends the military hierarchy, until he catches venereal disease. Dos Passos strives for a modernized, expressionistic style which catches and enacts the rhythmic mechanization of life and the reduction of men to functionaries in an antlike collectivity. But he cannot quite forgo the subjective mode and assert an objective historical significance for the story. The war becomes simply an 'unbearable agony' and a choice between self-abnegation and desertion. By suppressing, with his harder style, those flares of romantic

and aesthetic subjectivity which are the reason for opposing
war, Dos Passos appears to move away from his own needs.
The papers that blow around Andrews's room at the end of the
novel, as, in full self-knowledge, he silences himself and waits
for the military police, appear like an image of Dos Passos's
personal self-abnegation.

Dos Passos's real breakthrough to modern style came in
Manhattan Transfer, a remarkable novel set not in war but in
that other key metaphor of both naturalist and expressionist
writing: the great modern city. A book consonant with the
developing principles of European modernism, it belongs among
the great urban classics—James's *The Princess Casamassima*,
Conrad's *The Secret Agent*, Joyce's *Ulysses*, Doblin's *Berlin
Alexanderplatz*, Biely's *Petersburg*—where the city is seen less
as a vast system or warring jungle of forces than a synchronic
environment of multiple consciousnesses, flickering impressions, contingency and variety. *Manhattan Transfer* adds to the
old naturalist city of determining and destructive mass the new
expressionist city, of energy, strange selfhoods in remarkable
juxtaposition, a modern Eros. The methods relate to those of
the massive urban novel like Biely's, where experience falls into
strange luminous units, as well as to the collage and montage
techniques of avant-garde film-makers like Eisenstein and
Griffith. The debt to Joyce is apparent (Dos Passos bought
Ulysses in Paris in 1922), but where Joyce presents his paralysed
Dublin as a city from which form can arise only through the
revelation of art, Dos Passos, in more constructivist fashion,
sees his Manhattan as a vast collective motion, a mechanical
womb, a machine both for giving and suppressing life. We may
see in his Jimmy Herf a figure of the sensitive individual defeated;
but what is displaced from the individual life is reinvested in the
operational city itself. Mechanism and destructiveness are dominant, and characters become like the impersonal environment
through which they move. At the same time the environment
has its own vast motion and vigour. As Jean-Paul Sartre said in
an admiring essay, what Dos Passos had invented was an 'author-
less novel' with 'characterless characters': 'acts, emotions and
ideas suddenly settle within a character, make themselves at

home and then disappear without his having much to say about the matter. You cannot say he submits to them. He experiences them.[2] Dos Passos's Manhattan is a dynamo filled with motion, an endless contention between the vitalistic and the mechanistic where—as in Hart Crane's long poem *The Bridge* (1930)—the mechanical takes on romantic powers in the world's most modern and most futuristic city.

But as the Twenties ended, and the direction of fiction markedly changed, Dos Passos's techniques changed too. *Manhattan Transfer* is spatial and synchronic, portraying a cyclical and purposeless history. But Dos Passos had been steadily moving towards communism and anarchism, ahead of most of his contemporaries. In the three-volume sequence of novels consisting of *The 42nd Parallel* (1930), *1919* (1932), and *The Big Money* (1936), collected together as *U.S.A.* (1938), he sought to use his spatial techniques in a historical continuum, and to treat history as process. *U.S.A.* is really a very Thirties history, which reads backwards into American life to cover the nation's evolution from 1900 through to the late 1920s. Seen from a Thirties radical viewpoint, the Twenties were the nadir, the discredited decade, dominated by commercialism and materialism, suppression of Radicals (culminating in the executions of Sacco and Vanzetti), and rising bull-market absurdities pointing towards economic crash. *U.S.A.* is therefore a negative history, a process towards integration (with progressivism) and then disintegration. Dos Passos draws on the techniques he had evolved in *Manhattan Transfer*, using pluralized narration, large ranges of characters, intersections between documentary matter and naturalistic materials, to create a massive modernist epic. Spreading over a large historical curve and a vast geographical span, the work's concern is not just with the interior but the international life of the United States in its evolution from power to superpower, and from simple to complex modern capitalism.

U.S.A. distils all Dos Passos's personal as well as formal concerns. It is not only a large vision of America corrupting itself over his own lifetime, distorting the psychology of its

[2] Jean-Paul Sartre, *Literary and Philosophical Essays* (1955).

citizens, running deeper into the capitalist morass and the profit-mongers' war, and then into a gross commercial peace, so losing touch with community and with language itself. It is also a great technical enterprise in which the attempt is made through presentational techniques to relate the subjective aesthetic life of the author to historical process. The book has four basic structural levels—the extended life stories of the many fictional characters; the factual biographies of actual public figures; the 'Newsreel' collage of documentary data, headlines, songs, speeches, reports; and the 'Camera Eye' sections, a stream-of-consciousness flow of perception from the novelist's own position. These technical levels interfuse, but each has its own implicit historiography. Thus the individual stories of Margo Dowling, Dick Savage, J. Ward Moorhouse, and so on are tales of types. Some of them intersect, others simply run parallel, some continue for the entire sequence, others drop from sight; but they make up a compound narrative of disappointment and failure, especially of progressive failure, or of corrupting commercial success. The portraits of actual historical individuals make up a radical hagiography of heroes (Big Bill Heywood, La Follette, Veblen, Randolph Bourne, Frank Lloyd Wright, protesters, artists, or dreamers) and of villains (Woodrow Wilson, J. P. Morgan, Insull, politicians and capitalists). The Newsreels, collected from documentary sources, function sometimes as a contingent collage, sometimes as a source of ironic juxtaposition, illustrating the conflict between rhetoric and reality. And the 'Camera Eye' sections follow a helpless narrator, existing in a pained isolation of images, self-dwarfing and self-abnegating, a man hungry for speech and clarity but unable to do more than register impressions until the Sacco–Vanzetti case provokes him into verbal outrage.

The work oscillates between two possibilities: a collectivist and expressionist epic of American life, and a modernist anti-epic—where the sum of the parts indicates not collective meaning but loss of meaning. Underlying the book is an ideal of America, based on past myths, collective hopes and desires, and the possibility of a great reformed technological civilization. The young man in the prologue who walks through the emptying urban streets sees disjunctive lines, but finds himself greedy for speech, hungry in Whitman-like fashion to master contradictions: 'U.S.A. is the world's greatest rivervalley fringed with mountains and hills, U.S.A. is a set of bigmouthed officials with too many bank-accounts. . . . But mostly U.S.A. is the speech of the people.' But by the end language cannot emerge from the growth of the nation, for it is run by other systems; hence it can only be turned against its process ('America our nation has been beaten by strangers who have turned our language inside out,' 'We have only words against'). The multiplication and division of consciousness are the technical processes of the book, and they also represent the damaged nature of modern experience. They change in function, from being the expression of at first a collective, and then a contingent, history. For in all the main lines of narrative there is at work a historical sequence of growing mechanization and dehumanization, a suppression of aesthetic hopes and radical possibilities, a defeat of organic potential and ideals of culture that underlie the book and make epic ambitions possible. But (much as in Ezra Pound's *Cantos*) juxtaposition turns to disjunction, connection to disconnection, and the attempt to celebrate the nation turns into awareness of the space between its real and ideal meanings.

The three volumes of *U.S.A.* thus explore three phases of a declining history. *The 42nd Parallel*, dealing with the years from 1900 to American entry into the war in 1917, presents twentieth-century hopes for the new nation, and moves rhythmically towards the rise of the progressive impulse and radical challenges to the capitalist system; it then takes us towards the European battlefields, ending with the enforced silence of the character Charlie as his ship approaches wartime France. In *Nineteen Nineteen*, the fulcrum volume, the war is seen as the 'plot of the big interests', as a place of horror, debasement, new sexual opportunity, and rising revolutionary momentum, culminating in the Russian Revolution. But no western parallel comes, and even 'separate peace' is not really possible. Everything ends in the corrupted idealism of the Versailles conference, while, back home, the general strike of 1 May 1919, which may be 'the first morning of the first day of the new year', collapses into the Red Scare, leaving open the path towards commercialism and superpower capitalism. *The Big Money*, set in the Twenties, follows this through, portraying a society economically cohesive, socially divisive, and emotionally and personally destructive. The emotional collapse of the main characters and the economic wasting of the system run parallel; the deaths of Sacco and Vanzetti mark the end of all progressive social hope. But Dos Passos is writing out of what comes after, and the growing myth behind the book—of a true idealism hidden in the people and in the timeless history of the continent, which is set against 'history the billiondollar speedup'—is a Thirties myth. It attends to economic laws and processes, but believes in something else—the endurance of the land, the speech of the people.

Dos Passos uses modernist techniques as a form of modern historicism. *U.S.A.* is not intended simply as an external history of a crisis, but the expressive *form* of a crisis within the writer's own aesthetics, his own capacity to generate myth or create language. He had written throughout of the man who seeks for reality and wholeness, but cannot quite succeed in finding it. His dealings with the American Communist party were analogous; he got in deep but always retained his independence, and he was, in the leftward swing of the 1930s, early in deciding that Communism was not the answer: rather the despotism of Henry Ford than that of Mike Gold. 'I think there's more life in the débris of democracy than the comrades do', he noted, and grew into an America Firster. His later novels, some of large ambition, like *Mid-Century* (1961), attempted to construct the myth that, in *U.S.A.*, history had been working to destroy. Paradoxically, they lack the power and invested technical complexity of his earlier, major fiction.

6.

Dos Passos was an important contributor to American fictional modernism, but perhaps the most crucial and exemplary figure of all was William Faulkner. Not all critics have shared that view of him. To many, he is pre-eminently a novelist of that distinct region of the United States, the South: a complex late product of its romance tradition, its celebrations of heroism and chivalry, its idealisms, its semi-feudal social institutions, its rooted struggle against industrialism, its defeats, pains, and anxieties. To others he is, rather, one of the great figures of international modernist experiment—a writer with the range, capacities, and formal preoccupations we associate with Joyce, Proust, or Virginia Woolf, an experimenter, a symbolist, a witness to modern exile. His own view of himself was as a private man and a farmer, a man of his region, a writer writing of enduring human values, honour, endurance, compassion, and sacrifice in a rhetoric bred, as he put it, 'by Oratory out of Solitude'. He did have a bohemian phase, but in the Southern capital of New Orleans, and never attended the expatriate feasts of Paris. He did fly as an airman in the war, but only as a trainee pilot in Canada. Though his writings draw on the primary methods of modernism—stream of consciousness, collage presentation, time shifts, and achronicity—he never fully explained, in his own aesthetic statements, the impulses that drove him to use those techniques. And, where many modernists probed ever further into experiment, Faulkner's most experimental writing occurred as a 'phase' in the middle of his career.

But these two views of Faulkner are not incompatible; rather they attest to his extraordinary complexity. It is largely when his work grows most Southern and, in that sense, most provincial or localized that his technical experiment emerges in its full force. Certainly Faulkner was very much a writer of the South; born in 1897, he grew up in Oxford, Mississippi, and spent most of his life there. Going early to New Orleans to pursue his ambition to write, he found there Sherwood Anderson, and a bohemian climate. His early work, much influenced by all this, was mostly in poetry, and its debts to the Romantics—especially Keats, but above all to the *fin de siècle* decadent poets—are notable. These early writings are packed with avaricious borrowings, the accumulation of a self-educated provincial catching at certain romantic and new modern texts (like *The Waste Land*) to define his aesthetic preoccupations and find his way. Like Fitzgerald, Faulkner saw himself as a romantic egoist, and knew that beautiful was damned; he saw the world of art hunger crossed with the wasteland of modern life. And he too saw the need for redemptive style, in the new decadent fashion. So, as he moved towards fiction, notions of the failure of history, the decline of the west, the degenerations of modernity, the narcissism of modern existence, the displacement of sexuality, the need to refine sensation, and the claims of bohemia were all part of his push towards a modern definition of art and the discovery of a modern style.

His first two novels, *Soldier's Pay* (1926) and *Mosquitoes* (1927), were thus works of the new decadence. The motif is clad in its modern garb, in figures like the death-hungry airman, the epicene new woman, the artist hunting stasis out of time. In *Soldier's Pay* the central figure is the scarred, blinded veteran, Donald Mahon, who comes home to find the malaise of postwar society in the sterility of the people around him, who are unable to connect desire and fulfilment. In this voided world symbolist spaces and enclosures abound. The virginal and unchaste are ever in contention, while time rots and wastes. *Mosquitoes* is set directly among artists in New Orleans; the Keatsian search in the book is for a timeless beauty that will both capture and transcend present reality, and for a mode of realization that is more than words or euphony, that is wrapped in life. In both these novels, Faulkner seems to adopt the style of the sophisticated and cosmopolitan writer, though there is much inner unease. But with *Sartoris* (1929), a great change came. Faulkner returned home, to discover that his essential materials were not simply contemporary. They had an extended historical and social dimension, emerging from his familiar Mississippi environment and its past. *Sartoris* is a far less arch, much more deeply textured novel, fairly conventionally presented; it is a novel of deep social investment, exploring a community at many levels. Out of the book comes Yoknapatawpha County, Faulkner's local, Mississippi version of Hardy's Wessex, a complex invented society overlaying a real one, which he was to rearrange, alter, and complicate through most of the rest of his fiction. With Jefferson as its county seat, it is a distinctive world of displaced aristocrats, carpet-baggers, sharecroppers and entrepreneurs, blacks, and standing chorus of town gossips. With its woods, pine-winey afternoons, bear hunts, and its own historical 'curse' coming from the possession of Indian lands, the history of slavery, and the deep lesion of the Civil War, Yoknapatawpha was gradually written into existence as a totally functional society, a community with its distinct class and racial structure, its own inward agonies, its own processes of historical transformation towards commercialism and industrialism.

Faulkner sets the present of *Sartoris* in the post-First World War world, in the uneasy and changing South to which the ex-flyer young Bayard Sartoris returns, uneasy about his manhood and his place, seeking his masculine death recklessly in modern machines. But one world evokes another: Bayard's is a latter-day version of the reckless courage of his Southern aristocrat ancestors. And one story evokes another; the present, in debased form, both releases and re-enacts the past. Two essential contrasts dominate. One is between the masculine chivalric cult of the Sartorises and the feminized world of the Benbows, delicate, intellectual, and finally narcissistic, at odds with action and time. The other is between those who have an invested historical and social sense, like the Sartorises, De Spains, and Compsons, and those who act according to entrepreneurial and commercial self-interest, above all the Snopeses. Out of these contrasts arises a third, between past and present, a past of action, a present of sterility, a world of men, a world of women. For class barriers now fade, aristocratic manners are superimposed on a commercial world, slaves have been replaced by sharecroppers, the women have learned to turn inward into their own lives and the men towards inner tragedy, and above all the machine age begins to dominate. Thus a special postage stamp of soil, haunted with its own history, institutions, and sense of modern tragedy, now began to be populated. 'I discovered', said Faulkner, 'that writing was a mighty fine thing. You could make people stand on their hind legs and cast a shadow. I felt that I had all these people, and as soon as I discovered it I wanted to bring them all back.'

But bringing them back seemed to involve a complex aesthetic introversion, as if the very fact of making his own characters part of a larger history and hence part of a pluralized narrative forced a new technical complexity onto his work. But so did other things: a deep sense of temporal disjunction, an apocalyptic sense of time; and a desire to penetrate the psychic myths underlying the needs and rituals of this society. It is in the work of the end of the Twenties and the Thirties that we can feel Faulkner's experimental power at full force: in *The Sound and the Fury* (1929), *As I Lay Dying* (1930), *Light in August* (1932), and *Absalom, Absalom!* (1936). These are works that involve a sense of history, but they are not necessarily historical novels. They reach—most of them—segmentally, in small selective units, into the Yoknapatawpha experience, yielding it up not as expository narrative but as units of perception. The underlying history—extending from the earliest point of settlement in the virgin new land to the contemporary, dislocated instant—is itself an imaginative fiction of Southern experience in America. It is constructed as a process where moments of concentration and dissipation occur both collectively and personally, where psychic time strangely crosses historical time, where chiliastic moments in the world and frozen instants of personal perception interweave, where the chance of human innocence is newly offered to the American, but where taint, corruption, and rape re-enact their historical and hereditary cycles. Faulkner's writing contains some of the most powerful moments of modernizing unease in contemporary literature. The intensity arises partly from the hard and terrible facts of Southern history: the South concentrated in a single event, the Civil War, a hundred years of western history, facing a modern exposure, a military and cultural defeat, a vast destruction of cities and human lives, and the process of industrialization all at once. Hence Faulkner's history is apocalyptic: it exists in the context of a fallen Eden, though its degenerating sequence—as land as spirit yields to land as property, woods to axes, gardens to machines, South to North—none the less contains instants of promise, renewed outside time and process in certain individual moments or individual lives.

In the books that Faulkner now undertook, an important form of Southern history emerges in American fiction, all the more remarkable for its use of modernist methods, appropriate to the sense of temporal disjunction and the broken relation between 'social' and 'subjective' consciousness. Faulkner's novels of the Thirties display a remarkable compendium of fictional strategies, structuring his work not through chronological or historical ordering but through alternative radical sequences challenging such orders and generating symbolic resonance. Faulkner's modernist techniques have very different rationales than do, say, those of Joyce or Proust. One of these is the historical interlocking of the stories; his characters have, so to speak, a reality outside the stories in which they occur. As Faulkner said of them: 'These people I figure belong to me and I have the right to move them about in time when I need them.' The same applies to the larger history of Yoknapatawpha: Faulkner does not give it to us as really 'there', but manifests the conditions under which he is inventing it on this occasion, in this particular novel. 'Time', the interlocking of present and past, personal and public histories, is actually an essential mystery in Faulkner's work. In these central novels and the related stories, there is a recurrent structure of a continuous present behind which are stacked up different layers of time, validated in the story by a variety of justifications. Thus, in the long story 'The Bear', in *Go Down, Moses* (1942), there are layers belonging specifically to the evolution of Ike McCaslin, the central figure, dealing with his life at 16, 18, and so on; and others having to do with a broad apocalyptic historical conspectus (*'Jun 1833 yr stars fell'*). In *The Sound and the Fury*, we have a noncausative or continuous present given us for mimetic reasons, because we are dealing with the perceptions of Benjy, an idiot with the mental age of 5, but we also have complicated strata of consciousness relating to the reasons for Quentin Compson's suicide. In *Light in August*, there is a stream of consciousness appropriate to Joe Christmas's present position as it relates to the crises of his childhood, which are there in his consciousness without their actually being 'known' to be there, and this helps us comprehend his confused psychic and racial identity. Yet beyond all this there is an experimental author extremely and self-consciously interested in his own rhetoric and structure, his own power to generate form.

These novels of the late Twenties and early Thirties are classics of spatial form. Each very different, and each work has its own rationale. There are, though, two recurrent paradigms. One is historical or exterior temporal intrusion into personal life; the other is the instant of wonder or personal renewal, or of delocalized vision, of Adamic self-discovery (as experienced, say, by Ike McCaslin in 'The Bear'), converted into an eternal moment within time. It is the conversion of this—the flow and the arrest, the process and the transcendence—into art that constitutes the distinct basis of Faulkner's history and his experimentalism. These key novels are modes of penetrating the symbol, the psyche, and the historical continuum. In *The Sound and the Fury*, the central story concerns Quentin's attempt to arrest both historical and subjective time and maintain Candace's virginity from psychic corruption and time's flow; the novel started, Faulkner has told us, from the single image of Caddy's dirty drawers. There are four layers of interlocking response: Benjy's tale told by an idiot in the continuous present holds the story and its images in the form of a timeless memory; Quentin transliterates the image into psychic and historical tragedy, in one form of cause-and-effect; Jason sees it all causally and empirically; and the black Dilsey offers an enduring continuity. Associative links, like the coincidence between Caddy's name and the caddie at the golf course, generate the process of multiplication. These inward psychic connectives permit Faulkner's primary concern with consciousness to develop; at the same time the story links outward to the larger 'objective' history of Yoknapatawpha, in which Quentin's suicide is a key event. *As I Lay Dying* shows a different experimental tactic. About the six-day funeral journey of the Bundren family, it is told through fifty-nine interior monologues, reflections on movement and stasis, living and death, the moving wagon 'with an outward semblance of form and purpose, but with no inference of motion, progress or retrograde', and the complicated and grotesque panorama of life surrounding it.

The early Thirties saw a change in Faulkner's preoccupations—a darkening of his themes, an increased concern with a sterile modern evil, with the destruction of men by either the corrupt and dirty sexuality of women or the challenge of their abundance and fecundity, and finally with the dark outcome of the South's history of puritanism and miscegenation. *Sanctuary* (1932) creates a figure of modern evil in Popeye, the emptied man who has 'the vicious depthless quality of stamped tin', and who revenges his impotence with his corncob rape of Temple Drake, the whore-woman whose decadent sexuality in turn defeats the sentimental sanctuary of innocence sought by Horace Benbow. *Sanctuary* is sensational, and was written largely with commercial intent; *Light in August* draws on similar themes for what is probably Faulkner's finest novel, a work of extraordinary experiment written through extreme narrative indirection. Here three essential stories interlock. The central narrative is about the black wandering orphan Joe Christmas, whose sexual dislocation brings about the murder of the woman who protects and taunts him, and so causes his final self-sacrifice to racial lynching. The story of the Revd Gail Hightower shows sterility in another form, as Hightower attempts to lock himself into one timeless Civil War moment when life had meaning, and, unable to relate either to love or violence, now seeks (like Christmas) his own crucifixion. Both these dark stories are enfolded in a third, that of the fertile and abundant Lena Grove, the country woman come to town to find the father of her child, who lives in a natural timelessness and endurance, a lasting autumn of natural sexuality, which is opposed to the rigidly puritanic world of the town. Faulkner produced in this period one more extraordinary experimental novel, *Absalom, Absalom!*, a work that fits more directly into his continuous history of Yoknapatawpha. It is the massive, historical, gothic story of Thomas Sutpen's 'design', of cursed land, old tragedies and crimes, of the interlocking of history and psychic disorientation and perversion. It is his last truly 'modernist' book, but it opens yet another phase of Faulkner's writing.

For by now, Yoknapatawpha County—'William Faulkner, sole owner and proprietor', 2,400 square miles of crossing histories, a web of dynasties and genealogies, taints and crimes, stories and storytellers—was becoming infinitely populous. Much of Faulkner's later work extends that populousness, as in, for example, the extraordinary stories of *Go Down, Moses*. They are a complex exploration of the transformation through taint, crime, and racial exploitation of the virgin American land into emptiness and void, though there are many images of redemptive timelessness. Faulkner found many tones of voice for his complex historical vision—from the bleak tragedy of *Absalom, Absalom!* to the comedy of his late Snopes trilogy—*The Hamlet* (1940), *The Town* (1957), and *The Mansion* (1959)—and to the spirited and light-hearted note of his last novel *The Reivers* (1962). In his later books, some of his complexity of manner went, or moved towards convention. But that complexity had always come from two visions. One was Faulkner's quarrel with history; his multiples of consciousness seem, like Eliot's fragments, to be of a piece with the loss of meaning and order that he saw in the lapsed Eden of the American South. The other was opposite: Faulkner was interested not just in the disorders of the psyche, but in its plenitude, its sentience and lyricism, its structures and myths. And because consciousness is creative, as indeed it is in the lyrical flow of prose within the author's own mind, then time need not always destroy. It can also be relived, passed on from one human being to another. The past is after all perpetuated, and so renewable; through consciousness itself history may become timeless.

In this the artist is central, and style his business. Faulkner learned to create a language that worked not through cause and effect, but through processes of imagistic distillation, through symbolist suspensions that work between motion and stillness, past and present, the advancing movement and the static centre, perception and the thing perceived. Such moments form the heart of his style, as in this from *Light in August*:

Though the mules plod on in a steady and unflagging hypnosis, the vehicle does not seem to progress. It seems to hang suspended in the middle distance forever and forever, so infinitesimal is its progress, like a shabby bead upon the mild red string of road. So much is this so that in the watching of it the eye loses it as sight and sense drowsily merge and blend, like the road itself, with all the peaceful and monotonous changes between darkness and day, like already measured thread being rewound on a spool.

Faulkner's sentences repeatedly work like this, producing not the 'scrupulous meanness' of modern style that Joyce advocated and Hemingway realized, nor that 'fear of abstractions' advanced by imagism, but a complex, prolix, lyrical modern rhetoric. That rhetoric is of a piece with Faulkner's conviction that the modern lapse is temporary, that in human lives there are transcendent powers of endurance, that the curse may be lifted, that history, past or present, retains the potential for becoming timeless myth.

In 1950 Faulkner won the Nobel Prize for Literature, and spoke of his belief in 'courage and honor and hope and pride and compassion and pity and sacrifice', the human material of this feeling for timelessness we find in his work. That work originates amid the anxieties of the Twenties, in its decadent despair, its attempt to create the novel as a modern and a modernist genre, a form for encompassing our understanding of the disorientations of, but also the possible artistic recoveries in, twentieth-century experience. Faulkner portrays a world in which history goes awry, and his central figures experience extreme disorientation or psychic damage, in which both time and person are grotesque. But, changing through striking switches of genre, from tragedy to comedy, from tales of sound and fury to stories of amused narrative loquacity, his work moves towards formal and mythic recovery. Both the regionalism and the modernism of his enterprise made him a central modern influence. He found Southern fiction without a real tradition, except perhaps in the work of Ellen Glasgow or Katherine MacDowell; he left it endowed with a fundamental regional vision and a literary landscape which was to pass on into the work of a number of major successors.

These included the group of 'Fugitives' or South Agrarians who played a large part in restoring the intellectual life of the South during the 1920s and 1930s, of whom the major novelist was Robert Penn Warren, also a poet and a critic. Warren produced a line of novels that shared with Faulkner's work both a vivid sense of the Southern locality and an awareness of historical and moral crisis: his *Night Rider* (1939) deals with the tobacco wars in early twentieth-century Kentucky, and in *All the King's Men* (1946) he explores the corrupt practices of a Louisiana state governor who is clearly based on Huey Long, his novels having like Faulkner's a deep sense of the burden of history on Southern lives and an exacting view of form. Equally the finely made work of Eudora Welty, a Mississippian like Faulkner, also glows with his influence and his clear sense of place. And, like Faulkner, Welty is as much a short-story writer as a novelist, writing in her first collection *A Curtain of Green* (1941) about the grotesque and often comic aspects of Southern life. With her novel *The Robber Bridegroom* (1942) she employed historical legend; the late novel *Losing Battles* (1970) is a long history of a Mississippi family; in material and writerly precision, her work shows her a true inheritor of the Faulknerian tradition and has been a guide for many Southern writers since. But indeed the whole still-active landscape of Southern Gothic fiction—in the work of writers like Carson McCullers and Flannery O'Connor, and then James Purdy and James Dickey—would hardly be conceivable without Faulkner's work. He also had a great effect on writers not from the region, such as the surreal experimentalist John Hawkes. Indeed his way of developing modern form as a means for representing the psychic and temporal disturbance of disordered consciousness, and portraying the existential dislocation felt by modern minds, has made him an international influence (he was, for instance, to have as much effect on the French as the American tradition). Eudora Welty has rightly said that he was one of those writers able to convey his own place by uniting a gift of pure and truthful representation with a world that can live purely in the imagination.

Faulkner's was thus a major contribution to what seems the central enterprise of Twenties American fiction: its endeavour to explore the modern both as a distinct historical situation, and a new aesthetic condition. Out of its portrayal of new mores and its hunger for new styles, this generation created a whole new spirit in American fiction. It is often said that the aesthetic intensity of their work came from their withdrawal from the puritan, commercial, materialist Twenties, and this is partly true. But most Twenties writers expressed the deeper spirit of a decade that was divided between nostalgia and progress, love of tradition and avant-garde expectations. Even those writers who withdrew to Paris looked back, though sometimes through the long lens of critical irony, at their own American country and culture. They saw themselves as more modern than the times, only to be surprised by the modernity of changing American life over the decade. Certain that Americans would never understand their experimentalism, they often found themselves popular or commercially successful by the decade's end, when in any case the materialism so many of them condemned collapsed in the Great Crash of 1929. That crisis, which (as Fitzgerald saw) was not only economic but psychic and aesthetic, brought many of them back into mainstream American life again. By the end of the Twenties, when the great gaudy spree was nearly over, the experimental and modernist spirit that had developed in the new American fiction was itself becoming an accepted part of twentieth-century American culture, and the modern American novel had been transformed.

5
Realism and Surrealism: The 1930s

Where are the modern streets of New York, Chicago and New Orleans in these little novels? Where are the cotton mills, and the murder of Ella May and her songs? Where are the child slaves of the beet fields? Where are the stockbroker suicides, the labor racketeers or passion and death of the coal miners?

Michael Gold, 'Thornton Wilder: Prophet of the Genteel Christ' (1930)

I believe we are lost here in America, but I believe we shall be found. And this belief, which mounts now to the catharsis of knowledge and conviction, is for me—and I think for all of us—not our only hope, but America's everlasting, living dream. I think the life which we have fashioned in America, and which has fashioned us—the forms we have made, the cells that grew, the honeycomb that was created—was self-destructive in its nature, and must be destroyed. I think these forms are dying, and must die, just as I know that America, and the people in it, are deathless, undiscovered, and immortal, and must live.

Thomas Wolfe, *You Can't Go Home Again* (1940)

1.

As the Great Crash of 1929 developed, over the next years, into a deep-seated national and world Depression, it grew quickly apparent that the social and cultural mood which dominated the Twenties was over for good. By 1931, as the banks and factories closed, farming collapsed, industrial plants worked to 12 per cent of capacity, millions of unemployed walked the streets, and destitution, poverty, and pain were widespread, Fitzgerald signalled the closure of his own 'Jazz Age': 'It ended two years ago, because the utter confidence which was its essential prop received an enormous jolt, and it didn't take long for the flimsy

structure to settle earthward. . . . It was borrowed time anyhow.'
In the same year, in his remarkable work of instant history *Only Yesterday*, the social recorder Frederick Lewis Allen looked back to see the Twenties as 'a distinct era in American history', its styles and attitudes already past and remote. It was a change quickly written into the novel. In Paris, the cheques had ceased to arrive, and Europe was also moving into economic and political turmoil; those expatriate writers who had remained through the surrealist 'Revolution of the Word' now made what Malcolm Cowley has called an 'exile's return' to the revolution of the world. They came back to an America turned in on itself and its economic and social problems. Progressive values and political passions had not been entirely submerged in the Twenties. The argument for 'proletarian literature' had penetrated from post-revolutionary Russia, and was taken up as early as 1921 by Michael Gold. Radical voices had been sounding in Jewish immigrant fiction, starting with Abraham Cahan's *The Rise of David Levinsky* in 1917, and in the black fiction of the Harlem Renaissance, like Jean Toomer's *Cane* (1923). In 1927 intellectuals found a clear political cause protesting the execution of the anarchists Sacco and Vanzetti. But it was not really until the stock-market frenzy of 1928 was followed by the collapse of a financial system built on over-spending, over-capitalizing, and over-borrowing that the need for a new accounting seemed evident.

Now progressive attitudes renewed themselves, the languages of naturalism, documentary, and muckraking were called back, writers engaged or re-engaged themselves politically, and well-known figures like Sherwood Anderson, Upton Sinclair, Theodore Dreiser, and John Dos Passos took up radical causes or wrote in the rising new radical journals of depression, unemployment, urban despair, rural deprivation. The rhetoric of social identification now became important: 'There is one thing about being a writer,' wrote Anderson, reporting a unionization struggle in a Southern mill town. 'You can go everywhere. . . . I am accepted by working people everywhere as one of themselves and am proud of that fact.' So, while castigating an economic system, one could identify with the 'real' America; while challenging the political order, one could celebrate the nation. A mood of nationalist celebration replaced cosmopolitan distance, taking on an epic note: 'America' was in all the titles, and the desire to embrace the disordered American totality drove writers like Dos Passos and Thomas Wolfe. But this did not end the problem of the writer's obligation. Attachment to the cause of the 'toiling masses', usually no longer toiling, might help generate an epic naturalism, but beyond that was the classic problem of literary 'commitment'—a problem made sharper by the fact that, however much the writer might agonize in bourgeois guilt, the American masses remained remarkably unpoliticized. Clear answers were on offer. Mike Gold, editor of the Communist paper *The New Masses*, which had risen again from the débris of radicalism in 1926, had throughout the Twenties attacked the political 'imbecility' of American writing. Now he urged authors to 'go left', become workers identified with the workers, experience and record and radicalize the proletarian world which provided a writer with 'all the primitive material he needs'. A violent attack by Gold in the *New Republic* in 1930 on the 'genteel' experimentalism of Thornton Wilder's bourgeois and aesthetic fiction struck home. To the critic Edmund Wilson, it represented the start of a new literary mood.

The year 1930 was certainly one for novels of social concern and committed naturalism. Gold's own radical East Side ghetto novel, *Jews Without Money*, appeared; so did Dos Passos's *The 42nd Parallel* (the opening volume of *U.S.A.*), and books with strong, telling, and political titles—Edward Dahlberg's *Bottom Dogs*, Mary Heaton Vorse's *Strike!*. In 1928 the *New Masses* had called for worker–correspondents and author–fighters; writers of working-class background, like Jack Conroy, or from immigrant or black stock, like Gold himself or Richard Wright, now came to notice. Right after the Crash, in November 1929, the *New Masses* sponsored in New York the foundation of a John Reed Club for younger writers, its slogan 'Art Is a Class Weapon'; by 1934 thirty such clubs existed across the nation with a total membership of over 1,200. Not all writers found the Marxist analysis convincing, but the leftward drift was powerful. It also quickly developed its own schisms. In 1934 the John Reed

Clubs sponsored what would be the major intellectual magazine of the decade, *Partisan Review*, edited and largely written by the radical New York Jewish intelligentsia, and intended to challenge debilitating liberalism in writing, re-politicize writers, and engage intellectuals in modern historical argument and above all in the class struggle. Like that of the first American Writers' Congress in 1935, the magazine's position was Stalinist. But by 1937, in the wake of the Moscow Trials, its editors were reacting against the 'totalitarian trend' inherent in the Marxist attitude to culture, questioning the preference for proletarian over modernist writing, and adopting increasingly sophisticated critical theories, recognizing—as William Phillips, one of the editors, later explained—that 'the imagination could not be contained within any orthodoxy'.

The dissolution of the radical synthesis towards a 'new liberalism' was to be a crucial development in American intellectual life. The debates over the Spanish Civil War, the impact of the Moscow Trials, the relative success of Roosevelt's New Deal, and above all the signing of the Nazi–Soviet Pact in 1939 fractured the Marxist standpoint. In a spectacular defection from the Party after the signing of the pact, that great promoter of proletarian writing Granville Hicks noted: 'However much strength and influence the [American] Communist Party has lost remains to be seen, but it is my belief that the events of the last few weeks have largely destroyed its effectiveness.' By the time the Thirties in turn ended in the spectacular collapse of American isolationism following the Japanese attack on Pearl Harbor in 1941, which plunged America into a new world war, most of the writers who had been on the Left during the decade had rescinded their old politics. Turning now against pacificism, they frequently used the documentary skills they had developed in the Depression to report the battlefields—Dos Passos did so in the Pacific, Hemingway and Steinbeck in Europe—in the interests of American democracy in its war against Fascism.

It is sometimes argued that the return to realism and naturalism, and above all the move towards 'proletarian literature', was the essential direction of Thirties American writing. But this is too simple. For one thing, many of the best writers of the

Thirties had begun their careers in the Twenties, and new social emphases did not fully displace their modernism. Hemingway and Fitzgerald indeed changed direction and expressed new social and historical concerns, but did not cease to be aesthetically experimental. And if Faulkner's work in the Thirties grows more despairing, gothic, and historically anxious, the decade also sees his most complex and modernist novels. Dos Passos's remarkable *U.S.A.*, perhaps the decade's key work, employs a latter-day radical expressionism that remarkably links the period's documentary passion with the desire for formal experiment. Many younger writers, certainly, turned to proletarian themes and realistic techniques, and entered the places of poverty, social displacement, and ghetto alienation. They sought immediacy and engagement, a language that assaulted and violated, an account that was also an attitude; but in so doing they often found themselves in a complex quest for new forms. For some, like James T. Farrell, a massive objective documentary was the answer; for others, like Thomas Wolfe, the need was for a comprehensive subjectivity. Some, like John Steinbeck, tried to recover epic myth as a language of commitment. For others, like Djuna Barnes and Nathanael West, the quest for rational and orderly myth was illusory, and what was needed was not epical realism but grotesque surrealism. The Thirties began, for novelists, as a pressing subject-matter—a world of bread-lines and ghettoes, working-class anger, bourgeois self-doubt—that was a challenge to existing ideas of form. But, as the quest for new form became more complex, as the need grew for a new language to deal with the displacement, alienation, and deep unease generated by urban, technological, capitalist American life, a new aesthetic portrait of American fiction developed which would shape the novel not just in the age of the bread-line but in that of wartime economic recovery and subsequent cold war affluence.

2.

At the start of the Thirties, the dominant literary debate was about 'Proletcult', and its great proponent was Michael Gold, who described himself in 1930 as 'the first writer in America to herald the advent of a world proletarian literature as a concomitant to the rise of the world proletariat'. Assuming that modernism was discredited, an irrelevant deposit from the aesthetic, subjectivized, apolitical Twenties, Gold offered, in another article of 1930, his model of 'Proletarian Realism'. Its works should, he said, display not pessimism but revolutionary *élan*. They would deal with working-class life, and real conflicts and sufferings rather than private bourgeois agonies; they would have social themes, and go for swift action, clear form, a direct line; they would express the new poetry of materials and the spirit of the worker moulding his own world. Gold wrote with confidence, for there were a growing number of books that expressed the spirit he sought to define—not least his own *Jews Without Money*, which had come out earlier in this crucial year of 1930.

Like a number of the newer writers, including Waldo Frank and Ludwig Lewisohn, Gold was Jewish and came from recent urban immigrant stock. *Jews Without Money* is his ghetto novel, set among Romanian-Jewish immigrants on New York's Lower East Side around the turn of the century, when the Eastern European influx was at its highest. It may be 'proletarian realism', but its techniques are often fantastic and hallucinatory. And its more obvious place is in the lineage of the developing Jewish-American novel, with its basic theme of the conflict between Old World values and new, between ethnic and religious identity and secular assimilation. Abraham Cahan's *The Rise of David Levinsky*, published in 1917 (the year of the Bolshevik Revolution) can be read as the starting-point of such a line; his classic tale of the Diaspora Jew hungering for the promised land and seeking it in its modern mythical location, America, is a fable of economic success and moral catastrophe. Levinsky leaves the old land, Lithuania, and the *shtetl* life, already doubting his faith and sensing the appeal of the new, hoping for 'marvelous transformations' in America's 'distant, weird world'; arriving in New York with four cents in his pocket, shaving off his beard and his earlocks, he follows the path from rags to riches and becomes doubly a millionaire. The Columbus myth becomes a Jewish rite of passage, a shift from one state of history to another, from a rooted and religious life to a new world of secularism, alienation, complex sexuality; yet Levinsky's sense of 'reality' remains in the old world, and he never succeeds in connecting desire and fulfilment. Cahan's success was not just to record an essential Jewish experience—the move from Old World to New—but to find a striking fictional form and language for dealing with the consequent alienation.

Jews Without Money offers a more political version of this fable. It is the story of the intelligent Jew who stays poor and finds Marx. A highly autobiographical, indeed confessional, work, it is a series of sharp thematic sketches about Gold's own upbringing and coming to consciousness. Gold completed the book in 1928, but it is more a novel of the opening years of the century than a work about the 1930s. It has naturalist themes, picturing the gangsters and prostitutes, the sweatshops, rotting tenements and bedbugs, the newcomers arriving straight from Ellis Island into urban chaos and religious inertia, the political despair and the disappointed dreams going to waste in street violence, political corruption, and Tammany Hall exploitation. The 'unreal city' is a 'jungle' and a 'prison' and defeats all wonder, all desire to make it a 'circus' of joy and pleasure; it is 'a devil's dream, the most urbanized city in the world. It is all geometry angles and stone. It is mythical, a city buried by a volcano.' In the promised land of beginning again the utopian promises fail, and the old communal and traditional life collapses under pressure of greed and selfishness, generated by competitive and individualist principles. In such a city, its wonder corrupted by harsh working conditions, disease, depravity, and sexual distortion, apocalyptic messages are in order. Thus politics must come in to restore the dream and replace the wasted faith. The old religion is tainted, and a new secular one is necessary: the narrator, identifying with the true Jews, the 'Jews without money', becomes a Communist. In most of the book, the method is imagistic, depicting a life suspended between memories of the Old World and the facts of the new one in the 'Land of Hurry Up'; to such scenes political comment provides no more than a rhetorical aside. But in the final lines the writer undergoes his revelation and conversion, to Marxism, the new transcendent religion ('O workers' Revolution, you brought hope to me, a lonely suicidal boy. You are the true Messiah'). Cahan's story of alienation is redeemed; the utopian future is given back in new form.

Gold's committed, angry, and autobiographical naturalism links his book with works like Edward Dahlberg's also very poetic *Bottom Dogs* (1930), the story of Dahlberg's own young life in orphanages and as a wandering hobo in the pre-war years. And it is a tale from the underside—like, again, Jack Conroy's *The Disinherited* (1933), about a young Missouri worker who leaves the coal mines for the auto lines of the boom, and then in the Depression discovers his class allegiance and hopes for a violent upheaval that will apocalyptically renew the city and the American dream. Apocalyptic renewal was truly the decade's great preoccupation, and it turned writers away from the cause of a pure raw realism. But, as *Jews Without Money* (which is far better as a group of sharp vignettes than it is as an act of ideological structuring) suggested, this left writers looking for a new redemptive language appropriate to the times—a theme very exactly realized when, five years after Gold's novel, Henry Roth published *Call It Sleep* (1934), which might almost be read as a subtle commentary on Gold's book and his cause. Like *Jews Without Money*, it is the story of a boy's growing up on New York's Lower East Side amid Eastern European immigrants before the First World War, and it too deals with the collapse of the myth of the American promised land. Roth had Marxist sympathies, and he draws on the techniques of urban naturalism to present the bleak, violent streets, the debased sexuality, the embittered father, the life-giving mother, and the corrupted rabbis that Gold had drawn. But Roth's subject is finally not the loss of a faith nor the need for a secular religion, but the loss of a language and the need for a sign, a new gift of tongues. His book encounters the polyglot destiny of the immigrant and sees in it the need for new creative form. The result is a major novel.

Not surprisingly, the *New Masses* reviewer attacked it: 'It is a pity that so many young writers from the proletariat can make no better use of their working-class experience than as material for introspective and febrile novels,' the reviewer complained.

In fact *Call It Sleep* is a work of complex urban expressionism that bridged the space between social and political naturalism and fictional rediscovery. Roth concentrates on three years of David Schearl's childhood and tells his story from the perspective of his consciousness, that of a child growing up in a 'world that had been created without thought of him'. But this world is eminently a world of speech, of an endless pidgin street-talk which expresses the chaos and fragmentation of the outer world and permits no adequate inner language of desire and awareness. What David seeks is a language of the self that will give him psychic and emotional wholeness in a fragmented world. The book's climax comes when he seeks his gift of tongues by plunging a milk ladle into the electrified crack in the streetcar tracks, hunting a revelation that will defeat the babel of politics and obscenity filling the street world around him. Shocked into unconsciousness, sliding towards sleep as the book ends, he is left in a new silence which has pentecostal promises, because it relates to a new inner awareness, a sense of triumphant acquiescence. And just as David's quest is for a linguistic revelation, so the writer's task is to press through the barrage of discourse that surrounds him with a chaotic multiplicity of messages, towards symbolic form. *Call It Sleep* is in consequence a work of great experimental force. Undoubtedly the best Jewish-American novel of the decade, it also led the way towards the Jewish-American fiction of the 1940s and 1950s.

Roth conducts a quiet formal revolution of the radical Jewish-American novel; Richard Wright was to do much the same for black fiction. Born in rural Mississippi, moving to Chicago on the eve of the Depression, Wright was unprepared, he said, like so many fellow blacks, for the modern city. He was one of a number of black writers to feel encouraged by the Harlem Renaissance movement of the Twenties; another was Zora Neale Hurston, author of *Their Eyes Were Watching God* (1937), a book that has influenced several recent black women writers. Wright, drawn into political protest, entered the Chicago John Reed Club, became its organizer, and joined the Communist Party in 1934. His first book, *Uncle Tom's Children* (1938), five indignant novellas about life in the brutal racist South, goes back to his Mississippi origins. But the encounter with the city was the theme of a documentary novel, *Lawd Today*, he began next. This was finally suppressed because it did not meet party criteria, and was not published until 1965, after Wright's death. The material, however, opened the way to his one major novel, *Native Son* (1940), the story of Bigger Thomas, who grows up in the Chicago slums, kills a white woman, flees, murders again, is tried, defended as a political victim, and executed. The situation resembles that of Dreiser's *An American Tragedy*: Bigger is the murderer as victim, the product, as the lawyer Max argues at his trial, of social forces, and, as James Baldwin was later to say, the book uses the form of 'everybody's protest novel'. Its naturalist credentials are clear: Wright explained later that he wrote it from a scientific standpoint, inventing test-tube situations in which to place Bigger Thomas. Yet the book's remarkable power stems more from Wright's success in making Bigger not so much the sacrificial victim as the figure of modern identityless man. He is a man without essence; his condition is fear, his situation confinement, his reaction violence. He is the outsider, who feels he lives on 'the outside of the world peeping in through a knothole in the fence'. His essential experiences are of flight, capture, and trial; he finally identifies himself as one of 'suffering humanity'. But what we follow is his attempt to realize an existence, discover an ego, create a self. He makes the attempt at first through diabolic action, murder, but also in his endeavour to resist the role of social victim. It is others, and not Bigger himself, who see external forces as the rulers of his existence. For Bigger this is another form of invisibility; his primary need is to become visible to, real to, himself.

The theme in short is existential, and indeed Wright himself pursued that connection by moving to Paris and associating with the French existentialists. His novel *The Outsider* (1953) has not only a Camusian title but a directly philosophical intention. In it Wright displays some unease of tone, but its story of the black rebel hero, Cross Damon, contesting a meaningless world, is clearly an endeavour to make the black into a modern metaphor, the essential type of contemporary man, 'the twentieth century writ large'. Cross Damon is a Bigger Thomas vastly more

conscious of himself. He elects his own invisibility, pretending
to be killed in a subway accident when he is threatened with
blackmail and jail. Reborn without an identity, he is rebelliously
free to invent himself. He too commits murder, and the story
presses to the limits of his demoniac personality, pursuing the
question of moral responsibility in a world of eliminated identities.
The two novels Wright published in his lifetime may start close to
naturalism, and their existential spirit is to some degree contained
and qualified by it. But their essential theme, of a man's will to
move from non-being to being and at the same time to see an
exposed modern emptiness within such self-hunger, was to pass
on to the best black fiction of the 1950s. The spirit of proletarian
realism helped bring such books into being, but quickly that spirit
came to seem too narrow to contain them. Roth and Wright
represent the transliteration of the kind of novel Gold celebrated
into a new fictional possibility, and a decade later Jewish-
American and black fiction had already evolved into central forms
for the expression of American modernity.

3.

But naturalist intentions and the aspiration towards a documentary inclusiveness did mean much to the writers of the
Thirties. That was apparent in the work of James T. Farrell,
another Chicago writer of Marxist sympathies whose subject
was also to be working-class immigrant life. Farrell's background
was Irish Catholic, and he had personal experience of the
Chicago streets, working in shoe stores, cigar stores, and filling
stations before he began, at the University of Chicago, a sketch—
about the wake for a young man who has died suddenly of
drink—which was to become his most famous work, the 'Studs
Lonigan' trilogy. *Young Lonigan* (1932), *The Young Manhood
of Studs Lonigan* (1934), and *Judgment Day* (1935) began from
a small seed, but they grew into a massive construct through what
Farrell later explained in an essay as the 'objective' principles of
naturalist composition: Studs, 'a normal young American of his
time and his class', growing up 'several steps removed from the
slums and dire economic want', was carefully chosen 'not only

as a character for imaginative fiction, but also as a social manifestation'. What he manifests is not so much economic as spiritual poverty, and in this respect the Lonigan books share with the work of Gold, Roth, and many other writers of the period the conviction that the immigrant dream has failed not only through economic depression but through the corrupt and deadening pursuit of material wealth. Farrell's novels are an indictment of the empty culture of Irish Catholic family, community, and religious life, and their main story deals not with the Depression years but what precedes them, until Stud's brutalized life ends with his death in August 1931, at the age of 29.

Studs is a figure at the centre of a large map of sociological and historical insufficiencies, and his story is told against a drab historical backcloth. He sneeringly leaves a school which has scarcely affected him just as Woodrow Wilson, who has promised to keep the nation out of war, is again nominated for President. He enters the jungle of the streets just as war erupts, becomes a drunkard in the lawless era of the Twenties, and dies as the revived radicalism of the Thirties hints at the possibility of change. In every area of his life, home, school, church, and work, cultural enfeeblement exists. Farrell explained that he was opposed to a theory of total environmental determinism, such as Dreiser's work seemed to express. Social causation had, he said, always to be translated into individual motivation, or 'character', so that the reader had a centre in experience with which he might identify. Hence what surrounds Studs is less a pressing body of conditioning and determining forces than a massive and senseless contingency, a cultureless culture invested with no weight or meaning. He lives in a naturalist world because there is nothing better, deeper purposes and intentions in cultural life having all become debased. In the absence of substantial culture, he falls back upon and exploits brutal aggressiveness and physical and sexual prowess. His main qualities in Farrell's mode of characterization are those of movement, desire, and embittered vitality. This characterization makes him the natural centre of a heavily mapped world of events and random detail, to which he responds in primal ways. Studs may be an exemplary social type, but he is also the sensory receiver of Farrell's large documentary ambitions, the reference-point of a vast reportorial task.

Farrell's writing is Depression writing in more than one sense. It is a writing that untangles the crude social ambitions and expectations, and the betrayed historical promises, that have pointed the way to an economic collapse which is also spiritual. It also responds to failing times with a sense of failure, and sees the essential choice in life as between living out an enfeebled social existence in a mis-made world and a self-destructive vitalism. In this enclosed world Studs's is an unconscious and primitive rebellion, and it is inevitable that attention must fall upon the accumulated power of event and experience, on the unremitting expression of the realness of real life as well as its emptiness. As a result, his landscape of raw fact seems curiously style-less; what claim this fiction makes on our attention is through the writer's detailed acquaintance with a milieu. Farrell seemed conscious of this problem when he moved on to a new and yet longer sequence of semi-autobiographical novels devoted to Danny O'Neill, the more intelligent and creative hero of *A World I Never Made* (1936), *No Star Is Lost* (1938), *Father and Son* (1940), *My Days of Anger* (1943), and *The Face Of Time* (1953). These are books of obsessive self-accounting, displaying O'Neill's urgent need to record and report the world he has left behind him. They also suggest that, for Farrell as for many Thirties writers, his main possession was a subject calling endlessly for recording. He made that subject, the brutalized immigrant city, into one of the convincing settings of modern American life. But, because he treated it as subject rather than as form, we turn back to his work now mostly for its documentary rather than creative interest.

If there was James T. Farrell to create, for the Thirties, the brutalized city, there was also Erskine Caldwell, to create the brutalized countryside. A Southerner from Georgia, Caldwell offered the base underside to the Southern Agrarianism that developed as a cultural and literary tendency during the 1930s. *I'll Take My Stand*, a collection of essays expressing a strong social faith in the South's distinctiveness and traditionalism, appeared in 1930. Thereafter a new Southern Renaissance displayed itself during the next years as a whole group of writers, younger than Faulkner, explored with careful formality of style a complex landscape of social and psychic extremity. Novelists like Caroline Gordon (*Alex Maury, Sportsman*, 1934), Allen Tate (*The Fathers*, 1938), and Robert Penn Warren (*Night Rider*, 1939) linked modernist concerns with a sense of an ancient and traditional history whose heritage of blood and pain needed a mannered recording. There is no such formal or social elegance in Caldwell's work; in fact it functions by reversing this image. A radical who had published documentary works on social problems, and some working-class fiction, Caldwell made his reputation with two novels that dealt with sharecropping life in Georgia in a mode close to grotesque comedy. *Tobacco Road* (1932) and *God's Little Acre* (1933) mixed Depression documentary with sensational sexual themes. As Kenneth Burke once said, Caldwell's naturalism comes from the way he 'puts people into complex social situations while making them act with the scant, crude tropisms of an insect'. Social seriousness is present: these are tales of worn-out land, exploited farmers, a culture of deprivation, and Caldwell said his aim was 'describing to the best of my ability the aspirations and despair of the people I wrote about'. But the realistic mode is cut across with the tradition of Southern humour; the life of the poor is treated as a culture of degeneracy, primitivism, and cunning. The realism turns to melodrama. Lust, avarice, and hope—Jeeter Lester's dream in *Tobacco Road* of winning a good tobacco crop from neglected land, Ty Ty Walden's in *God's Little Acre* of finding gold under useless soil—are the main subjects. Caldwell's primitive naturalism became sensationalism, striking less because of its social report than its raw shock value.

The naturalistic reporting of working-class life was only one urgent literary task of the Thirties. Another was realistic exploration of the disorders of the troubled bourgeois world in an age of economic fears and declining certainties. These found their best chronicler in John O'Hara, a novelist of, as Lionel Trilling said, 'exacerbated social awareness', who converted the traditional mode of bourgeois realism into a powerful discourse for Depression times. O'Hara's fiction is built, with an exacting precision, on the patent, material solidity of society—the weight of things, the detailed appurtenances of possession, the symbolic value of goods, the problems of rank, class, wealth, and religion. But, just like Fitzgerald, whom he recognized as a fellow parvenu to whom social advancement offered the true and magical subject of fiction, O'Hara wrote when there was rot at the centre, and when that solidity was no longer solid. His main setting, 'Gibbsville, Pennsylvania' and the surrounding 'Region', was his own background, a territory of exact knowledge where elaborate social demarcations and discriminations prevail. O'Hara catches all this just as its substance collapses under historical pressure. His novels—among the best are *Appointment in Samarra* (1934) and *BUtterfield 8* (1935)—form an essential chronicle of Thirties America, probing the gap between the social and the private self. *Appointment in Samarra* is exemplary: in it Julian English, convinced his social position is secure, fails to respond to the pressure of a changed time in which no one owns the road he travels on, and so encounters tragedy. O'Hara's tragedies come in many ways, but they turn on the perception that individuals both rest in and rebel against their social being, imperilling themselves as a result. Above all, it is sexual desire that threatens social cohesion; O'Hara's typical hero is the respectable reprobate fleeing unsatisfactory monogamy, who then crashes tragically through the ice of social stability. It was a theme that caught exactly at Depression anxiety, though O'Hara was to sustain it onward into his novels of the 1950s and 1960s.

4.

During the Thirties, there was proletarian realism and bourgeois realism, urban realism and rural realism, WASP realism and Dustbowl realism, white realism and black realism. This was a decade when the forms of realism and naturalism once more came to seem the 'natural' or appropriate way to record a changing and troubled society. What is striking in retrospect is that so much of this writing was not, in fact, directly concerned with the experience of the Depression. Both Mike Gold and

Henry Roth, along with Richard Wright and Zora Neale Hurston, wrote mostly of the world of childhood and upbringing, deprivation and heritage. John Dos Passos and James T. Farrell wrote of the first part of the century to give a critical angle on an America that had now reached this pass. The changed preoccupations of the Thirties, the growing politicization of writers, and the decline in formal and aesthetic experiments (now often judged to be bourgeois methods for evading the harder realities), in fact provided a means by which many subordinate or alternative histories of American lives could be written. In retrospect, the fictional direction of the Thirties bears some resemblance to that of the Eighties, when after a period of formal experiment a reckoning of the multifarious, multicultural realities of changed American life needed to be taken in a sobered and uneasy time. The often playful spirit of the Harlem Renaissance of the Twenties gave way to the growing black anger of the Thirties; the exploration of immigrant life as a pathway to the American dream by the Jewish-American novelists of the Twenties, like Lewis Lewisohn or Anzia Yezierska, yielded to the political exposés of Jerome Weidman (*I Can Get It For You Wholesale*, 1937) or Budd Schulberg, whose *What Makes Sammy Run?* (1941) is a remarkable portrait of the pressured Hollywood of the Thirties, where the dreams and nightmares ended up. The Depression and the political awareness it brought caused Americans to look again at their America, and find that it was not only the world of Babbitt and the booboisie, of Midwest innocence and East Coast wealth. If the Twenties saw an aesthetic cosmopolitanization of American writing, the Thirties saw, increasingly, its social cosmopolitanization.

There was one writer who did devote himself to the myths of the Depression itself, and attempted to do so in the light of a serious naturalism systematically concerned with a biological and deterministic account of human nature. This was John Steinbeck, who was born in 1902 in the Salinas Valley of California, the region and state where many of his books were to be set. Steinbeck liked to present himself as a 'real poor kid', though his parents were a flour-mill manager and a teacher, and as a self-taught product of the school of life and biological observation, though he had some formal education at Stanford University. But he had been carpenter, surveyor, department-store clerk, chemist, a clerk in a sugar factory and a ranch hand, and all this went into his writing. He owed a great deal to the earlier, turn-of-the-century tradition of California naturalism— the work of Frank Norris, whose *The Octopus* (1901) and its portrait of land-ownership struggles influenced him, and the nature-fiction of Jack London—and came to share their desire for an explanation of man's primal biological nature. He found his guide and guru in a marine biologist called Edward F. Ricketts, versions of whom, as a sage-like figure explaining the larger operations of human destiny and intention, occur in a number of his novels. Ricketts, with whom Steinbeck was to collaborate, offered him a 'scientific' and neo-biological account of human and animal destiny which was to provide an idealized and transcendent philosophy we can trace within Steinbeck's fiction. For his ambitions were both scientific and prophetic; Steinbeck sought in his novels and stories to explain the corporate or collective biology of human action, to see in it a spiritual intention and a drive toward some ultimate destiny. And from this much of his great popularity stemmed, once he moved from the early exotic writings of the Twenties (his first published novel, *Cup of Gold* (1929), is a ripe historical romance about the buccaneer Sir Henry Morgan) to more familiar and popular subject-matter he found in the life around him.

Steinbeck's subjects were always popular, but he invested them with large mythical concerns. His next two books, *The Pastures of Heaven* (1932) and *To A God Unknown* (1933), follow a collective motion and myth, the 'westering' movement of Americans across the continent from the settled past towards the paradise of the California valleys, where these human wanderers instinctively seek their primitive roots. Increasingly he wanted to show that those roots lay not in individual satisfactions, possession of property, or regard for conventional morality. 'The fascinating thing to me', he wrote in a letter of 1933, 'is the way the group has a soul, a drive, an intent, an end, a method, a reaction and a set of tropisms which in no way resembles the same things possessed by the men who make up the group.' The 'phalanx of human emotions' was now, he said, the essential subject of his fiction. The notion arose for him from biological and to some extent political naturalism, but in his central work it emerged as primitive mysticism. That work is his California novel *Tortilla Flat* (1935), his 'strike' novel *In Dubious Battle* (1936), the powerful novella *Of Mice and Men* (1937), various stories, such as *The Red Pony* (1937), the tales of *Cannery Row* (1945), and above all *The Grapes of Wrath* (1939). This last, a book that for many sums up the Thirties, was his classic tale of 'Okie' migration in the Depression Thirties from the Oklahoma Dust Bowl to the California valleys, a vast novel that follows out that same 'westering motion' and its underlying myth through a world of natural and economic disaster. All these works are sometimes read as social realism, though this is not what they are. 'I never had much ability for nor faith nor belief in realism,' Steinbeck explained. 'It is just a form of fantasy as nearly as I can figure.' His concern, he said, was with the 'streams in man more profound and dark and strong than the libido of Freud', the biological and sociological determinants of being, the emotions below consciousness or control, which made life into a collective mystery involving primitive and pagan powers.

Steinbeck therefore also belongs to the line of American transcendentalism—the Emersonian idealism of those who saw a unified soul in man and nature, and who sought that soul's deliverance in a new America seen as paradisial Eden, where life returns to innocence and to its primal sources. Steinbeck's are novels of human participation in society and nature; moral crimes occur when human needs are blocked by institutions. Natural comradeship is the theme of his first successful novel, *Tortilla Flat*. Based on the myth of the chivalric comradeship of the Arthurian round table, it lushly celebrates the spontaneous, moneyless, propertyless lives of the Paisanos (Mexican-Americans) of Monterey. *Of Mice and Men* is a tragedy about the collapse of just such another 'natural' community, brought about when Lennie, the idiot 'unfinished child', commits an 'innocent' act of murder. *In Dubious Battle* (1936) takes its title and myth from Milton. The 'dubious battle' is the conflict between capitalism and communism in the heavenly California valleys, during a strike among fruit-pickers in the Torgas Valley. This novel contains some of the bitter social indignation of Norris's *The Octopus*, with which it can be interestingly compared. It also shares something of Norris's transcendental detachment, his belief that human suffering is part of a greater 'romance'. Steinbeck's political sympathies are clearly with the radicals, but they too are attempting to impose a system on nature: 'I don't believe in the cause, but I believe in men,' says Steinbeck's sagacious Doc Burton, expressing the spirit of the book.

And this, too, is the spirit of *The Grapes of Wrath*, the book Steinbeck wrote after travelling westward with Okie migrants from Dust Bowl and foreclosure by the desperate banks. A work expressing social despair and political indignation at the way failure and decay breed a harvest of wrath, it is in fact one of the most optimistic of modern American novels—an epic narrative mural, its figures expressionistic and larger than life, the momentum mythical, and the foundation a biological evolutionism expressing Steinbeck's theories of instinctive collective existence. Two myths govern the book. One is that of hopeful American westering, seen as the journey from bondage to the promised land; the other is of heroic evolution, mankind's vital journey from solitude to selfhood in community. The Joad family's progress is from the aridity of the Oklahoma Dust Bowl, which is caused as much by the bank as by drought and the tractor, to the Californian Eden where, despite the Hoovervilles and social opposition, old signs of promise remain, not least in the Joads' own motion from nuclear family to participation in a vaster 'we'. At times, these two journeys seem to conflict or contradict. Sometimes this motion appears a rational, moral voyage towards a utopian form of human collectivity; sometimes it is a blind, amoral, instinctive process revealing not individual will and choice but an animal-like natural endurance. Sometimes Steinbeck is the political writer, celebrating in large rhetorical sweeps the need for human beings to transcend selfishness, form the human family, become one; at other times he becomes the observant scientist, indifferently watching the biologically blind actions of living systems pursuing survival. So the key scene, in which the maternal and redemptive girl Rose of Sharon suckles the starving man after she has lost her own child, may be read as symbolic of political love and action, or (as Steinbeck himself stressed in a letter) of pure biological survival, life ensuring its own continuity.

As the political ferment of the Thirties died, it was the latter vein, of mythic naturalism, that Steinbeck carried on into the work for which he was awarded the Nobel Prize for Literature in 1962. His late epic novel *East of Eden* (1952) reverts to his key theme, of the American West as Eden, the virgin land where the classic dreams and struggles of man are re-experienced. The central character, Adam Trask, travels west from Connecticut to the Salinas Valley, where his sons repeat the Biblical Cain and Abel conflict that brings death into nature. By now Steinbeck's politics had changed, and his theme points not towards the making of an ideal human collective but to ideas of Jeffersonian independence cursed by mankind's fallen nature. By now some of his more obvious weaknesses had grown more apparent. There is his sentimentalism, which cannot now quite capture the complexity of the evil he senses within human nature, and his devotion to the natural world, which means that he has little grasp of the process of industrialism. Steinbeck had always strained toward pure wonder, mythic scale, and grandeur, the vast process rather than the historical fact. Yet beyond that are his strengths: the signs remain of that powerful transcendental hope that had made *The Grapes of Wrath* not an evanescent novel of social protest but a genuine modern epic driving onwards towards an Emersonian oneness with the world.

Steinbeck shows us that an epic transcendentalism was often there to counterbalance the bitter social critiques spawned by the Depression conditions of an uneasy and political decade. The times did not still the epic desires so strong in American fiction, as is clear from the novels of Thomas Wolfe. For Wolfe, though, the great transcendental epic was to be a Whitman-like Story of Myself. Wolfe came from a Scots-American background and the Appalachian South; he was born in 1900, the son of a stone-cutter in Asheville, North Carolina. This was to be the 'Altamont' and 'Libya Hill' of his vast and autobiographical novels when he grew up to become, as he always meant to, a

Great Writer. His novels record the quest that this involved—
first study at the University of North Carolina, then to Harvard
to take writing classes, then experience of the great city of New
York, then onward to the troubled and dangerous Europe of
the interwar years. For Wolfe, the writer was always the modern
lyrical traveller, ever moving onward and catching up as he
went the spirit of the times, the place, the people. It was his aim
and destiny to write, he said, of 'night and darkness in America,
and the faces of sleepers in ten thousand towns; and of the tides
of sleep and how the rivers flowed forever in the darkness . . . I
wrote about death and sleep, and of that enfabled rock of life we
call the city.' From the flow of life came the flow of his novels,
epics of self-discovery which were spread across the contemporary
landscape of boom and slump, city and nature, flux and force.
The aim, he said, was to make this world 'enfabled', turning life's
ebb and flow into a myth at the centre of which was the author's
perceiving, feeling, romantic self. Wolfe may not have been a
great writer; his work is far too prolix. But he was certainly a
Great Writer, an author who placed himself at the centre of the
most ambitious literary dreams. 'The writer's task', he noted, 'is
rather for us to write "why?" across the scroll of our being, and
there to answer the question we have raised.' The question, and
indeed the answer, may have been innocent, but the project was
marvellously successful. Wolfe became one of the most celebrated
and admired writers of the Thirties before his sudden early death
from a brain infection following pneumonia in 1938.

Wolfe's fiction was always a fiction of its author's own being
and becoming. He established the theme in his celebrated first
novel *Look Homeward, Angel*, which came out in 1929, just six
days before the Wall Street Crash that changed his and everyone
else's world. Like Fitzgerald's *This Side of Paradise*, it was a
work of youthful autobiography, only partly distanced and dis-
guised. He explained in the preface: 'All serious work is autobiographical . . . The book was written in simpleness and
nakedness of soul . . . It is a book made out of my life, and
represents my vision of my life to my twentieth year.' Wolfe
appears as Eugene Gant, and his story is taken onward in a
second volume, *Of Time and the River*, published in 1935. Like

many heroes of the Teens and Twenties, Gant is an artist growing up in a sterile and provincial, though also a deep rooted, world, this time in the American South. His task is to break free and sail the deeper waters of experience, to encounter new places, make new discoveries, explore the Northern cities and the greater world further on. By virtue of his sensitivity and special powers, such an artist must remain isolated, his appetites must be 'gargantuan', and he must try to register all that can be known, felt, and suffered. The hero of life is the artist himself; art is the compact made between the hungering artist and 'life'. As Wolfe put it in a letter: 'There are few heroic lives; about the only one I know a great deal about is my own. This is boastful, perhaps, but as it is true, I see no cause to deny it.'

Throughout the large body of writing he was to produce, Wolfe never did deny it. His books were to become a vast outpouring of personal experience, which he found difficult to organize into publishable form. Maxwell Perkins, the editor at Scribner's who stayed home while his famous authors, including Fitzgerald and Hemingway, took on life and Europe, virtually co-authored most of his novels. He completed and shaped the writing process, taking the great life record and editing it into manageable books. Meanwhile Wolfe attacked and recorded the experience, taking on happiness and unhappiness, love and the confusions of the city, action and reverie, and drawing from them those large meanings of which Eugene Gant becomes the gargantuan focus:

It seemed to him that all this incredible miracle of his own life and fate had ordered all these accidental facts into coherent and related meanings. He felt that everything—the powerful movement of the train, the infinite mystery and lonely wildness of the earth, the feeling of luxury, abundance and unlimited wealth that was stimulated by the rich furnishings of the Pullman, and the general air of affluence of these prosperous men—belonged to him, had come out of his own life, and were ready to serve him at his own behest and command.

With such feelings, of course, any experience will serve both for self-enlargement and as fictional material; even things not directly experienced by Gant may be freely added to enlarge the myth ('At just this moment the train had entered the State of Virginia, although, of course, none of the men who sat there talking knew that'). It is the sign of bad writing that it is always enlarging itself into significance through rhetoric; Wolfe's gift was to find a logic to justify the extravagance. The Gant novels are the story of just this sort of acquisitiveness: about Gant's sensory, emotional, and imaginative upbringing, about the 'cyclic curve of a family's life—genesis, union, decay, and dissolution' which surrounds him, about the growing sense of isolation from others, and about the sterility and paralysis that drive the artist ever onward.

Look Homeward, Angel, subtitled 'A Story of a Buried Life', explores the life of the family and of the Southern town that provides Gant with a rooted world, offering him both the ancestral, natural setting he needs and the prison from which, as an artist, he must escape. Archetypal conflicts of this kind—stasis and motion, web and rock—fed the Wolfean myth, further enlarged in *Of Time and the River*, which takes Gant to the Northern world of change and cosmopolitanism, to Boston, New York City, Oxford, France. The city is seen as a place of wonder, confusion, and contingencies, but is also 'life' in its fullest form; Gant's quest is to reach 'the city of myself, the continent of my soul'. The novels are novels of search—the search, Wolfe said, for a father, an organizing principle, an idea of art. This theme becomes manifest when in the city Gant begins a love affair with an older woman who offers to shape his life. This is the key to his endless pursuit of something that will turn chance experience into transcendence, transform pure time into form. The problem is that of the modern artist; life starts in tradition, in the 'realism' of home life, but cannot be contained there, for, as the artist in man grows, so must the world he experiences. So Wolfe starts in the traditional novel of community, the world in which men have ancestors, live densely in families, and take the past as the guide to the present; he moves onward into the modern novel of naked quest, for self-exposure within a disorderly urban world that yields up endless experience which he cannot quite make into knowledge. Emotionally and technically, Wolfe sets himself the task of fusing the novel of community and the existential fiction. His books become the answer, their danger being that frequently the space in between is filled with a hungry selfhood expressed as a tireless rhetoric of wanting and desire—a rhetoric sometimes splendid, sometimes uneasily loaded with empty resonances and vague, hyper-literary echoes.

The two Gant novels made Wolfe famous. Now his problem was what should follow. Like Farrell, he went back to the beginnings, inventing a new surrogate self, George Webber, his history very close to Gant's, who however becomes rich and famous. In *The Web and the Rock* (1939), we find him in the middle of the love affair with the older woman, but this collapses as he discovers the corruptions of the artistic life they live. He moves on to larger historical corruptions in Germany; in *You Can't Go Home Again* (1940), he does go home again, returning to a Depression America of despair, failure, and 'the ruin of the human conscience'. None the less he finds a new social hope that the nation will lead the way from decadence to fresh humanity. From pain, corruption, decadence, and solitude, innocence can be recovered, epic hope re-won. These books differ somewhat from the earlier sequence, not just because, posthumously, they were cut and put together by a different editor, Edward C. Aswell, with a different view of Wolfe's intentions. Wolfe himself emphasized the difference. It was partly derived from the longer distance taken up from his North Carolina past and a deepened sense of historical change, partly from a stronger political vision, partly by his desire to give more symbolic or mythic weight to autobiographical material, so producing a much more complex time-scheme. In some ways more documentary, they are also more 'modernist', in that the juxtaposition of elements—past life and present, large symbolic entities like the web (of traditional society) and the rock (of the city)—is made far more oblique. For earlier and often clumsy narrative techniques, Wolfe substitutes far more complex techniques. The logic of memory alters, the tonalities of symbolism are stronger, and there is a greater satiric and parodic distance from his material. However the autobiographical element firmly persists—these novels are epics of self, life, and America, three vast enterprises—and so does Wolfe's very American hunger for an affirmative, transcendental confession born of his claim to have passed through crucifying experience, which could make all things epical. He writes of the defeat of the Depression, the world dominance of satanic greed, but, given his instinct for abstract rhetoric, there was little doubt what his discovery would be, a grand prophecy: 'I believe that we are lost here in America, but I believe we shall be found.' Art and confession lead to prophetic wisdom, a pure vision of truth. And the ultimate aim becomes to produce the bookless book that would see and say everything anew.

5.

Wolfe was not the only writer of the Thirties with ambitions to transcend the book:

This then? This is not a book. This is libel, slander, defamation of character. This is not a book, in the ordinary sense of the word. No, this is a prolonged insult, a gob of spit in the face of Art, a kick in the pants to God, Man, Destiny, Time, Love, Beauty . . . what you will. I am going to sing for you, a little off key perhaps, but I will sing. I will sing while you croak, I will dance over your dirty corpse.

So began *Tropic of Cancer* (Paris, 1934; New York, 1961), the first of the 'Tropics' sequence of Henry Miller, a writer who in many ways aimed to reverse or affront all the tendencies and values of the decade. In a time when the expatriates came home, he wrote in expatriate Paris, and his books were printed there, not to be published in the USA until the 1960s, excluded not because of their avant-garde content but because of their sexual explicitness, violent eroticism, and apparent perversity. Miller's refusal to write a 'book' was a deliberate assault on all established concepts of art, and above all to the notion of literary responsibility and social allegiance. Miller is a crucial reminder that the novel of radical extremity took other than directly social form in the Thirties; he is rightly seen now as a forerunner of post-war experimentalism and post-modernism. The Thirties notes are present: a strong naturalist content, especially in the evocation of his immigrant childhood and life as an urban rogue in Brooklyn; a large transcendental intention, very American, though based on a grand dissent and on Taoism, surrealism, and European anarchist as well as American philosophies; the need for the book that does more than a book can, confessing, prophesying, transforming and touching life's 'reality' directly. However, conventional politics, progressive and optimistic views of history, and celebration of America were not for Miller. The burdens American writers were taking up Miller hoped to leave behind when, in 1930, penniless, he moved not to atelier but to *clochard* Paris and made his own distinctive contribution to the new surrealist arts of outrage and atrocity.

Miller's novels were to be Thirties anti-novels—even though, as Leslie Fiedler once said, they are genuine Depression novels too, written out of a sense of economic chaos, historical lesion, and political pain. At the same time they react against all the conventional and responsible attitudes and judgements—liberal humanism and bourgeois guilt, political radicalism or utopian expectation. It is easy to glimpse in Miller's writing the proletarian novelist he might have been, but refuses to be. He was born in Brownsville, Brooklyn, New York, son of a tailor of German immigrant stock, and spoke German himself until he went to school. He grew up the street-wise city boy in the ghetto, in a world of deprivation and excitement, grossness and possibility, where violence and sensitivity, sexual adventure and romantic literariness, were always in combat. Miller had radical attitudes, admired Jack London and Emma Goldman, and was attracted to theosophy and anarchism. He took up, much as Steinbeck had, the endless round of menial odd jobs and rapid hirings and firings that now seemed required for any literary career. He was variously a clerk, an employee in his father's tailoring shop, a ranch hand in California, a garbage collector, bellhop, statistician, editor, and through a trick, personnel manager of the messenger service at Western Union, where he himself now wildly hired and fired, in fury against 'the whole system of American labor, which is rotten at both ends'. He hated the place he was born in, and everything his parents endorsed or approved; an assiduous reader, he found that books inflamed him to further revolt. He turned to manual labour and vagabondage, resolving to reject books and make a living with his hands, but felt ceaselessly suspect, betrayed by his language and his ideas. 'I had no principles, no loyalty, no code whatsoever. . . . I usually repaid kindness with insult and injury. I was insolent, arrogant, intolerant, violently prejudiced, relentlessly obstinate,' he explained later in *The Time of the Assassins* (1956), a study of his literary hero Rimbaud which is even more a study of another literary hero, the author himself.

This autobiographical history was to be recorded in his second 'Tropic' book, *Black Spring* (Paris, 1936; New York, 1963) and yet more in the third, *Tropic of Capricorn* (Paris, 1939; New York, 1962), then again in his later series *The Rosy Crucifixion* (made up of *Sexus*, 1945; *Plexus*, 1949; and *Nexus*, 1960), written when some partial reconciliation with his homeland had occurred and his desire to outrage had softened. But Miller's initial tale was one of dissent, severance, and withdrawal from a home he disliked, a New York he detested, an America with whose culture and citizens he felt nothing in common, a capitalism he was happy to undermine with a rancorous sexual energy. In 1924, abandoning his job with Western Union to become at last a writer, Miller felt confirmed in his view of himself as the one true artist, the dispossessed genius cast aside by all—the gangster genius of the dissenting, romantic-anarchic tradition he would always celebrate, of those who 'lived like scarecrows, amid the abundant riches of our culture'. The artist had to be the eye outside, the outsider and undersider, and his task was self-ejection: 'All my life I have felt a great kinship with the madman and the criminal . . .,' he observes in his 'Brooklyn Bridge' essay in *The Cosmological Eye* (1945). 'To me the city is crime personified. I feel at home.' If social indignation was strong, his attitude excluded a direct political solution, and it led to no humanistic message: 'Today I am proud to say I am *inhuman*,' he would write in *Tropic of Cancer*, 'that I belong not to men and governments, that I have nothing to do with creeds and principles.' Nor was he prepared to be a writer of American celebration. He saw America as the 'air-conditioned nightmare', a 'huge cesspool', the heartland of modern sterility, and himself as the writer totally deracinated—as he put it in *The Cosmological Eye*, he was not an American but a 'cosmological' writer. This all logically led to expatriation, and expatriation led to *Tropic of Cancer*, his first, most affronting, and still surely best book.

Tropic of Cancer is the story, more fictionalized than it looks, of Miller's poverty-stricken life as an amoral genius in Paris, where he found other writers of sexual and radical exploration, especially Anaïs Nin. Paris is satisfying above all because it is not America: 'America three thousand miles away,' he cries, 'I never want to see it again.' Paris, though, while itself eaten away with cancer and excremental flow, permits the new art which is not art, and 'One can live in Paris—I discovered that!—on just grief and anguish.' Behind the book are many Thirties ideas: of modern historical debasement and sterility, the waste land and the dead city confirmed by economic apocalypse; of the reality of the obscene; of the need for a subjective anarchistic surrealism that works towards self-liberation, in terms of a new psycho-history that is built on Groddeck and Rank, and encapsulated in the image of the double womb—the womb one regresses into, avoiding rebirth; the world as womb, permitting a rebirth of consciousness. This surrealistic sexual historiography has much of the occult in it. The prevailing sense of universal corruption is necessary for the enterprise. Culture—especially American culture—has broken down, the ecstatic man has disappeared, 'The world is pooped out.' This apocalyptic world, 'a world used up and polished like a leper's skull', calls for an obscene resurrection, a mystery recreated around the complex psychic mystery of the vaginal hole: 'If anyone knew what it meant to read the riddle of that thing which today is called a "crack" or a "hole", if anyone had the least feeling of mystery about the phenomena which are labelled "obscene", this world would crack asunder. . . . If there is only a gaping wound left then it must gush forth though it produce nothing but toads and bats and homunculi.' In fact what gushes out is not only a confessional cry hunting its way towards prophecy, but a wild vision, like a surrealist painting, in which the flow from the womb and the flow from the city alike pour out images of sex and death, sterility and birth, excrement and flowers.

Paris was more for Miller than a setting for poverty-stricken expatriation, an alternative city for his rebellion, a place of sexual freedom and surreal fantasies. It provided an unexpected rootedness, 'a soil so saturated with the past that however far back the human mind roams one can never detach it from its human background,' to contrast with the American void. It also gave him much from its own dominant experimental movement, surrealism. In *Tropic of Capricorn*, Miller, trapped in the *fourmillante cité* of dead souls, New York, recognizes himself as 'perhaps the unique Dadaist in America, and I didn't know it.' His enterprise, like the surrealist one, went beyond literature into post-literature, beyond art into outrage, beyond reason into the flooded unconscious, beyond form into an apocalyptic randomness, a second-order chaos that was to echo the chaos of the existing and open to the chaos of the new, transformed world. His prose becomes passionate, visionary, often incoherent, always comic, drawing on bawdy and invective both for outrage and authenticity. Miller's books are sometimes read as frank sexual realism. In fact they are books of the grotesque, and the writing seeks often to follow the chaotic flow of consciousness ('chaos is the score upon which reality is written'), which is made occult by the violations the 'I's of his books can score against the cancered environment. A central iconography is of sex, death, excrement, and resurrection, with sex portrayed as a destructive act, a violation of this particular regressive female womb, in the interest of the visionary recovery of the male self. The condition of rebirth—or of rebirths, for Miller is reborn rather more frequently than the surrounding environment might suggest is possible—is of course the persisting sterility and corruption.

Tropic of Cancer ends, like most of Miller's books, with a visionary recovery, even raising the possibility of a return to America. *Black Spring*, a set of apocalyptic scenes reaching back into his American past, attempts more elaborate prose experiments. *Tropic of Capricorn* then reaches even further into his American past, starting from the existential premise that 'Once you have given up the ghost, everything follows with dead certainty, even in the midst of chaos.' The book begins in a mixture of cunning acquiescence in and rage with the American system ('in the bottom of my heart there was murder: I wanted to see America destroyed, razed from top to bottom . . .') and is dominated by the sexual imagery of 'The Ovarian Trolley'—the diseased ovaries of Hymie's wife, the vaginal wound that spawns the paradoxes of 'The Land of Fuck', the land of life and of death, of the womb as corruption and resurrection. Beginning in social rage, Miller gradually learns to look on everything that is happening around him in America as if he were a spectator from another planet, picking up a cabbage leaf from the gutter to hold it in his hand and see it as its own universe, finding the city insane and himself a great witnessing eye above the world, a man shedding his skin in a succession of layers. The structure of the telling is loose, disorderly, associative; the aim is clear—the creation of a new life, where 'Equilibrium is no longer the goal—the scales must be destroyed.' Capricorn, 'renaissance in death', can now balance Cancer, 'the extreme point of realization along the wrong path'. And life becomes a hairline walk between the two.

The energy and obscene vitality of Miller's early novels are sustained through their power of apocalyptic fantasy; in them the underdog becomes exploiter-redeemer because he has nothing to lose and everything to gain. With the war, Miller returned to the States, assaulting it in *The Air-Conditioned Nightmare*, a record of his travels round the continent. He finally settled, in 1944, at Big Sur in California, where he wrote extensively. As his earlier books were no longer banned in the States, and were now being republished there, he became a guru of the new radicalism, the Beat Generation, the voice of American romantic anarchism. *The Rosy Crucifixion*, re-covering the early ground from a more speculative point of view, is largely a text of visionary celebrations. Miller came to be seen as the type of post-Marcusean man, detached from the conservatism of the maternal womb, free to enjoy bodily and spiritual consciousness. As such, his work deeply influenced many writers of the late Fifties and Sixties, reopening the path of visionary surrealism. This was one Miller, but another is the view of George Orwell's early essay on him, 'Inside the Whale' (1940). Orwell saw Miller as the typical writer of the collapse of the Thirties—the new quietist, the writer in a dead and corrupted world, enduring and recording the world process without political solutions, a 'completely negative, unconstructive, amoral writer', a 'Whitman among the corpses'. Both views of Miller are enlightening. He was a potential optimist, his mysticism and metaphysics finally pointing the way back to American transcendentalism. But in his notable early work the tension between nihilism and self-discovering vitalism is the key, and it is there that he creates both a remarkable obscene comedy of despair and a striking surrealist form.

Miller was not the only American writer of the Thirties to look at European surrealism for a way to write the times. So did Djuna Barnes, another expatriate, in *Nightwood* (1936), a complex, dense fantasy-novel of psycho-pathological disturbance and tragic horror. So did Anaïs Nin, the author of *House of Incest* (1936) and much erotica, a recording, she said, of 'my thousand years of womanhood'. And so did Nathanael West, whose apparently eccentric work proves now to belong firmly in the tradition of American comic grotesquerie, and who shared with Miller a vision of a world of total inhumanity hovering between dream and nightmare, and ever on the edge of apocalypse. Born Nathan Weinstein, the son of Jewish immigrants, in New York in 1903, he went to Brown University, acquired a talent for dandified imposture, and took the name West on moving to Paris in the late Twenties. His was a brief expatriation, but it confirmed his avant-garde disposition and his interest in surrealism—though a part of his comic-satirical talent undoubtedly owes much to his friendship with the American humorist S. J. Perelman. In Paris West worked on *The Dream Life of Balso Snell*, a parodic text published there in 1931. It is a surreal comedy about an American poet innocent who wanders into the womb-world of the Trojan horse through the posterior opening, and finds it 'inhabited solely by writers in search of an audience'. This opens the (rear) door to pastiche and parody of many literary styles, a generalized mockery of art that dislodges past forms and even recent modernism, including the work of Joyce. It is a creative writer's notebook, a striking act of apprenticeship. West was always to be an idiosyncratic writer, with some obvious limitations: his desire to mock, undercut, make art into a kind of comic strip with puppet-like agents, often looks like bad writing, and at times, as in parts of *Balso Snell*, it is. Yet exactly those qualities, which displace prior artistic conventions and ideas of art's humanism, were to prove his real resource, as his work developed through three more novels—*Miss Lonelyhearts* (1933), *A Cool Million* (1934), and *The Day of the Locust* (1939)—before it was cut off by his sudden death in a car accident in 1940.

It is with *Miss Lonelyhearts* that West achieves a coherent vision, a lasting tone, founded on a perception of the pain and anguish underlying the myths of American society. *Miss Lonelyhearts* is a black farce about a newspaperman who actually (and disastrously) tries to respond to the sufferings displayed in the letters he receives from readers of his agony column. But grotesquerie is not just a condition displayed by the sufferers; it is also the dominant fictional device. West dissolves any direct concept of character, turning all his agents, including Miss Lonelyhearts, into rhetorical figures or objects, comic automata whom we see through the jerks of their flesh, the independent, broken life of their bodies, which come to seem masterpieces of bad design. Yet this too becomes a basis for pain and pathos, for the human figure itself is seen as inadequate for the suffering it is invited to bear. Meaningful being is divided off from the absurd actions of the body and the impulses of the will; hence his characters live in a state of semi-crazed illusion, a collective dream of desire which readily tips into violence. Of all this Miss Lonelyhearts, the sensitive man, is the focus, becoming a maddened and inadequate Christ, unable to offer any true redemption to this sad and distorted world. Against his failed Christ is set the Antichrist, the witty, indifferent, predatory editor Shrike, who mocks the hero into attempting the 'miracle' of bringing love to one of the surrounding victims, the crippled Doyle—an attempt that leads to Doyle's useless and absurd death. The book offers a soft centre and a hard face. Throughout pathos is both created and taken away, generating a black comic tone that resembles some of Twain's late work, and that some of the black humorists of the Sixties were to echo. West's theme is clearly human yearning, as much in its grotesquerie as its pathos— a natural enough theme, he implied, for a society where dreams of success and desire were prevalent, yet emerged in distorted and freakish forms, above all in the world of Depression and urban deprivation.

The sense of historical pain and political disaster implicit in *Miss Lonelyhearts* becomes the clear theme of his next book, *A Cool Million*. A satire on the lore of the American dream and the Horatio Alger success myth of rags to riches, its 'hero' is a classic fictional innocent, Lemuel Pitkin, the American good boy who never loiters on his way home from school. Parodically told in a variety of mock styles, the book reverses the ancient American-success plot, substituting misfortune for fortune. His home foreclosed upon by a wicked squire, who wants to sell it to an interior decorator, Lemuel seeks the good offices of 'Shagpoke' Whipple, former President of the United States and president now of the Rat River National Bank, who explains that, since he is poor, honest, and born on a farm, this applicant cannot but succeed. But Lemuel is then quickly robbed, imprisoned, and has his teeth taken out—the first of a series of dismemberments as he tries to pursue his innocent fortune in the land of the great American dream. He loses an eye, a thumb, his scalp, a leg, and is finally shot at a political rally. 'Through his martyrdom the National Revolutionary Party triumphed,' Whipple announces, 'and by that triumph this country was delivered from sophistication, Marxism and International Capitalism. Through the National Revolution its people were purged of alien diseases and America became again American.' The all-American boy thus wins his final apotheosis. A satire on nativist politics and myths, the book depends on a fictional energy where violence, dismemberment, and distortion are, again, not only the subject but the artistic method: all the harshness and abstraction of satire is drawn upon. West's most political book, *A Cool Million* penetrates the distortions of society, the process by which dream becomes corruption, exploitation, and violation of innocence, myths become misleading legends. The theme leads naturally to West's next novel, about the great American dream-factory, Hollywood.

The Day of the Locust is West's finest book, inevitably compared with Fitzgerald's *The Last Tycoon*, since the two Hollywood

novels were written about the same time. and from similar
experiences of working as a screenwriter. Fitzgerald's book,
however, is primarily about the studio world, West's about the
frenzied and bitter dreamers who surround it—the crowds that
pour into this city of American possibilities, fantasies, myths,
and religions, all expressed in their most extreme and artificial
form. Towards Hollywood come the distorted, strange creatures
of a dislocated American life, themselves fantasists. Their overwhelming boredom, as they grow gradually 'tired of sunshine
and oranges', moves towards violent frustration, with themselves as well as with the illusory world about them. They are
unsatisfied dreamers in the land of false dreams, hungry for
ever more sensation and emotional release, bored and repressed
by poverty, lovelessness, anger, or disability. Like Sherwood
Anderson's grotesques, they feel denied and held down by
repression, but they are far more violent, sterile, and extreme,
with their 'drained-out feeble bodies and their wild disordered
minds'. *The Day of the Locust* thus begins at the fantasy's heart,
on the studio sets with their illusions and their stars, but it
quickly moves out into the equally fantastic world of Los Angeles
beyond—a world of sensations and sports, cults and sects, clowns
and circuses, excesses and extras, narcissistic promises and
flaunted life-styles. It is fed by a daily news-diet of 'lynchings,
murder, sex crimes, explosions, wrecks, love nests, fires, miracles,
revolutions, wars', all of them somewhere between actuality and
sensational dream. Its citizens are both lost and bizarre; Abe
Kusich is a pugnacious dwarf, Homer Simpson has a murderous
body, like a 'poorly made automaton'. The sex symbol Fay
Greener offers an ambiguous sexual invitation which is not to
pleasure but to struggle, 'hard and sharp, closer to murder than
to love', while her father Harry is a 'bedraggled Harlequin'
whose clowning is a pathetic attempt to win sympathy. All are
creatures of caricature, but West is less interested in portraying
sympathetic figures or inner consciousness than in capturing the
spirit of collective Hollywood and California themselves, the
land of unsatisfied dreamers. He portrays wild collective action,
the nervous and instinctive behaviour of a world where life is
both a necessary yet a meaningless performance, and where

everyone under the California sun is seeking sensations and living fantasies that grow daily ever more extreme.

At the centre of it all West puts the figure of the artist, Tod Hackett (the violent associations of his name are clearly intended), who assumes the task of trying to depict such a world. A set designer with artistic ambitions, Tod wants to paint an apocalyptic modern canvas called 'The Burning of Los Angeles', about the world of frustrated desire around him that is waiting to be galvanized into existence. Tod wants to portray the absurdity of the crowd, but also to 'paint their fury with respect, appreciating its awful, anarchic power and aware that they had it in them to destroy civilization'. Finally, at a picture premiere, the mob breaks loose, and begins rioting, looting and burning. The apocalypse has come, and Tod, though hurt, is able to finish his painting—an elaborate, surreal 'Guernica', depicting both the enraged mob trying to purify their land, and the artist himself, present but apart. We can take this as a clear commentary on West's own attitude and methods. Tod's expressionistic cartoon art has its equivalent in West's own caricature, his short-takes technique, his fictional use of cartoon animation. Like Tod he is drawn into pathetic sympathy with the situation but also stands apart; though he shares the contemporary sadness, he also has the satirist's satirical delight. *The Day of the Locust* is thus a comic-surreal canvas with dreamlike qualities and filled with apocalyptic images—the cock-fight, the dead horse in the swimming pool, the riot that burns the dream landscape and ends the book. In fact this is a basic work of American black humour, a Gothic comedy of a world that, driven to frenzy by extreme desires, seeks solace in absurd and apocalyptic dreams. West's tragi-comic method would pass on into the post-war fictional tradition, when the sense of extremity grew yet stronger; but it reminds us that the fiction of the Thirties was itself by no means all realism, naturalism, and reportage. Like Hollywood, the great American dream-factory itself, it encompassed an ever wider variety of myths, dreams and nightmares, forms and genres, which expanded, complicated and criticized the novel's portrayal of American life and took it beyond the so often hopeful modernism of the Twenties.

6

Liberal and Existential Imaginations: The 1940s and 1950s

Guiltlessness. Our fat Fifties cars, how we loved them, revved them: no thought of pollution. Exhaust smoke, cigarette smoke, factory smoke, all romantic. Romance of consumption at its height. Shopping for baby food in the gaudy trash of the supermarkets. Purchasing power: young, newly powerful, born to consume. To procreate greedily. A smug conviction that the world was doomed. Beyond the sparkling horizon, an absolute enemy. Above us, bombs whose flash would fill the scene like a cup to overflowing.

John Updike, 'When Everyone Was Pregnant', in
Museums and Women (1973)

He asked himself a question I still would like answered, namely, 'How should a good man live; what ought he to do?'

Saul Bellow, *Dangling Man* (1944)

1.

WHEN the Japanese attacked the United States at Pearl Harbor in December 1941, they did not simply precipitate America into its second world war of the century. They also transformed its economy, redirected its national purpose, and set it on its role as the great post-war superpower. The Depression era ended as military spending boosted the national economy, and the United States emerged from the war as a nation of growing material affluence. The war united Americans against the totalitarian cause, and the left-wing and Marxist attitudes of the 1930s died along with the social causes that had produced them. The United States emerged in 1945 as the war's one outright victor: it was the nation that had initiated the nuclear age, when it dropped atomic weapons on Hiroshima and Nagasaki, and it now had to assume a world role in the tense era to follow. There were, as even the writers and intellectuals conceded, many things to value in the new post-war America, as in a short time real incomes doubled, the material rewards of a mass consumer society spread ever further, and America became a land of unprecedented affluence, an example to others. But the age of affluence was also an age of materialism and conformity. And America's new world role implicated her in the deep disorders and conflicts of the modern world; this time the nation could not, as in 1918, withdraw within her own continent and mind her own business. When the hot war ended, a cold one began, and America's international role was in part ideological; she represented individualistic capitalist democracy against the other major twentieth-century ideology, collectivist communism. With whatever misgivings, Americans were now in the historical mainstream, and this sense of entering the bloodied arena of late modern history was soon to show itself in American fiction.

The American novel itself took on a new world role as the conflict ended and the age of American hegemony began. American writers were internationally read and increasingly studied as the great examples of a late modern literature. In all the western cultures there was an obvious sense of fracture, as writers adapted to a sense of profound historical change. Modernism had, in effect, ended: several of its great figures had died around the outbreak of war (Yeats and Sigmund Freud in 1939, Joyce and Virginia Woolf in 1941) and others from Céline to Pound had adopted Fascist loyalties. German and Italian writing had to begin again, British fiction was adapting to the new post-imperial and welfare-state age, French fiction reassessed the modern responsibility in the existential fictions of Sartre and Camus. American fiction also lost some of its experimental figures: Fitzgerald and Nathanael West died within a few days of each other in Hollywood in 1940, Anderson died in 1941, Stein in 1946, still asking on her deathbed 'What is the question?' Other notable figures from the 1920s and 1930s wrote on, and Hemingway, Faulkner, and Steinbeck all won Nobel Prizes in the 1950s and early 1960s, reflecting the new international significance and power of American fiction. But though their modernist spirit became better understood, influencing many in the new generation, they were largely past their best work. Meanwhile the political sympathies that writers had espoused in the 1930s had to be reassessed, and they had to adjust to the conditions of an international, anxious, yet neo-conservative age. The red-baiting campaign of Senator Joseph McCarthy suggested that a new era of anti-intellectualism was forming, though of more significance was the fact that the new era looked to its intellectuals to influence international liberal opinion, to teach in universities, and to leave behind their avant-garde past. American writers, asked to express the entry of America into the centre of the new world history, were also asked to support an age of materialist conformity.

To critics from the 1930s, the promises were poor. John Aldridge in *After the Lost Generation* (1951) argued that American writing was now deprived of its energies, too bereft of moral, mythological, or artistic certainty to create a serious art. Malcolm Cowley in *The Literary Situation* (1954) claimed that the co-option of writers by the academic treadmill would produce an age not of creation but of dull literary criticism. Even in 1959, when a new generation of American novelists was clearly evident, the influential Irving Howe observed in an article called 'Mass Society and Post-Modern Fiction' that it was virtually impossible to produce an art of literary integration in affluent-society America, 'a relatively comfortable, half welfare and half garrison society in which the population grows passive, indifferent and atomized'. To Howe, the age of modernism was indeed over, and the novel was struggling to find a new form, though he questioned whether it had the experimental power to do so. By now, however, it was apparent that a new fiction was developing in America, and that it had been shaped both by the heritage of American social realism in the 1930s and by the growing exposure of American writing to international influences, especially those of European modernism. Of the writers most clearly exposed to that double influence, many were Jewish, often involved in Thirties radicalism but now painfully Europeanized by the experience of their fellow-Jews in Europe during the 1930s and the terrible facts of the Holocaust. Aware of the heritage of modernism, they were equally concerned with creating the moral record of a terrible age and with constructing a new spirit of liberalism.

By the beginning of the 1940s, when the left-wing attitudes of the 1930s began to fail under the impact of the Nazi-Soviet Pact, this new mood was already becoming plain. Saul Bellow sharply caught this new tone in his first novel *Dangling Man* (1944), the story of an anti-hero who has lost all his Thirties moral and political certainties as he awaits wartime military induction. He retreats into himself, but this quest for existential recovery fails, and he welcomes army life with relief, crying 'Long live regimentation!' The age of regimentation dominates Norman Mailer's war novel *The Naked and the Dead* (1948) and his post-war novel *Barbary Shore* (1948), which depicts the ideological vacuum of wartime persisting into the chilly peace, leaving the hero adrift in 'the air of our time, authority and nihilism stalking one another in the orgiastic hollow of this century'. War produced many notable war novels, from old and new writers, born from the experience of young Americans within the military machine, on the battlefronts of the Pacific, or in the dismaying 'zones' of war-torn and blasted Europe. They include John Hersey's *A Bell for Adano* (1944), Gore Vidal's *Williwaw* (1946), John Horne Burns's *The Gallery* (1947), Irwin Shaw's *The Young Lions* (1948), James Gould Cozzens's *Guard of Honor* (1948), John Hawkes's *The Cannibal* (1949), Herman Wouk's *The Caine Mutiny* (1951), James Jones's *From Here to Eternity* (1951) and J. D. Salinger's moving *Nine Stories* (1953). Much of this fiction was written as naturalism and reportage, and in 1954 Malcolm Cowley could fairly complain that where the First World War had produced fiction of great technical experiment, the Second World War had produced conventional realism. Yet such was the impact of the war and its aftermath on post-war American consciousness that the theme continued virtually to the present; it would not be too much to say that it gave contemporary American fiction its most potent image of modern crisis. Much of this later fiction—Joseph Heller's *Catch-22* (1961), Kurt Vonnegut's *Slaughterhouse-Five* (1969), Thomas Pynchon's

Gravity's Rainbow (1973)—was far more experimental, as naturalism gave way to the postmodern spirit.

And even in the 1940s and 1950s that naturalism seemed largely bereft of moral conviction or ideological consciousness, depicting rather a world in tragic disarray or, as Salinger called it, 'squalor'. Books like *The Naked and the Dead* were less about war than the emergence of a world where both liberal optimism and political activism seemed powerless before the massing of bland but ominous forces—military, political, industrial, technological, commercial—swamping all the certainties of morality and the very confidence of the self. There was a similarly dark naturalism in the new novels of modern urban life in the new neon city of violence, disorder, and psychic extravagance—Willard Motley's *Knock on Any Door* (1947), Nelson Algren's *The Man With the Golden Arm* (1949), Chandler Brossard's *Who Walk In Darkness* (1952). Though in some ways works of high realism, these are also explorations of urban landscapes of horror and nightmare in a society that seems alienating and historically lost. In these books we see the darker side of American affluence, the remnants of poverty, the figures of alienation and revolt. In much of the new fiction critics began to notice persistent themes: of alienation, a separation between the self and a massed society, a dissent or despair that gave this fiction a different mood from Thirties naturalism. The Forties and Fifties also saw a marked revival of Gothic writing, especially in the South. Some of the most remarkable of this work was by women writers: Carson McCullers's *The Heart Is a Lonely Hunter* (1940) and *The Member of the Wedding* (1946); Eudora Welty's *A Curtain of Green* (1941), *The Robber Bridegroom* (1942), and *Delta Wedding* (1946); and Flannery O'Connor's *Wise Blood* (1952), *A Good Man Is Hard to Find* (1955), and *The Violent Bear It Away* (1960) all mixed a formal experimentalism with a dark vision of decadence and evil, producing a Gothic vision that has persisted powerfully in more recent women's writing. Set mostly not in the urban but the rural world, in the decline of the South rather than the affluence of the North, often among children, neglected women, or the physically damaged or disabled, this fiction—touched with the 'tragic sense of life' that marked the times—was less concerned with sociological report than with the exploration of human loneliness and the eternal problem of evil. Broken communication and failed love are prevailing conditions. Loneliness can lead to pure existential exposure, or perhaps to a saving religious awareness, in which knowledge of human evil becomes a step towards truth. A similar sense of the grotesque is found in the fiction of Truman Capote (*Other Voices, Other Rooms*, 1948; *Breakfast at Tiffany's*, 1958), William Styron (*Lie Down in Darkness*, 1951), James Purdy (*Malcolm*, 1959; *Cabot Wright Begins*, 1964), and Walker Percy (*The Moviegoer*, 1961), and it persists through much contemporary American fiction.

The American novel as it developed after 1940 was to be very different from much of the work that went before. It left behind the large mythic themes and modernist experiments of its predecessors, and equally the optimistic naturalism of writers like Steinbeck. In some ways it appeared even more alienated than the writing of European contemporaries, and was much concerned with moral uncertainty and metaphysical complexity. The darkened mood was sometimes described as the 'new liberalism', the spirit of an age after ideology, shaken by awareness of the holocaust, atomic anxiety, the fact of human evil. In the essays of *The Liberal Imagination* (1950) the critic Lionel Trilling saw the spirit of the age moving away from simple ideologies and into the moral complexity of the novel, where the human mixture of good and evil could be faced with what he called 'moral realism'. Trilling explores just this theme in his own novel *The Middle of the Journey* (1947), which looks back on the ideological world of the Thirties. Here he contrasts the pure radicalism of Nancy Croom, with her 'passion of the mind and will so pure that, as it swept through her, she could not believe that anything that opposed it required consideration', and Maxim Gifford, a Communist Party renegade who converts to Catholicism and replaces his vision of proletarian innocence with one of universal sin. Caught between the two is the book's hero, John Laskell, who accepts the contingency of experience, the general shapelessness of life, the eternal mingling of human good and human evil, just as Trilling suggested the novel itself should. A similar sense of the moral and ideological confusions of the age runs through the wonderfully satirical works of Mary McCarthy, who casts her cold eye over the *naïvetés* of American radical liberalism and utopian optimism in a remarkable series of novels. *The Oasis* (1947) deals with a utopian colony of the high-minded who are confronted with the fact of human evil and wrong-doing; *The Groves of Academe* (1952) is an excellent campus novel about a teacher who falsely claims Communist Party membership to protect himself under the liberal shield against dismissal for incompetence; *The Group* (1963), is about the girls of the Vassar Class of '33, and their naïve hopes of 'the idea of progress . . . seen in the female sphere'. Like that of other powerful American satirists such as Alison Lurie, McCarthy's irony is a sharp expression of the moral realism that marks much of the writing of the time. It represents a revolt against naïve ideological interpretations, uses liberalism not as a faith but as a vision of human complexity and the basis of moral satire, and surveys the contemporary situation with ironic detachment. If liberal realism had returned to the American novel, it had returned in a complex and sceptical form.

2.

It is significant that some of the very best of the post-war American writers were those who had acquired their political education in the left-wing atmosphere of the 1930s and were now in process of coming to terms with the atmosphere of moral ambiguity that ran so strongly through the post-war, cold war atmosphere of the late 1940s and 1950s, when writers throughout the west felt writing needed to begin again. Among these American writers were some who had very good reason to think of themselves as survivors of war and holocaust, and whose entire intellectual heritage had been transformed by the dark wartime events of 1941–5. Jewish intellectuals had often followed the radical path into and out of Communism, had been preoccupied by European intellectual life and its modernist arts. It was they who could speak most validly for the six million victims of the old world order, see the dangers of totalitarianism in politics and art, express the argument for a new humanism. By the Fifties, a significant new group of Jewish-American novelists had appeared. Their work drew on the Yiddish tradition (brought to the States particularly by Isaac Bashevis Singer) and on Russian and European modernism—especially that part of it concerned with the dismantling of the self by an intolerable modern history. In Saul Bellow, Norman Mailer, Bernard Malamud, and Philip Roth, one can see the transformation of the older tradition of Jewish-American writing. Now the theme was no longer the immigrant victim struggling for place and recognition in the New World, rather that of the Jew as modern victim forced by history into existential self-definition, a definition that was not solely religious, political, or ethnic. As Leslie Fiedler said, in this fiction the Jew now became the type of modern man, 'the metropolitan at home, though expert in the indignities, rather than the amenities, of urban life'. Many of the titles—*The Victim*; *Goodbye, Columbus*; *A New Life*—allude to the old myths, either of ultimate promise or of fear of victimization. But the books became complex explorations of the individual's place as beneficiary or exile in the contemporary world, and are largely conducted as metaphysical enquiries, speculations on the predicament of disoriented modern man in a world of urban anonymity, behavioural indifference, and the totalitarian massing of social force. Humanism was the aim, but it was hard to forge in the face of disjunctive modern experience. The desire was to link the history of single individuals with the larger processes of society, but those individuals were also seen as alienated, victimized, dislocated, materially satisfied but spiritually damaged, conformist yet anomic, rational but anarchic. The mood of these books went beyond the rural innocence and epicality of earlier American writing, exploring the dark modernity of post-industrial society in an attempt to face Bellow's question: How should a good man live, what ought he to do?

There were similar developments in black fiction; following on from Richard Wright, the black too became an image of the existential and displaced hero, the other in American culture. Ralph Ellison's *Invisible Man* (1952), owing clear debts to Dostoevsky's *Notes from Underground*, evoked the nameless-ness and exposure felt by the modern black, but not only the black ('Who knows but that, on the lower frequencies, I speak for you?'). Ellison's outstanding novel mixed naturalism, expressionism, and surrealism. A work of liberal sympathies, it is also a novel about the disappearance of self and the collapse of moral perspective, and it ends in an apocalyptic riot that both expresses and seeks to purge American disorder, in response to the narrator's comment that 'the mind that has conceived a plan for living must never lose sight of the chaos against which the pattern was conceived.' The book explores moral problems, yet, says the unnamed narrator, 'When one is invisible, he finds such problems as good and evil, honesty and dishonesty, of such shifting shapes that he confuses one with the other, depending upon who happens to be looking through him at the time.' Ellison's obvious successor was James Baldwin, writing a new black novel of violence, suffering, and despair. *Go Tell It on the Mountain* (1953) portrayed the attempts of a suffering black family to find hope through religion, and *Giovanni's Room* (1956) is a sensitive exploration of a homosexual relationship between a black and a white in Paris. By *Another Country* (1962), however, Baldwin's intensified political indignation had made his fiction into an indictment of the racial gangrene at the centre of all things.

In most of these works, angry or despairing, a humanistic desire is present. As with the Jewish writers, the books are dominated by a sense of the absurd situation of the self, the individual's need to withdraw from a history which silences, makes invisible, and is beyond his or her capacity to control or master. Yet this absurdist theme is persistently tempered, in liberal fashion, by a desire for civility, a desire to re-attach the individual to society, and so give him a value beyond that of mere determinism or victimization. There was a new tension between the claims of alienation and accommodation, between the discrete, separated individual and the system, the victimized or comic self and a disordered history. The result was a fiction deeply conscious of alienation and anomie, often voiced in the despairing intonations of modernism, yet also turned towards society, and moving back towards realism. Its heroes were often 'philosphical' heroes, seeking to make sense of lives made absurd by society and history; yet that society and history needed to be registered in· all their new and commanding detail. Earlier naturalism had been largely raw, accumulative, denotative, driven by a deterministic picture of individual lives. Earlier modernism had often shown the individual as a discrete consciousness and had sought form and insight outside history. Now the elements seemed to merge, in a complex equation of absurdist existentialism and self-doubting liberalism. The result was frequently an oblique realism—a fiction of tragi-comic disorder and displacement that still insistently alluded to a real external world.

Thus did a new and very distinctive generation emerge over the 1940s and 1950s, and of such power as to give post-war American fiction a remarkable international reputation. Their writing caught the very flavour of the new America—affluent, urban, liberal yet conformist, technologically advanced, a consumer mass society—that was having such influence in the world. The very portrait of that changed America was to some degree sufficient to establish the significance of the new American novel. Despite critical fears that the Great American Novel was now in decline, the fiction of the period actually came to seem the central form in which both the aspirations and contradictions of the changing American culture was expressed. It was a fiction that had moved a long way from the generation of Hemingway, Faulkner, Dos Passos, Fitzgerald, and Steinbeck. It was multiethnic as never before: there were the Jewish-American writers (Bellow, Malamud, Roth, Wallant, and Chaim Potok), exploring the trivialization of evil in the age of affluence; the black writers like Wright, Ellison and Baldwin, portraying blacks less as social victims than figures of modern existential alienation; the émigré writers from an unsettled Europe, from Isaac Bashevis Singer to Vladimir Nabokov, writing of a new modern diaspora. There was the Southern grotesque of McCullers, Welty, and Capote, with their sense of an age of moral conflict; a writing of secular displacement in the work of Updike, Salinger, and Cheever. As the Fifties developed, there emerged a growing writing of expatriate dissent and radical experiment, the fiction of Kerouac, Burroughs, and Paul Bowles. Over the post-war era, the fiction of liberal compromise with difficult times turned towards a more extreme, fantastic, and experimental form, which would evolve through the writing of the Sixties. However the years from 1941 to 1959 were indeed a remarkable period of American fiction, from which emerged many outstanding new writers who were to establish the American novel in a position of international influence and world-wide appeal.

3.

The rise of Jewish-American fiction in the years immediately after the Second World War was the development of a tradition that went back to the 1890s and to writers like Abraham Cahan. But its remarkable efflorescence in writers as various as Bellow, Malamud, Roth, Lionel Trilling, Edgar Lewis Wallant, Chaim Potok, Herbert Gold, Stanley Elkin, Arthur Miller, Joseph Heller, E. L. Doctorow, Grace Paley, Tillie Olsen, and Cynthia Ozick indicates the extraordinary revival and indeed the new dominance of this tradition in post-war American culture. For this there were several reasons: the far more central role of educated Jews in metropolitan intellectual and political culture; the cosmopolitan historical alertness of American Jewish culture in an age of growing internationalism; the persisting preoccupation of Jewish fiction with the conflict between ethical responsibility and purely material success—a key theme of the age of affluence, which led to a radical questioning of the all-too-easily celebrated American dream; a concern with victimization and alienation; and above all, the task felt by the Jewish-American writers of being responsible survivors of the Holocaust. It is thus in Jewish-American fiction that we find the strongest link between the European tradition, in forms as various as Eastern European fable and cosmopolitanized modernism, and the lineage of the American novel tradition.

This is nowhere better exemplified than in the work of Isaac Bashevis Singer, then a relatively recent immigrant from Poland who came to the United States in 1935. Singer always retained his European roots and rabbinical sources; in fact he largely continued to write in Yiddish, and contributed much of his writing to New York Jewish periodicals. Some of his books, like the novels *The Family Moskat* (in English, 1950) and *The Magician of Lublin* (1960) and his many short stories (*Gimpel the Fool*, 1957), were slow to be translated. Singer's work remarkably crosses the seemingly timeless peasant and ghetto world of his native Poland (with its magical themes and supernatural faiths) with the smarter, secular, metropolitan world of modern America, producing bizarre and ironic contrasts of a kind we have come to call 'magic realism'. His work helped many younger writers link the stock of Jewish fable, narrative, and metaphysical preoccupation with their secular American condition, and encouraged them to reach back into their background in European experience—often, as in the later novels of Philip Roth, in surprising ways. Appropriately Singer's story 'Gimpel the Fool' was translated into English by one of the most significant of the novelists to emerge in America in the 1940s, a writer who like Singer himself would win the Nobel Prize for Literature, Saul Bellow.

Bellow was born in Canada in 1915 of immigrant Jewish parents and as a child moved to Chicago, the city about which he writes most; the homemade world of Jewish culture in the 1920s and 1930s is a repeated reference-point in his many novels. Bellow was a contributor to the influential left-wing literary-political journal *Partisan Review*, and published his first story there in 1941. His novels have always been rich in political and philosophical ideas, and touched with the heritage of modernism. But above all his work displays a deep Jewish humanism—a concern to affirm mankind, to explore moral and metaphysical questions, to confront the characteristic Jewish themes of victimization and alienation, and of the need in a material world for transcendental perceptions. The heritage of European philosophical thought shapes most of his heroes, who are normally themselves men of thought and heirs of modern romanticism, always concerned to defend their inner claim to self against a modernizing world where man seems to have lost his place, and where beyond the individual is the massive, determining transforming city, the world of human diminution. Often in Bellow's books the world and consciousness split apart, but his heroes (usually but not always Jewish, and nearly always male) are driven by mental and emotional desire to reforge their pact with others, with the human condition, with the universe in all its scale: as Bellow's Henderson cries: 'the universe itself being put into us, it calls for scope.' In his work our social and historical existence struggles with our mythical and metaphysical existence, a conflict that Bellow reconciles in the form of a complex modern comedy, where in every situation or material fact there is always the prospect of an anguished or a joyful idea.

His books also reflect the distinctive decades in which they were written. His first novel, *Dangling Man*, appeared in 1944 as the war continued, and can indeed be called a war novel, though it is set not on the battlefield but in a denatured wartime Chicago. Its central character, Joseph (the Kafkaesque association is surely deliberate), waits to be drafted. A Communist sympathizer in the Thirties, he is a marginal man whose aim is to know himself: 'to know what we are and what we are for, to know our purpose, to seek grace'. But the world—politics, the city, human relations—gives him no answers, and he withdraws into his own private rooms, where 'the perspectives end in the walls'. Joseph is an existentialist anti-hero, who finds his existence without essence in a hostile world. But, he accepts, 'we have history to answer to,' and the world demands a moral response to the question, what should a good man do? Bellow confessedly drew on Dreiser's naturalism for his portrait of the machine of the city, but also on the soul-searching literature of modernism—the work of Dostoevsky, Kafka, above all Sartre and Camus, whose existentialist novels *La Nausée* and *L'Étranger* were now having considerable influence on American writers. But Bellow's novel is also an anxious backward answer to the already-dead Thirties. Joseph finds no solution either in the inward withdrawal of modernism or the social action of the political writers. So he turns to the enforced existence of army life, and in effect cancels his empty freedom. The ending is ambiguous: it can be read as a stoical acceptance of social responsibility or a dangerous compromise with force (much the dilemma Norman Mailer explores in *The Naked and the Dead*). But what distinguishes Bellow's writing, here and subsequently, is its powerful vein of Jewish rhetoric, and its desire to discover what Joseph calls *le genre humain*, a metaphysical hunger that makes the book far more than a fable of tragic self-nullification.

Bellow's struggle between determinism and humanism persists into his first post-war novel, *The Victim* (1947), set in the other major city of his fiction, New York. Amid its oppressive, heat-ridden, mechanical jostle, Asa Leventhal lives irritably in a world of offices, street crowds, and urban anonymity, the familiar environment of recent American urban fiction. His city is an agglomeration of competition and misery, governed as he sees it by mysterious blacklists and arbitrary decisions, and survival is a Darwinian battle. Gradually the novel establishes a thread of distant connection and hence moral responsibility between Leventhal, the petty-bourgeois Jew deeply uncertain of his place in the world, and Allbee, a Gentile who rises suddenly from the urban crowd to blame Leventhal for the loss of his. Leventhal, considering himself as the true victim, at first refuses all responsibility, but gradually comes to acknowledge the human link. This lesson is learned partly through a key central chapter in which a group of Jews discuss the measure of man, trying to discover not what is more than human, or less than human, but human exactly. The question had become Bellow's own. In the novels that followed he was to seek an answer not through tight, determinist, or existentialist fictions, but by turning toward exuberant and picaresque comedy, a form that would allow him to move from the comedy of suffering to the exploration of an idea of human grandeur.

With his books of the Fifties, *The Adventures of Augie March* (1953), *Seize the Day* (1956), and *Henderson the Rain King* (1959), Bellow suddenly displayed a new stage in his writing, which became ebullient, elaborate, and increasingly picaresque in form. *Augie March* begins in the James T. Farrell-like world of Depression Chicago ('just plain brutal and unmitigated') but Bellow's hero Augie is a great self-creator who believes a man's character is his fate. Determined to be a Columbus of the near at hand, he breaks out of his universe in quest of the 'axial lines' that might guide us. He confronts history (by meeting Trotsky) and struggles with nature, declaring 'It takes some of us a long time to find out what the price is of our being in nature, and what the facts are about your tenure. How long it takes depends on how swiftly the social sugars dissolve.' Augie is the first of Bellow's heroes to be larger rather than smaller than the world he lives in, and his picaresque adventures are given us in a rather loose structure but with great comic power. *Seize the Day*, a novella, has a tighter form; it tells of one day in the life of Tommy Wilhelm, failed actor, feeble husband, *schlemiel*, who meets a confidence man, Dr Tamkin, who promises to set his life in order. This he finally does, by taking all Tommy's money but revealing to him his membership in mortal humanity. *Henderson the Rain King*, Bellow's most ambitious Fifties novel, unites the picaresque and the formal in the story of Eugene Henderson, an extravagant WASP millionaire with a careless energy but a desire to serve, who, feeling he is unfit to live among men, goes to Africa and meets two exemplary tribes. Returned to his primal base in nature, the animal kingdom, and the bases of culture, Henderson learns to employ his 'grun-tu-molani', his will to live, and, having journeyed through his complex origins, returns to America via, appropriately, Newfoundland, to end up still the comedian of his own self-assertion, but the most success-ful hero Bellow has ever depicted.

The Sixties saw another shift in Bellow's writing, as indeed it did in the work of his near-contemporaries Norman Mailer, Philip Roth, and J. D. Salinger. In 1963 in his essay 'Some Notes on Recent American Fiction', Bellow observed that the modern novelist now appeared to feel defeated by a vast public life which dwarfed him as an individual, and encouraged him or his characters to become giants in loathing or fantasy. The humanism of the novel was now in question, in part from the influence of contemporary European philosophies. This was to prove part of the theme of *Herzog* (1964), Bellow's next and best novel. Its central character is Moses Herzog, a distressed Jewish intellectual with a complex family and marital history, and a 'suffering joker' who believes he is going mad. In letters composed in his mind he quarrels with the insignificant living and with the great dead ('He wrote to Spinoza, *Thoughts not causally connected were said by you to cause pain. I find that this is indeed the case . . .*'). A historian of romantic thought, he quarrels with nihilism and abstract historicism, and attempts to throw off the influence of those 'reality instructors' who claim the inalienable right to alienation and psychic extravagance. Yet Herzog himself is suffering a romantic agony, his inner pain matching the outward suffering of the two dark cities of New York and his hometown Chicago. In this learned and demanding book, Bellow sets himself the task of defining a notion of modern selfhood that does not yield to fashionable romantic nihilism, or any of the 'five cent syntheses' that form popular answers to the troubles of the age. The boredoms, pluralisms, and self-conscious despairs of the time move formlessly through Herzog's own mind, and the book itself possesses some of the same formlessness—until, finally, Herzog and the novel itself reach beyond the chaos of words and messages towards a transcendental silence. Bellow thus ends the book affirmatively, and Herzog settles for a contentment to remain in human occupancy and accept the oneness of things, his thoughts silenced, his letters stopped, his mind for the moment at peace.

Bellow's next book is a rather more bitter portrait of the rising spirit of nihilism he saw in contemporary American life, though it does not lack humour. *Mr Sammler's Planet* (1970) is a bleak and ironic novel about a one-eyed survivor of the German holocaust, in which he has been left for dead. Now, almost beyond his human life-span, in a state of kindly earth-detachment, he finds himself in the New York city in the age of revolutionary consciousness, black power, florid romanticism, irrationalism, and 'hyper-civilized Byzantine lunacy'. This is an apocalyptic novel about a modern New York that has turned to a wasteland breeding revolt, violence, and corruption, and hungry for sexual potency. It is also about the planet itself in the moonshot age, its consciousness mysteriously transforming as it adapts to the age of interplanetary space, so that 'finalities are demanded, summaries'. Weighed down both by the heavy burden of a cruel twentieth-century history and by the late modern world of psychic excess, Sammler tries to redeem the remnants of civilization, and reconstruct the essence of the stony planet on which he still survives. The book marks Bellow's evident disenchantment with the radical and romantic apocalypticism of late Sixties, ego-ridden America, and it is the book in which he comes closest to social and political disillusion. But the comic euphoria persists, and so does the belief in transcendental discovery, the need to explore the nature of the human tenure and allow the facts of our own mortality to feed back into the meanings of life. Again Bellow affirms, and perhaps in more transcendental and universal terms than before, the power of the human contract that binds us in common mortality and compels us to forge a worthy connection with the universe.

The award of the Nobel Prize for Literature to Bellow in 1976 honoured both his humanism and his by now clearly central place in contemporary American fiction. He took the occasion to object to the personless works of the *nouveau roman*, and assert his own belief in the humane potential of fiction, even in a world where, as he put it in *Humboldt's Gift* (1975), the more *it* means the less *we*. In his later books some of the darkness dissipates, and Bellow has become the great explorer of the late modern world of material excess and Byzantine superfluity. *Humboldt's Gift* is set in an affluent but divided Chicago where even the wives of mafiosi are taking Ph.D.s, and the cops are psychiatric experts in modern alienation. The book deals with two generations of American writers. One is exemplified by Von Humboldt Fleischer, a 'Mozart of gab', an anguished, modernist, intellectually omnivorous poet who dies poor in a flophouse (and is reputedly based on the poet and story-writer Delmore Schwartz). The other is his protégé Charlie Citrine, who survives to become rich in the Chicago of the materialist Seventies, suffering the calamity of his own sexual desires and the confusions of the relation between art and success. Like many of Bellow's late heroes, Charlie defeats the chaotic materialism of his world and the emptiness of morality by finding a late life gnosticism. So does Albert Corde, in Bellow's next and bleaker novel, *The Dean's December* (1982). This is a tale of two cities, set in 'free' Chicago—a city of 'wounds, lesions, cancers, destructive fury, death'—and enslaved Bucharest, where, none the less, a decent family life still seems possible. Corde himself is left trying to reconcile two modes of knowledge: his own experience as a city journalist, which leads him to despair, and the astrophysical knowledge of his Romanian wife Minna. At the end of the book we find him trying to bridge dull terra firma and the world of space as he ascends in the elevator at the Mount Palomar laboratory, still trying to defeat, as Bellow's heroes do, the emptiness of death. With *More Die of Heartbreak* (1987) Bellow returned to a more comic form, in a novel which shows how intellectual life is constantly and inevitably subject to sexual absurdity, since after all 'more die of heartbreak than of radiation.' Bellow, always a novelist of both the power and absurdity of the human intelligence, has always been a mixture of Von Humboldt Fleischer and Charlie Citrine.

By now Bellow was a novelist of four decades, over which the Jewish-American novel had developed from ghetto-like beginnings to a national and international form. It had produced many major figures over several generations, and writing that ranged from a documentary realism (Edgar Lewis Wallant, *The Pawnbroker*, 1960), to the wild black humour of Joseph Heller or Stanley Elkin (*A Bad Man*, 1967). Amongst its most important performers were Bernard Malamud and Philip Roth, who took its themes and preoccupations in contrasting directions: Malamud as a novelist of the more traditional Jewish world, Roth as an explorer of its extremities and absurdities in the permissive mood of the Sixties and Seventies. Malamud's work is touched both with naturalism and the tradition of Jewish mysticism; in it, life is generally an imprisonment which has to be transcended. At the same time it is greatly preoccupied by the challenge of art, the strange transcendence produced usually out of dross and misconduct. Thus his best work is usually a form of symbolic, and comic, realism, where mythic processes are at work behind a seemingly solid surface, as in the marvellous stories of his collection *The Magic Barrel* (1958). Malamud's first novel, *The Natural* (1952), is seemingly his least Jewish book, set in the very American world of baseball and reworking the Grail legend. The book teases the great quests of American fiction, from Ahab's to Huckleberry Finn's, but it is also concerned with the 'Jewish' theme of the renewal of life through suffering, the passage from 'the life we learn with and the life we live after that'. This is also the theme of his much more naturalistic and brilliant next novel *The Assistant* (1957), the story of a poor Jewish grocer, Morris Bober, who tries to live a decent life in a small store in the New York ghetto, and slaves away to make a loss. Into his world of absurd decency comes a small-time Italian hoodlum, Frankie Alpine, who first holds up the store, then guiltily returns to work for Morris. At first he despises the grocer's passivity and willingness to suffer ('the one that has got the biggest pain in the gut and can hold onto it longest is the best Jew'), but through wrongdoing, lust, and self-loathing he comes comically to Jewishness himself—falling into Bober's grave, accepting circumcision, and taking on the grocer's role. Similarly in *A New Life* (1962), S. Levin, 'formerly a drunkard', goes to teach in a college in the now suburban pastoral of the American West coast, hoping to find freedom. Again the story moves from victimization to absurd redemption; Levin does find a new life, but it is by running off with a less than glamorous heroine who promises only new cares and dull domesticity, but offering Levin a tattered hope.

In his next book, written in the Sixties, Malamud turns to a far more political theme. *The Fixer* (1966), a historical novel set in the pograms of Tsarist Russia before the First World War, is about a Jewish handyman or fixer, Jakov Bok, who leaves the *shtetl* seeking a new life in the city of St Petersburg, only to be falsely accused of the ritual murder of a Christian child. Though imprisoned, Bok refuses to surrender to his fate, and he acquires a revolutionary Jewishness which takes him into the Bolshevik Revolution. The novel explores the dark sense of victimization and suffering beneath Malamud's more comic themes, but rarely addressed so directly. Indeed the linked stories of *Pictures of Fidelman* (1969) are more typical of his work. Fidelman is an artist and forger wandering in Italy, the golden land of art, and the stories variously tell of the deceits, corruptions, and trickeries out of which art comes. Like Bellow, Malamud then ironically compared art's double role, as aesthetic satisfaction and political action, in *The Tenants* (1971). In a crumbling tenement block the Jewish writer Harry Lesser attempts to make up for past failures by creating masterpieces; he confronts the black revolutionary Willie Spearpoint, who sees art as action and a form of radical violence. Gradually the two change roles, Lesser being caught up in the violence and sexuality of Willie's black world, and Willie withdrawing into aesthetic creation. The book ends in energetic hatred, the destruction of manuscripts, and the murder of each writer by the other, while Malamud's own text collapses into the repeated word 'mercy'. The books that followed grew more meditative. If *The Tenants* seems to doubt the role of art to reconcile the tensions of life, Malamud was to compensate for this in *Dubin's Lives* (1979), the story of an elderly biographer, a rabbinical, sorrowful figure in a marriage 'more happy than many but not as happy as some', who records the lives of others because he cannot live one of his own. Then Dubin falls in love with a commonplace young girl, recovers sensually, and discovers that art is indeed achieved at the expense of lives—one's own, or those of others. Malamud died in 1986; his last book, *God's Grace*, is a bleak memorial—a darkly apocalyptic though often comic story about the end of humanity, an unexpected work from a writer whose greatest gift had been for a painful comedy of endurance against the trials of the age.

If Bernard Malamud is a writer of 'ethical Jewhood', the much younger Philip Roth is a writer exploring the world of its collapse; one of his novels is very appropriately titled *Letting Go*. Roth made his mark with the novella *Goodbye, Columbus* in 1959, a searing portrait of affluent Jewish life in the post-war 'swamp of prosperity' and the era of the full refrigerator, a life which the hero momentarily mistakes for the true fulfillment of the American dream. With *Letting Go* (1962) and *When She Was Good* (1967), two novels set in the Midwest, one around a Chicago graduate school, the other in the classic American small town, and both about the struggle between traditional ethics and the desire for personal freedom, he appeared to have the aims of a neo-Jamesian literary formalist, but as he later made clear in *The Great American Novel* (1973), Roth's relation to the G.A.N. was always ambiguous. In an essay of 1961, 'Writing American Fiction', he had reflected on the unreality and absurdity of contemporary American history and the task it posed for the writer—'the American writer in the middle of the twentieth century has his hands full in trying to understand, describe and then make *credible* much of the American reality'— and the belief he expresses there that contemporary American experience has made formal realism impossible was soon reflected in his works. Nothing made this clearer than *Portnoy's Complaint* (1969), a *succès de scandale* about the predatory Jewish mother and her mother-disabled son, the endlessly masturbating Alexander Portnoy. Roth described the book as his revolt against the 'moral seriousness' of the fiction of the 1950s, in his own work as well as that of others, and so it is. Portnoy fulfills all the expected social aspirations according to the old Jewish joke ('my son the doctor is drowning'), but cannot escape from the narcissistic sexual prison to which he is condemned. Nor can he create his own story as a formal development, only as a cry or confession, a tale told to his analyst, Dr Spielvogel. Where Malamud's *The Tenants* ends with a repeated cry of 'mercy', *Portnoy's Complaint* ends on a scream, followed by a 'punchline', as Dr Spielvogel starts the whole story again ('Now vee may perhaps to begin. Yes?').

We can also say that it is here that the later Philip Roth himself begins, testing and retesting the relationship between the fictional and the story of his life, or lives like his own, between the novel as form and the novel as confession. Roth now proved a playful user of many resources, from the materials of political satire (*Our Gang*, 1971) to Kafkaesque fantasies like *The Breast* (1972), about an emasculated Jewish professor who turns into a gigantic female breast, and another story about the relation between Jewish sexual guilt and the desire for permissive sexual expression. While Roth makes this an intensely Jewish theme (full sexual expression seems reserved for Gentiles; it was the Jewish Freud who mapped repression and the unconscious, and the Jewish Kafka who explored the humiliation that could only be relieved by metamorphosis), his enquiries belonged to the contemporary problems of fiction in general. Like Malamud he was concerned with the way we might make art out of the dross of life, moral truth out of confession. *The Great American Novel* is his attempt at a self-conscious or reflexive fiction, using, as

Malamud did in *The Natural*, the myths of baseball to play with and parody the stock of American fiction. But more successful was his *My Life as a Man* (1974), which is refracted confession. Here, in the persona of Peter Tarnopol, Roth reflects on his own previous 'moral seriousness' and his dependence on fictional ideas of how life should be lived, and considers how 'useful fictions' both guide and disguise the issues of an author's personal life. Yet even Tarnopol is himself what Roth would call a 'ghost writer', a fictional disguise, however much he attempts to approach truth, as he does in the last story. Here art and its pursuit of moral seriousness are seen as a disguise, 'literature' is what the writer must escape from (it is what got him into this mess, and must get him out again), and realism is a formal self-concealment hiding revelation.

Like other writers of the Sixties and Seventies, Roth now saw the novel as a precarious bridge between reality and falsehood—one that his later fiction plays with both with flamboyant display and moral seriousness. He stressed his theme was the breaking of personal inhibition, the hungry freeing of identity, the fragmenting of fixed images of self or gender. Here many of his characters reappear in strange and unexpected combinations of the reportorial and the fantastic, sometimes seen in the frame of a previous fiction, sometimes in the light of an autobiographical reality. In *The Professor of Desire* (1977) the narcissistic central character of *The Breast*, David Kepesh, is taken to Prague and introduced into the real, or external, world of Kafka as it attempts to survive under Communism. He is taken to Kafka's grave, introduced to 'Kafka's whore', the extraordinary figure who shows the ambiguity of the modern muse and the sexual prompts behind the difficulties of art. The book is also an acknowledgement of debt to Eastern European writers like Bruno Schultz and Milan Kundera, to whom, indeed, his next novel, *The Ghost Writer* (1980), is dedicated. This book resurrects another alter ego, Nathan Zuckerman, condemned by his father for corrupting Jewish experience, and living in the house of an elderly Jewish writer closely resembling Isaac Bashevis Singer, who imagines himself making love to a resurrected Anne Frank. In *Zuckerman Unbound* (1981), Nathan returns to struggle with his rising fame and the criticism it has attracted for falsifying the Jewish experience, and in *The Anatomy Lesson* (1983) he seems in illness to forswear his writing—only to reappear in new guise in *The Prague Orgy* (1985), where he returns to Czechoslovakia to recover a Yiddish literary heritage, and in *The Counterlife* (1986), where he dies and then, through the buoyant freedom of narrative, is reborn, to examine his responsibilities to Israel. Ambiguous refractions, juxtapositions of fact and fiction, realism and fantasy, report and displacement, mark all his recent books. They are filled with ghostwriters, the writers or fictions of the past who might guide or deceive us, who plot our lives, shape our tales, pass on our imaginative freedoms, stimulate our desires, and leave us as new hunger artists striving to tell an original tale out of our own endless and often misdirected passion. Roth's later fiction is both an unravelling of the literary heritage both of American and of international Jewish fiction, and a personal and ever changing attempt at its reconstruction. His work has had its impact on writers as various as E. L. Doctorow, concerned with the ambiguous border between historical truth and fiction, and Stanley Elkin, with his demonic and painful Jewish black humour. Roth's theme is the Jewish writer in crisis, having always to probe and re-probe the literary, sexual, autobiographical, historical, political and psychic content of his materials, and define his patrimony. In his recent novels he has become a quintessential voice of late modern unease, a witness to the pressure of unreality on the writer's always ambiguous desire for reality.

4.

What Roth makes clear is that the moral and realistic novel of the 1950s was always a novel in strain, under pressure from ethical change, sexual expectation, and changing attitudes to personal fulfillment, and above all from the ever-complicating American reality. Perhaps no writer expressed this sense of tension more than J. D. Salinger, a writer whose path took him from early fame to silence. In some ways his first novel, *The Catcher in the Rye* (1951) can be said to be the strongest novel of the Fifties; it caught its mood and became a universal student classic. The first-person story of Holden Caulfield, the middle-class adolescent expelled from his prep-school whose foray to New York reveals to him the fragility of innocence, it captured the dismay of those who saw the spirit of human decency corrupted by an age of hypocrisy and self-deceit. The book partly owed its success to its idiom: like Mark Twain's *Huckleberry Finn*, Salinger's novel captures the perfect vernacular voice for seeing through the falsehood of the adult social world, creating a moral universe out of a plain-speaking childish vision. Holden is in fact adult and sophisticated enough to find his way around the Manhattan world, with its pick-up bars, its smart hotels, its various confidence men and 'phoneys'. But Holden remains on the childhood side of the fall into adulthood, and his love is for the innocent remnants of his boyhood: his young sister Phoebe, the ducks on the lake in Central Park, the Natural History Museum, the things that are 'too damn nice' to damage. For these things he creates not simply a love but a half-articulated and semi-religious sanction, and the book is an endeavour to discover a lyrical religion of innocence that can be set against the corruption of adult society. Holden does not, in the end, save those who are about to fall over the cliff into adulthood, catch them in the rye; he ends under medical treatment, refusing to grow up.

The terrible stress on those who are fragile in a terrible age is also the theme of the powerful tales of *Nine Stories* (1953),[1] which again portray the adult world as corrupt and damaging, a place where love is always sacrificed to squalor. One of the stories, 'A Perfect Day for Bananafish', tells of the suicide of Seymour Glass, who was to appear in the group of stories about the Glass family that were collected as *Franny and Zooey* (1961) and *Raise High the Roofbeam, Carpenters and Seymour: An Introduction* (1963). The Glass family are the wise, inter-dependent, fragile children of two vaudeville entertainers, and have won public acclaim on a radio quiz show. The stories largely turn on a series of neo-Buddhist revelations from Seymour, the oldest and wisest of these whizz kids, and aspire to a philosophy of total spiritual inclusion of the stuff of the universe. But their religious precocity

[1] In Britain this book was originally titled *For Esmé—With Love and Squalor*.

is gained at the expense of neurosis throughout the family and the early death of Seymour, leaving others, notably Zooey, to explain his message—thus he tells his sister Franny that the world is the ugly Fat Lady out there, and that that cancered Fat Lady is 'Christ himself, buddy'. Yet the family themselves are a withdrawn Elect, living outside the world in their apartment with a philosophy of almost total exclusion of others, and the role of Seymour as saint and guru involves such a degree of romantic inflation that the author seems to have problems in controlling it. Indeed the Zen-religious dimension of Salinger's work, deeply popular with its *New Yorker* audience at the time, becomes a little cloying, though the complexity and formality of the art is considerable. Salinger's highly speculative style, alternating moments of vivid description with layers of multiple narration, is part of the general anxiety to break through the potential dishonesty of fiction toward an absolute truth or vision. Thus the principal narrator, Buddy Glass, is assigned the task of bearing responsibility for relating the matter to the manner. As Seymour aspires to a condition of transcendent silence, so Buddy himself eventually falls silent, and thereafter did his author. It was as if the psychic tension of living in a self-corrupting world, and the stress of precision, exactness, and honesty, were simply too great to sustain. The persistent rumours of a later novel from Salinger continue, but his movement to silence is itself a manifestation of the sense of crisis that has passed through so much modern writing.

By contrast Salinger's fellow *New Yorker* writer John Updike has been one of the most prolific, and engaging, of the novelists who came to notice during the 1950s. Born in Pennsylvania, Updike studied at the Ruskin School of Drawing and of Fine Art in Oxford, and then worked at the *New Yorker*; a concern with aesthetic precision, of the revelation of form amongst the contingencies of life, has always shaped his writing—which has none the less gone on to form a major record of the social and moral history of post-war America. Both story-writer and novelist, Updike came to attention in 1959 with the novel *The Poorhouse Fair* and the story collection *The Same Door*. In 1960 he published *Rabbit, Run*, a novel about an ordinary American *homme moyen* sensuel, Harold 'Rabbit' Angstrom, an ex-basketball player and man of spontaneity who is now caught up in the domestic ordinariness of his married world. Rabbit did indeed run, and the four volumes of what is now the Rabbit sequence—*Rabbit Redux* appeared in 1971, *Rabbit Is Rich* in 1981, and *Rabbit at Rest* in 1990—themselves form a sufficient and vivid record of the thirty years over which Updike has been writing. In various stories of the Sixties and in the autobiographical novel *The Centaur* (1963)—based on Greek myth, about the father–son relationship in the modern world—he dealt with his rural Pennsylvanian background in his imaginary Ollinger. In his stories, as in Salinger's, runs the theme of lost sacramentalism, a feeling that we have fallen into a shabby world which art might redeem by the recovery of vision, through the moment of love or insight, through the creation of form. During the 1960s Updike's themes became increasingly metropolitan, and he became the exemplary story-writer of the 'guiltless Fifties' and age of consumption, exploring middle-class young matrimonies and adulteries and the confusions of love and work. At the same time he showed a great experimental and parodic vigour, as in *Bech: A Book* (1970), which, by telling of a Jewish-American writer travelling through the countries of Communist Eastern Europe, allowed him to reflect both on modern political experience and on the Jewish-American novel as a form.

The form is not exactly his own: Updike is essentially a novelist of the white middle-class, and he built up a clearly delimited world—of modern couples, solemn, sexy, and delicate, living in New York attics and lofts, visiting museums, bringing home bottles of wine after work. Often themselves artists or writers, they share their author's taste for vision and epiphany, for bright and vivid rewards won from domestic life and marital turmoil, defying the emptying of life in an age of religious loss through the use of domestic and social rituals. A precise recorder of social and historical change, Updike's fiction too began to change as the Sixties developed. The domestic scene increasingly begins to shatter and apocalyptic feelings intensify in the age of moon-shot and the Vietnam war. His stories largely move in setting from New York to the well-heeled Connecticut and

Massachusetts shoreline, where the houses are Old Colonial, babysitters no problem, but marriages grow fragile and adulteries and divorces increase. *Couples* (1968), set in the earlier Kennedy era, erotically describes a troubled world where, against growing historical disturbance, adultery turns into a complex blasphemy, a substitute for lost faiths. By *Marry Me* (1976) the new ritual of the age, in 'the twilight of the old morality', is divorce, as the now older couples try to recover through 'Bodily Ascension', sex as sacrament, the old mystery. But Updike always has larger themes, about the more general history of the age; *The Coup* (1979) is set in the dry African republic of Kush, and is the story of an anti-American dictator reflecting on American follies, as Updike himself, a writer of considerable irony and a fine critic, has always done.

Updike's often domestic novels are thus registers of a general social anxiety and a secular unease, and can be read as works of what he once called 'instinctive realism'. Yet his work of the Eighties increasingly revealed that behind the realism is a deep debt to the tradition of the American romance, and above all to Hawthorne. *A Month of Sundays* (1976) and more especially *Roger's Version* (1986) showed him adapting the themes of Nathaniel Hawthorne's *The Scarlet Letter*, of faith tested by adultery and the need for independence, to the modern secular world of science and computing. *The Witches of Eastwick* (1984) is an ironic view of modern feminism, as the divorced 'witches' bring the devil back to puritan Rhode Island and release the evil that never lies far below sexual conflict. Updike's more than thirty volumes show him as a writer both of strong metaphysical obsessions and serious realism, of great historical curiosity and a belief in the salvations of form and art. His work compares well with that of other writers like John Cheever, who in *The Wapshot Chronicle* (1957), *The Wapshot Scandal* (1964), *Bullet Park* (1969), and above all in *Falconer* (1977), explores the shattering encounter between the seemingly stable world of middle-class white America and the life of psychic extremity and historical nightmare that lies beyond. Updike represents the tradition in modern American fiction which has attempted to retain an art of formal elegance and compactness, of moral judgement and careful vision, in a time of considerable fictional change, and done so with remarkable success.

5.

If one part of modern American fiction during the Fifties and Sixties was concerned to retain a realism of subject and a morality of form, it persistently portrayed that realism as under strain, disturbed by the complexity and enormity of post-war American history. As one critic, R. W. B. Lewis, put it: 'It is as though these novelists, and the characters they create, have been shaken loose by the amount and the violence of the history America had passed through (America, it must be remembered, has until late been unaccustomed to history).' The sense of discontinuity between society and the individual, between the historical tremors and the individual life, was evident in all the above writers, and it greatly intensified in their work of the Sixties: in Bellow's sense of the mind surrounded by a growing Byzantine madness, in Roth's vision of form having to yield to confession and desire, in Malamud's growing sense of art as a sphere of conflict, in Salinger's silence, and Updike's world of secular loss. It was also there in the growing rage of James Baldwin's black fiction as he moved from the formal elegance of *Giovanni's Room* to the social fury of *In Another Country*, a novel of apocalyptic rage. The problems of containing the sense of a rising modern extremity within a formal or moral frame were clearly considerable, not least for one of the most notable and promising of the writers of the time, Norman Mailer, a novelist who consistently offered to incorporate within his work and indeed within himself the disturbed psycho-history of the post-war age.

Mailer, as remarkable as a journalist as he has been as a novelist, has consistently offered himself as a writer in search of a new order of anarchistic consciousness in the face of a history that seemed to him destructive of feeling, sexuality, and realized being. From the essays of *Advertisements for Myself* (1959) onward he put on record his struggle to be a writer not of purified art but of existential consciousness and historical engagement.

His war novel of the 1940s, *The Naked and the Dead*, was formally naturalistic, reporting on war's violence, nature's intractable indifference, and the repressive victimization of the military machine. But it is also intercut with the experimental mechanism of the 'Time Machine', interlocking the Pacific battlefield with the equally jungle-like world of American society back home. Mailer follows the naturalist convention of taking basic social types—the Southern cracker, the Brooklyn Jew, the Montana wanderer, the New York liberal—and putting them into the machine of war, where 'the individual personality was just a hindrance.' But he stressed that the book was 'a parable about the movement of men through history', and the encounter with that larger history was to remain his main theme. The book begins his lasting concern with the massing of modern power and its psychic consequences: General Cummings thus explains that the war is not a matter of ideals but a 'power concentration', and 'You can consider the army as a preview of the future.' The failure of the liberal mind to grasp the consequences of 'power morality' is displayed in the collapse of Lieutenant Hearn; in Mailer's coming world liberalism will be persistently weak and powerless. Only through immersion in totalitarian energies can power be dissipated and resisted, and Mailer's work moves onward from this away from liberalism and toward a concern with violence, structures of power, and neo-sexual anarchism.

His next book, *Barbary Shore*, explored the political wasteland of post-war America. With *The Deer Park* (1955), at one point intended as part of an eight-part sequence of box-in-box novels, he began to seek a connection of new circuits, through a path of existential self-discovery primarily won through sexuality and apocalyptic violence. Set in the Hollywood of the McCarthyite anti-Communist purges, this novel identifies the politics of the movies with the chaos of national politics, and the Californian desert spaces around Desert D'Or with contemporary American history. As Mailer explained, his aim in both books was to build a contemporary psychology of politics, a union of Marx and Freud. The writer's task was, he said, to unite the subjective with the historical, the sexual body with the social body. At the centre of the project was the image of the romantic-revolutionary savage who is at once sexually harmonious and historically evolutionary; the figure is, inescapably, Mailer himself. *Advertisements for Myself* shows him squaring up to Hemingway's existentialism and commitment to style through action, and to Faulkner's technical complexity, and trying to merge the two in order to take on responsibility for the evolving style and consciousness of his own generation. Form or craft as such is no longer the essential issue; 'Craft is very little finally,' he said, for consciousness and performance were the great necessities. Writing was a merging of self-awareness and a report on the psychic and social workings of a cancerous history. Mailer's attempt to become the writer as immersed historical performer reached its strongest expression in his essay 'The White Negro' (1957, reprinted in *Advertisements for Myself*), where he explained that the age called for a new hero, the White Negro or the 'hipster', to react against the totalitarian order: 'One is Hip or one is Square (the alternative which each new generation is beginning to feel), one is a rebel or one conforms, one is a frontiersman in the Wild West of American night life, or else a Square cell, trapped in the totalitarian tissues of American society, doomed willy nilly to conform if one is to succeed.'

The essay dramatizes the Manichean struggle into which Mailer felt the writer must throw himself in modern American culture. One fictional outcome was *An American Dream* (1965), an unselfconsciously obscene, semi-autobiographical novel told in the first person by Stephen Rojack, 'a personality built on an abyss', a man both of wild inner desires and large political ambitions. The book becomes a sex-and-power fantasy, seeking to draw into Rojack's responding consciousness both those political and psychic forces that order and shape American society, and the extra-territorial and supernatural powers of salvation and damnation at work in the world. Mailer's concern is again with the fantastic interweaving of the psychic, sexual, and political worlds, and *An American Dream* is a dark nightmare that turns towards an apocalyptic redemption. Another possible mode was fictionalized journalism; Mailer developed it most fully in *The Armies of the Night* (1968). Subtitled 'History as a Novel, The Novel as History', the book, about an actual protest march on the Pentagon over the Vietnam war, seeks to merge reportage and the novelistic dramatization of the active consciousness of one participant, Mailer himself, which alone can give an accurate perspective on what is recorded by the media as 'historical fact'. The relation of fiction to history was to become an insistent theme of writing during the 1960s and 1970s, and from this time on most of Mailer's best work has been in the form of journalism and reportage, in which he has portrayed many of the conflicts of recent American public and political life. Another notable novel, *Why Are We in Vietnam?*, appeared in 1967, metaphorically relating a bear-hunt in Alaska to the violence and psychic disorder of the war in Vietnam, while the later *Ancient Evenings* (1983) is an historical novel (about Egypt) of massive ambition. Mailer remains the writer who has most powerfully sought to portray the link between history and the disorder of the social and individual psyche. By moving between fiction and reportage, the dream-world of sex and violence and the actual violence of American life, he has been a leading explorer of the deeper politics of the age.

Appropriately it was Mailer who signalled, in 'The White Negro', the marked change in cultural consciousness that was to have great impact on writing at the end of the 1950s. The essay portrayed what was to be called the 'counter-cultural' rebellion of the end of the decade, and in it Mailer suggested that a new form of writing was already arising from new behavioural experiment, from a growing romantic disaffiliation, from youthful protest, and the underground culture of drugs and homosexuality. The voices of what Mailer called the 'frontiersmen in the Wild West of American night life' were indeed already making their underground mark on Fifties culture. In 1952 Paul Bowles, an American expatriate living in Tangier with his writer wife Jane Bowles, brought out the novel *Let It Come Down*, a powerful work about degenerate exhaustion and exposure, drugs, and violence set in a vacant North African landscape. Like his earlier *The Sheltering Sky* (1949), it was a forceful image of the irrational and nihilistic energies that Bowles saw behind modern culture. In 1953 another writer living in Tangier, William S. Burroughs, brought out under the pen-name 'William Lee' a novel, *Junkie*, about drug addiction and homosexuality, which would become an underground classic. In 1955 another American expatriate writer, J. P. Donleavy, living in Ireland, brought out (in Paris, where Burroughs's book also appeared) his novel *The Ginger Man*, a work of comic sexual anarchy, set in Dublin, which won an erotic reputation. The anarchistic-expatriate tradition of Henry Miller clearly had not died. Meanwhile at home a new culture of disaffection and 'inward expatriation' was developing under the name of 'beat'. The term was reputedly coined by Jack Kerouac in or before 1952; Kerouac explained that it was associated both with the spontaneous beat of jazz music and the beatific joys of oriental mysticism: 'Beat means beatitude, not beat up'. Also in 1952, John Clellon Holmes was recording the life of the 'Beat Generation' in his novel *Go*, and then linking it with the world of jazz in his novel *The Horn* (1958). Over the 1950s, 'beat' writing, and the radical life-style that went with it, became part of the spirit of a generation that was in growing revolt against the conformity, respectability, and materialism of Lonely Crowd America, and was ready to express its despair in deviance. The strongest expression of 'beat' came in a new, free-form, spontaneous poetry, and above all in Allen Ginsberg's long poem *Howl*, about the 'madness' of a generation, in 1955.

In the novel, the parallel text was undoubtedly Jack Kerouac's own 'spontaneous bop prose' novel *On the Road* (1957). Kerouac was a friend of Ginsberg and other Beat poets, who figure in the novel; part of the theme of the book was self-celebration of the generation itself. The book also extended well beyond Salinger's fragile, and influential, zen mysticism in its interest in Eastern philosophy, and the attraction of drugs. But above all it celebrated the free-wheeling, defiant journey west across America, on the road, out of the technological city and into the freedom of one's own spontaneous nature. Kerouac's book marked the beginnings of the 'hippie' movement, and its dreams of inner journeys and physical and political freedom gained through jazz, drugs, sexual freedom, and pure movement. Kerouac took these themes further in *The Subterraneans* and *The Dharma Bums* (both 1958), moving deeper both into the drugs and drop-out culture and into oriental mysticism. He published several more novels and some poetry before he died in 1969. Today *On the Road*, his best book, seems less interesting for its experiments with prose 'spontaneity' than it does as a record of a cultural episode which changed the intonation of much American writing. By the early Sixties, this new romantic anarchism, emphasizing spontaneity, instinct, open style, and free expression—often rejecting the security and fixing of print for the immediacy of performance—became a new aesthetic, though the revolution was as much one in behaviour as it was in literary form. 'Beat' writing and fluid prose were of a piece with improvised poetry-and-jazz, the happening, the multimedia performance, the freewheeling global-village sensibility. Kerouac's own prose style, suitably loose, influenced other writers like Hubert Selby (*Last Exit to Brooklyn*, 1964) and John Rechy (*City of Night*, 1963), who were to take far further his sense of human extremity and his quality of hallucinatory naturalism.

But of far more importance as an experimenter was William S. Burroughs, the dedicatee of *Howl*, whose work came to represent Beat fiction at its surrealist, avant-garde edge. Following on from *Junkie*, Burroughs began to win scandalous attention with the sequence *The Naked Lunch* (1959), *The Soft Machine* (1961), *The Ticket That Exploded* (1962), and *Nova Express* (1964). His books were sufficiently scatological and outrageous for *The Naked Lunch*, also published in Paris, to be delayed in its American publication until 1962. But the place of publication was appropriate; Burroughs owed much to French writers like Céline and Genet, and the surrealist movement of the 1930s, which mixed collage presentation with fantastic, hallucinatory, dream-like systems. Burroughs defined his technique as the 'cut-up, fold-in method of Brion Gysin' (Gysin was a friend and collaborator), and it owes much to collage and chance association, depending on 'junk' in two senses: junk as drugs (especially heroin, from addiction to which Burroughs was releasing himself), and junk as cultural rubbish randomly collected. Thus Burroughs's work used drug-like or drug-induced states to assimilate the floating detritus and loose images of contemporary American life, which he saw with a bitter and anarchistic rage resembling Henry Miller's. The *dreck* of newspapers, the flashing images of media systems, fantastic motifs from science fiction, are merged through the cut-up, fold-in method with the author's own homo-erotic fantasies and anxieties, which are used in the sequence to create the surreal imagery of the 'Nova' universe. Burroughs's novels are also works of political dissent, and he liked to call them 'satires', though the term suggests a control and a clarity of position which their very form denies. They see, and challenge, a world of oppressive, authoritarian systems, run by policing forces who seek to deny and persecute the free play of consciousness. In this respect, they satirize a distorted, psychotic, plot-ridden, and science-managed age. But Burroughs also describes himself as a 'cosmonaut of inner space', and his fictional world of violent plots, disfiguring obscenities, and sadistic degradation also coincides with his own inner fantasies. It results in a satirical grotesquerie in which, however, there can be no stable object of indignation, since the author's ostensible outrage is also an indulgence of the sadistic homo-erotic fantasies of the self. Burroughs's books are consciously works of a post-humanist age, unstable and free-form texts that attempt to penetrate at various points a world far gone in obscenity, barbarity, technological systems, and violence which dissolves the human subject, but also to explore an imagination itself in a similar condition of dehumanization. These books, and their later successors like *Cities of the Red Night* (1981), break open the difficult frontiers of fantasy, and represent a powerful transfiguring of the surreal tradition into the paranoid style of post-humanist fiction that played its part in the radical mood of the American 1960s.

Around the same time in the Fifties that Burroughs was beginning to write experimentally ('In my writing I am acting as a map maker, an explorer of psychic areas . . ., and I see no point in exploring areas that have already been thoroughly surveyed'), another writer of even greater importance was challenging the realist conventions of the day. 'Reality is neither the subject nor the object of true art, which creates its own special reality,' Vladimir Nabokov observed in his 'novel' *Pale Fire* (1962), which is presented to us in the form of a long symbolist poem surrounded by a scholarly commentary. Nabokov had been born in turn-of-the-century St Petersburg of a distinguished Russian family which was exiled in 1919, at the time of the Bolshevik

Revolution. He wrote novels in Russian and German in the various European cities to which exile took him, until, as a result of the Nazi invasion of France, he began a second exile in the United States in 1940. By this time he had already begun his first English-language novel, *The Real Life of Sebastian Knight* (1941), where an effort to write a 'true' biography dissolves into the paradoxes both of human identity and literary representation. Now began his 'love affair with the English language' which was to result in an important sequence of experimental novels. They include *Bend Sinister* (1947), which he described as written by 'an anthropomorphic deity impersonated by me'; the remarkable *Lolita*, which was first published in Paris in 1955 because of its erotic theme and its decadent sensibility, and did not appear in the USA until 1958; a fine comic novel of émigré academic life *Pnin* (1957); *Ada or Ardor: A Family Chronicle* (1969); *Transparent Things* (1972); and *Look At the Harlequins* (1974). During the 1960s Nabokov returned to Switzerland, and died there in 1977, the most inventive, urbane, and cosmopolitan of experimental novelists.

Nabokov comes clearly out of the Russian tradition. His work owes much to the tradition of Russian comic grotesquerie, particularly to Gogol, to the imagination of Pushkin, on whom he wrote, and above all to the climate of Russian symbolism in the pre-Revolutionary years, which was preoccupied with the elusive relation of word to world. A scholar as well as a writer, Nabokov was also fascinated by the linguistic enquiries taking place in Europe during the 1930s, such as the work of the Vienna Circle. But though his earlier fiction has been subsequently translated into English, it was his second life as an American writer that established him as a major figure. His books collectively amount to a major investigation into the nature of fiction, fictionality, and symbolic representation, as well as into the nature of the modern artist. In these novels of games and labyrinths, the word often does not allude to the thing, and the types and genres of fiction are subjected to pastiche and mockery. Narrators may be madmen, liars, or experts in linguistic deception, the names of characters may be emblems, anagrams, or puns. Plots develop through complex codes and games, such as acrostic or word golf. The artist himself is an exile from his own language, and the central characters—the Humbert Humberts, Pnins, Charles Kinbotes, and Van Veens—are found in a world of chaotic disorder and historical displacement which extends to the émigré world of the United States. Nabokov is the novelist as nominalist, the writer who believes that the world is literally named into existence, is born of the play of language. Art is both a comic and a cosmic game of knowledge, or a fictive acrostic with transcendental properties. Such notions go back to the climate of decadence in the symbolist arts at the turn of the century, and their complex culture of narcissism, where the labyrinthine, the mirrored, the doubled, the enigmatic, and the fleeting are the stuff of art. His heroes are obsessive game-players who are chasing the butterflies of transcendence with the net of language, and they are usually in search of some elusive imprint of reality, some held moment of identity or beauty, from which they are none the less perpetually exiled.

Both Nabokov and Burroughs inherit the novel as a parodic storehouse of forms. Unlike Burroughs, Nabokov is an explorer of the fictional impression itself, and an interpreter of the intertextual, the parodic, the rewritten nature of all literary art. But an essential faith in the novel form remains, because of the very fact that the form displays the way we construct the sense of 'reality'—a word, he points out in his comments on *Lolita*, that means nothing except in quotes. Nabokov's faith is in the artist as maker, and the need to invent fictions and live in the labyrinthine pleasures of the mind is what makes his heroes and his stories. The novel is a self-analyzing form of perception, constructing not an external truth but a compositional truth that is its own. The task is comic, the comedy being based on the sheer absurdity of reality and the obsessive and even psychotic nature of our attempts to pursue and grasp it. Much of this comes from the aesthetics of modernism, out of which Nabokov's theories and attitudes emerge. In this view, art becomes the last paradise, the world we are alienated from by our human imperfection, but to which we seek to return. Like Samuel Beckett and the Argentinian story-writer Jorge Luis Borges, two other non-American authors who were to have a massive influence on American fiction in the

1960s, Nabokov represents a major link between the earlier European stages of the modern movement and the development of that kind of writing in the United States that came to be called 'postmodern'.

Of the books of Nabokov's American phase, the best and most powerful is *Lolita*, a story, told from prison by a decadent, obsessive, and unreliable narrator, the ageing Russian émigré Humbert Humbert, of his pursuit of America and the English language itself. Humbert's sexual desires are stirred only by 'nymphets', those young women of a certain age who are briefly caught on the cusp between innocence and experience. The main part of the story is Humbert's chase across America after his obscure object of desire, a child-woman appropriately called Dolores Haze. The pursuit is also a pursuit of the elusive symbol that is art itself. Meanwhile he is also chasing or is being chased by his own double, Quilty, whom he violently murders, to become 'guilty of killing Quilty'. The book is a literary gallery of acrostics, puns, and allusions to works of American literature; Dolores Haze is a version of Edgar Allan Poe's Annabel Lee, and also a metaphorical substitute for the ambiguous and elusive myth of America itself. The America that Humbert crosses from motel to motel is a series of punning mysteries and clues that encourage the quest but also add up to a representation of American 'reality'. Humbert represents European experience, which is a kind of innocence; Dolores Haze represents American innocence, which is actually sophisticated experience. Among his later books *Pale Fire* is amongst other things a brilliant literary parody, while *Ada* is both a reconstruction and a deconstruction of an American story. It too is based on parody, pastiche, doubles, and mirrors. Ivan Veen incestuously loves his 'cousin' Ada Veen; the main setting, Ardis Hall, lies on 'the gentle eminence of old novels'; the story is set on the planet of Anti-Terra, where the landscape consists of motifs mixed from the heritage both of the Russian and the American novel. The parodic method has, of course, a serious point. The task of the writer is to know his own literariness, understand his own instruments, genre, language, and symbol, and defeat the world both of conventional time and place, and imprisoning fact.

Fiction needs to see itself as fiction: a humanly created world of language and symbol constructed by a questing artist who may reveal but cannot copy reality.

6.

Nabokov is one of the great tragic ironists of modern fiction, and
an important international writer. But his impact on American writing largely coincided with a time when the spirit of grotesque and black humour was growing in American fiction, along with the belief that it was becoming ever harder to record the American realities of the 1960s. Like Burroughs's, his work suited a climate in which the spirit of realism and naturalism was increasingly coming under question. Where, however, Burroughs suggests that the human subject and the political reality were disintegrating under extreme pressures, Nabokov explores the eternal scepticism of the nominalist about whether a sign or image can ever be anything more than itself. Both writers indicate the dissolution of convention and the playful breaking down of genres and representational methods that marked the writing of the early Sixties, when it seemed that humanist representation, moral realism, and objective certainty were no longer easily available to the novel. Burroughs's spontaneous prose and grotesque satire, and Nabokov's exploration of the parodic status of a fiction in relation not just to other literature but to reality itself, were experiments with the potential of the novel, but they could also be seen as commentaries on a time of disordered history, threatening plots and systems, and anxieties about the very nature of language and signs themselves. By the later years of the 1950s, American fiction was already responding more experimentally, obliquely, and indirectly to the world of late-technological American life and contemporary materialism, to the 'junk' of American culture. And by the start of the 1960s, a spirit of fantasy and experiment, parody and dark humour, was already bringing a sense of stylistic change to the American novel.

7

Postmoderns and Others: The 1960s and After

Ghosts, monsters, criminals, deviates represent melodrama and weakness. The only horror about them is the dreamer's own horror of isolation. But the desert, or a row of false shop fronts; a slag pile, a forge where the fires are banked, these and the street and the dreamer, only an inconsequential shadow himself in the landscape, partaking of the soullessness of these other masses and shadows; this is the 20th Century nightmare.

Thomas Pynchon, *V.* (1963)

'I began to write fiction on the assumption that the true enemies of the novel were plot, character, setting and theme, and having once abandoned these familiar ways of thinking about fiction, totality of vision or structure were really all that remained.'

John Hawkes, in an interview (1965)

1.

NOTHING more clearly marked the end of the anxious, tranquillized Fifties than the election to President of John F. Kennedy in 1960. Kennedy was young, intelligent, and personable; with the Second World War at a distance and an era of space exploration to hand, he was able to speak hopefully of the New Frontier of American life. He was interested in ideas and the arts, and many writers and intellectuals gathered around the 'Camelot court' of his brief presidency. In his *Presidential Papers* (1963), Norman Mailer drew an optimistic new link between power and culture, the Kennedy administration and his own anarchistic radicalism, and in his novel *An American Dream* (1965), the hipster 'hero' Rojack, trying to fight the battle of good and evil in the American universe, has links with the Kennedy clan.

Much of the writing of the Sixties, particularly the Kennedy Sixties, was given to attempts to forge a significant link between intellectual life and American political power. If Mailer acquired political ambitions (Mayor of New York), Gore Vidal had presidential ones, and his elaborate and long-running series of Washington novels—*Washington, D.C.* (1967), *Burr* (1974), *1876* (1976), *Lincoln* (1984), and *Empire* (1987)—which deal with the courts of the various great American presidents, show his long-term political fascination. The theme persisted, and in Philip Roth's *Portnoy's Complaint* (1969), Bellow's *Humboldt's Gift* (1975), Jerzy Kosinski's *Being There* (1971), and Joseph Heller's *Good As Gold* (1979), the heroes are government political advisors, or have some important, if as time went on increasingly ironic, relation to politics and power.

If in the early Sixties a new alliance seemed to be growing between writers and the leaders and political direction of the nation, it was not to last long. Unease grew even during the Kennedy years, particularly over the Cuban missile crisis, and when Kennedy was tragically assassinated in Dallas in 1963 a brief era seemed to end. Next came the Johnson and Nixon presidencies, the escalating war in Vietnam, the rise (on and off the campuses) of civil rights, free speech, and anti-war protests, as well as black power, street violence, and the campaign to replace official politics with a radical, and sometimes revolutionary, New Left agenda. By the mid-Sixties, Norman Mailer, ever the indicator of cultural change, was asking in one of his novel titles *Why Are We in Vietnam?* (1967), and in two books from the key year of 1968, *The Armies of the Night* and *Miami and the Siege of Chicago*, he provided as a participant 'informal histories' both of the march of intellectuals on the Pentagon to protest the war in Vietnam and of the chaos and violence that surrounded the Republican and Democratic party conventions. By now the Sixties had seen the growth of an ever more confident 'counter-culture', in which the arts had a significant part. The Beat Generation grew into the hippie movement, which saw itself as a large-scale revolution of youth consciousness. New forms of expression from the rock concert to the happening, from bop prosody to the new 'black arts', from poetry-and-jazz

to performance and fringe theatre, declared the spirit of randomness and provisionality, of instantaneous experience and
communal radicalism, of generational conflict and racial anger,
that was the mood of the times. The arts themselves became
more expectant, more open, more outrageous and more experimental, taking their place in a greening of consciousness that
would change the spirit of America.

If the writings of the Sixties show a clear return to politics and
history, this was not expressed (as it had been for the Marxist
intellectuals of the 1930s) in the form of a clear ideology, nor in
a devotion to social or proletarian realism. The Sixties were a
transforming period in the American arts, and were marked by
a spirit of avant-garde revival. Techniques grew random, styles
mixed and merged, methods became increasingly provisional.
The tendencies that emerged acquired a variety of names—beat
writing, black humour, aleatory art, bop prosody, and so on—
but, in an age that likes to have even its most provisional arts
clearly labelled, it is well to settle, for a description of the general tendency, on the term 'postmodernism'. That elusive word
tells us two things: that modernism is over, and that the late
modern arts still function in its shadow. It assumes the arts
retain an avant-garde duty, but that the duty now has a lack of
definition; these are the arts of those who come after, but also
look before. The Sixties avant-garde revival was as behavioural
as it was aesthetic. It celebrated youth, the momentary event,
the instantaneous cultural experience, dropping out, taking
drugs. It distrusted established forms, genres, and canons, and
all official structures of power. It also provided a lively environment for serious artistic experiments, and from it grew a new
approach to all the forms of writing.

The excitement was new but, well before Kennedy's presidency
altered the national mood, it was clear that in fiction too the
times they were a-changing. Before the end of the Fifties, the
neo-realist spirit and existentialist anxieties that had dominated
the first part of the decade had already begun yielding to a new
tone of black humour and absurdism, which was taking fiction
away from realism. 'Men have learned to live with a black burden, a huge aching hump: the supposition that "reality" may only

be a dream,' Vladimir Nabokov had written as early as 1941 in *The Real Life of Sebastian Knight*: 'How much more dreadful it would be if the very awareness of your being aware of reality's dream-like nature were also a dream, a built-in hallucination.' Like Beckett and Borges, Nabokov handed to younger successors a sense of absurdity and narcissistic self-awareness that would hallmark much Sixties writing. But this new spirit was equally shaped by a pervasive feeling of the absurdity of American history itself, and the unreality of its reality. That perverse opponent of American power structures William S. Burroughs observed in *The Naked Lunch*: 'The world cannot be expressed, it can perhaps be indicated by a mosaics of juxtaposition, like objects abandoned in a hotel room, defined by negatives and absence.' Novelists increasingly saw around them a contemporary American history of vast plots and powers, which shrivelled, drained, and programmed the self, challenged the conventional codes of representation, and required new and experimental expression. In a famous essay of 1961, 'Writing American Fiction', Philip Roth declared that American realities were now growing so absurd and incredible they were the envy of any novelist, and his fiction, like that of others, began exploring the unreliable borders between the outward world of history and the imaginary life of fiction. In 1963 Saul Bellow observed in an essay, 'Some Notes on Recent American Fiction', that the forces of public power and energy were becoming so massed in American life that they drove the private self back into hiding, causing fiction to lose touch with its humanistic and moral function.[1]

Even before Kennedy's death, then, the new American fiction was beginning to present a portrait of history and reality which showed it not as a place of hope, opportunity, and humanity but as an arena of distorting power-plays, vast technological systems, conspiratorial structures, and apocalyptic threats to individual survival. In 1961 Joseph Heller published *Catch-22*, a novel ostensibly about American flyers in Italy during the Second World War. An absurdist's anti-war novel, it showed the war as

[1] Roth's and Bellow's essays are reprinted in Malcolm Bradbury (ed.), *The Novel Today: Contemporary Writers on Modern Fiction* (London: Fontana, rev. edn., 1990).

a set of illogicalities and conspiracies where battles were fought and lives lost for no intelligible reason. In the same year, the science-fiction writer Kurt Vonnegut published *Mother Night*, another absurdist Second World War novel in which the central character delivers propaganda for both sides and so serves 'good too secretly and evil too openly'. Vonnegut named his work 'black humour' or 'gallows humour', humour written in reaction to the horrors of life and society. By the decade's end, in *Slaughterhouse-Five* (1969), he made his theme even more explicit, mixing two genres—science fiction and autobiographical reportage—to relate the world of modern horror, exemplified by the fire-bombing of Dresden by the Allied forces in 1945, with the imaginary life of his distant planet Tralfamadore, from where human life could be observed as absurd. In *One Flew Over the Cuckoo's Nest* in 1962, Ken Kesey portrayed American society as a madhouse, controlling and repressing the anarchistic energies of the self. In 1963, Sylvia Plath published her fragile novel of disintegration *The Bell Jar*, and Thomas Pynchon, perhaps the most remarkable new writer of the time, attempted in his vast novel *V.* nothing less than a reconstitution of modern world history—seen as a disintegrative, entropic process working free of human intention and dissolving integral human identity into vast systems. If fiction was indeed being drawn back into the larger historical and political world, its fundamental images were strange and disquieting—images of power, pattern, process, and system, of the animate struggling against the inanimate, of self and character trapped within a universe of increased and mechanical force. Novelists might attempt to celebrate some unpatterned, resistant reaction to history, system, and code, or point to the entry of the system into the fragile centre of the self, making humanism impossible and life blackly—though sometimes comically—absurd.

After the Kennedy assassination, when dissent increased and American politicians appeared to lose touch with American dreams, this note of disquiet, absurdity, and extremity grew in the new fiction. Treatment of contemporary history grew more critical and surreal, and a surrealist writer like John Hawkes—who had been linking the landscape of historical violence to the world of inner disorientation and schizophrenia ever since his Gothic *The Cannibal* in 1949—became more central. In his earlier writing, John Barth had been concerned, in Fifties fashion, with existential crises in an absurd world. But now his fiction grew more self-examining and with *Giles Goat-Boy* (1966) represented the world as a great campus war of rival computers struggling to possess the 'revised new syllabus'. With *A Confederate General from Big Sur* (1964), Richard Brautigan created a mocking, open-ended form of fiction to contrast the solid world of established American history with the hippie spirit of provisionality. As American writers looked again to history, past or present, they played with it in a parodic and disruptive spirit, rewriting public legend, teasing the dream and the flag, playing at the ambiguous border between fact and imagination, official record and invented fiction, public sign and private symbol, thereby undermining familiar concepts of realism. Often their writing acquired the quality of mock-text, fantasizing actuality, cartooning character, and subjecting the objective world to a surrealist awareness of alternatives, opposites, and oppositions.

If some writers, like Saul Bellow, complained that American fiction was leaving behind its humanism and its moral responsibilities by mocking the self and its own sign, others argued that, the world outside being over-written and over-plotted, the novel could do nothing other than rewrite or deconstruct it. It became a postmodern convention to say that the conventional novel, with its fixed text, chronological development, claim to authority and to authorship, had become exhausted, overwhelmed by the glut of public narrative in the multiplying media, and the plurality of forms and styles available to the late modern writer. John Barth argued in an essay of 1967, 'The Literature of Exhaustion', that the contemporary writer now confronted the 'used-upedness' of the modes of fiction, had now to reassess all the conventions—authorial omniscience, narrative coherence, familiar outcome and conventional ending—and was left in the role of the playful inheritor of a world already made into a story.[2] Problems of political and historical representation beset the novelist—but in

[2] This essay is also reprinted in Bradbury (ed.), *The Novel Today*, cited in note 1.

a time which discouraged the notion that the word represented the world, that stories told direct and public truths, that fiction transcended its own fictionality. Hence for many the writer's task was now to break the conventional narrative boundaries, mix the historical genres (as Vonnegut mixed realism with science fiction), examine the relation of fiction to fact, and reconstruct the novel.

Now, broadly, the novel seemed to move in two contrary, yet related, directions. One was towards a new encounter with factual writing, a fresh model of reportage. Truman Capote called his *In Cold Blood* (1966)—a novel-shaped report on the actual murder of a Middle American farming family by two wandering psychopaths, which Capote represents as a symbolic encounter between an innocent and a corrupted, urban, and dark America—a 'nonfiction novel'. The genre was hardly original to the Sixties (it could indeed be traced back to Defoe) but it displayed the preoccupation with the borderline of fact and fiction, the problem of 'faction'. Norman Mailer similarly subtitled his personal report on the protest march on the Pentagon, *The Armies of the Night*, 'History as a Novel, The Novel as History', and his book deals not just with the difference between official and subjective reporting but with the boundaries of the real, which is often a fiction masquerading as a fact, and the fictive, which asserts its own principles of narration and perception. Mailer's point, that the writing of history, the journalistic reporting of events, the making of any record, is itself an enterprise in constructing a fictional narrative, was reinforced by the self-analysis of many Sixties historians and journalists. The 'New Journalist' Tom Wolfe—later to emerge as a novelist himself—made a double strike by claiming that the novel was irrelevant to the complexity of contemporary experience, but that journalism could take over all its sensitivities and techniques. 'New Journalism' could thus displace 'boring' novels as the imaginative record of the times, capturing fiction's methods—scene-by-scene construction, imaginative recording of dialogue, interiorization of viewpoint, detailed explication of social mores, concern with style—to record current culture (the 'crazed obscene uproarious Mammon-faced drug-soaked mau mau lust-oozing Sixties') with visionary accuracy.

Wolfe and other 'New Journalists' like Hunter S. Thompson, Joan Didion, and Seymour Krim stressed at once the subjective, creative novelty of their techniques and their social and political research. The claims seemed justified when two *Washington Post* investigative journalists, Bob Woodward and Carl Bernstein, explored the cryptic, conspiratorial world surrounding the Watergate break-in in *All the President's Men* (1976) and forced Nixon to resign as President. Breaking down the borders of the fictional, merging the genres of fact and fantasy, became a dominant theme of much Sixties writing. E. L. Doctorow's novels *Welcome to Hard Times* (1960), *The Book of Daniel* (1971) and *Ragtime* (1975) constantly cross and recross the borders of fact and fiction. He explained: 'The presumption of the interpenetration of fact and fiction is that it is what everybody does—lawyers, social scientists, policemen. So why should it be denied to novelists?' The method opened the door for a sceptical, often highly critical, return to past and present American history. Thomas Berger (who had written about the deceits of the American dream in wartime in his black humour novel *Crazy in Berlin*, 1958), dealt in *Little Big Man* (1964) with the Battle of Little Big Horn, largely seen from the Indian point of view. William Styron wrote in *The Confessions of Nat Turner* (1967) about an actual nineteenth-century slave rebellion, recreating the story from the black viewpoint, and Robert Coover offered a fantastic exploration of the trial and execution of the atomic spies the Rosenbergs in *The Public Burning* (1977).

While some writers self-consciously examined the conventions covering the boundary between fact and fiction, actual and imaginary, others explored in the opposite direction, examining the limits of fictionality. Many novels grew self-conscious and reflexive, treating fiction's subject as fictionality itself. This experimental enquiry has been given various names: Raymond Federman—author of the interesting experimental text *Double or Nothing* (1972)—called it 'surfiction', Robert Scholes 'fabulation', others 'meta-fiction'. Here the essential premise is that the novel constructs nothing other than itself, is at best an ambiguous and deceitful mirror of what we think to be reality, and can make no claim to represent it, to signify. This also is not entirely a novel issue in the novel; it goes back to fiction's origins in the eighteenth century and is a recurrent preoccupation of modernism. What distinguishes postmodern meta-fiction is its relation to the public and social fictions that surround it, and its attempt to find a mode of discovery and exploration within them. Here it is possible to distinguish two main tendencies. One is the exploration of fictiveness itself, in writers like Federman, Barth, William H. Gass, Robert Coover, and Donald Barthelme. In their self-reflexive work, the idea of fictionality is played with and parodied, and the elements of fiction made provisional, so that novel or story becomes an elaborate form of complicity between author, text, and reader. Narrative is often largely concerned with the metaphysics of writing, the options of story, or the problems of language ('What does language have against me—me that has been good to it, respecting its little peculiarities and nicilosities, for sixty years,' asks the narrator of one of Donald Barthelme's stories). The other is an increased interest in the fantastic, Gothic, and surreal—fantasy being, as modern critics have argued, not an escape from reality and the real, but a means for interrogating its conventions and breaking the rules of narrative familiarity.

Postmodern writing in the Sixties is therefore a remarkable and plural mixture of forms, ranging from the documentary to the reflexive, from historical narrative to grotesque and absurdist black humour and surrealism. If the bleak, extravagant notes of black humour played a large part in the writing of the early 1960s, with writers like Heller, Vonnegut, Berger, Terry Southern, Bruce Jay Friedman, and Stanley Elkin, the middle of the decade saw a clear turn towards meta-fiction. John Hawkes's *Second Skin* appeared in 1964, Robert Coover's *The Origin of the Brunists* and Jerzy Kosinski's *The Painted Bird* in 1965. 1966 saw Thomas Pynchon's fine *The Crying of Lot 49*, William Gass's *Omensetter's Luck*, and Barth's meta-fictional parable *Giles Goat-Boy*. 1967 saw publication of Brautigan's *Trout Fishing in America*, Donald Barthelme's anti-novel *Snow White*, and Susan Sontag's experimental fiction *Death-Kit*. In 1968, the key year of student radicalism, protest and near-revolution, there were Barth's intermedia exercise *Lost in the Funhouse* (subtitled 'Fiction for Print, Tape, Live Voice'), William Gass's *In the Heart of the Heart of the Country*, Jerzy Kosinski's *Steps*, Ronald Sukenick's experimental novel *Up*, and Steve Katz's *The Exagggerations of Peter Prince*. Most of this was avant-garde writing, marked with scepticism about generic types and categories, ironic inversion, disposition to pastiche and parody, and meta-fictional insistence on the arbitrariness of its own power to signify.

At the same time Sixties writing was influenced by the powerful ideas of the prevailing counter-culture: the interest in drugs, psychedelic experience, the new psycho-politics, the concern with alternative orders of being. The counter-culture was not solely political. It saw itself as a new avant-garde, reacting to the outward order and its violence with a new inward spirit, expressing the blanks and indeterminacies of materialist culture. Post-humanistic, messianic, often mystical, it was rooted in the youth or protest movements, in the media wrap of the new global village, in the new cultural melting-pot with its rich but random display of styles, messages, images, and goods. This mixture is apparent in the important black fiction of the times. Some is fundamentally political: the work of radical black writers like John Oliver Killens in *And Then We Heard the Thunder* (1963), John A. Williams in *The Man Who Cried I Am* (1967), or William Melvin Kelley, in *Dem* (1969) is a revolt of black consciousness against the world of white experience, drawing on black modes of speech. But there was also a new postmodern black surrealism: Ishmael Reed produced the free-form text *The Free-Lance Pallbearers* (1967) and the mock western *Yellow Back Radio Broke Down* (1969), while Clarence Major, in *All-Night Visitors* (1969) and other works, displayed a less parodic and more poetic mode of fictional experiment.

2.

By the end of the Sixties, it was possible to believe that an entire new tendency—a body of new forms and discourses—had entered American writing, as in painting and architecture. To some critics this new transforming spirit appeared as radical in its meaning and impact as the great revolution of form and consciousness mounted by modernism at the beginning of the century: hence the term postmodernism. But, unlike modernism, born in Europe, it appeared entirely American. So one critic, Alan Wilde, tells us in his *Horizons of Assent: Modernism, Postmodernism and the Ironic Imagination* (1980), that 'postmodernism is an essentially American affair'. This, though, was to domesticate what was already an international phenomenon, linked with experiments in other countries. As we have seen, American postmodernism was unquestionably influenced by writers like Nabokov, Beckett, and Borges, who provided a link with earlier European modernism, and it related to tendencies in other countries: the French *nouveau roman* (the novel of what Nathalie Saurraute named 'the era of suspicion'), the fiction of Peter Handke in Austria, Italo Calvino and Umberto Eco in Italy, B. S. Johnson, Ann Quin, and John Fowles in Britain. There were other important European intellectual influences, in particular the tendencies that followed on from French existentialism: structuralism, with its semiotic approach and its concern with the nature of the sign, and deconstruction, which argued that the structure had no structure, saw the sign as under erasure, and emphasized the inevitable slippage of all referents. Yet, just as over the century modernism had moved closer to the United States, so postmodernism did seem to have a special application to the land of late modern post-culture. By the 1970s deconstruction's most influential philosopher, Jacques Derrida, was finding his warmest following in the USA and declaring 'America *is* Deconstruction'. As the argument over what postmodern is, or was, intensified, most recently in the work of Jean-François Lyotard and Fredric Jameson, it has been increasingly identified with a capitalist, pluralist, multi-hegemonic society, of which the United States is the prime example.

Certainly at the high point of the late Sixties, new American writers appeared as the most inventive and daring representatives of the late modern aesthetic, and postmodernism often simply meant innovative American fiction read (or misread) with the methods and slippages of French deconstructive criticism. It expressed much of what was to be said about American

stylistic abundance, its plurality of cultural references, its inter-
fusion of many media techniques and many genres, its vast
consumption of style and mannerism. For cultural critics like
Christopher Lasch it displayed a parodic 'culture of narcissism'
based on the fading of moral and political certainties from
recent American life. The French philosopher Jean-François
Lyotard saw the 'postmodern condition' as marked by the collapse of all the great meta-narratives (Christianity, Marxism)
that presumed to truth, and their replacement by essentially
provisional and indeterminate forms of narrative, while Jean
Baudrillard in *America* (1986) saw the USA as the apotheosis of
a strange new age of technological futility and simulated reality he
perceives as postmodern. In its sheer technological superiority
and cultural heterogeneity, the USA has a distinctive late modern
culture unquestionably reflected or refracted in its writings, and
it has inevitably played an advanced role in creating the repres-
entations, styles, and mannerisms of the age.

American postmodern writing did have a certain distinctive
character of its own. It generally lacked the philosophical seriousness of French or Italian fiction, or the humanist preoccupations
of the British. If it was often pervaded by dismay and negativity,
it was also often touched with a quality of American optimism,
humour, and hope, what one critic has identified as 'cheerful
nihilism'. Donald Barthelme, a writer of great subtlety and
intricate irony, observed that he found the French *nouveau
roman* inimical for its deadly seriousness, while John Barth
remarked of his French contemporaries 'good for them, [but]
the *nouveau roman* isn't just my cup of tea . . . Scheherazade's
my *avant-gardiste* . . .'. And though some American postmodernism is a bitter response to American actualities, much of
it shows playful delight in the freedoms of the imagination. If
there were no absolute realities, no truths prior to fiction, if all
the discourses of fact—science, biography, journalism—were
also fictionalist narratives, then the novel now had the freedom
to try all the literary variants, make a virtue of the provisionality
of all discourse, and pursue a new reality—'open-ended, provisional, characterized by suspended judgments, disbelief in hier-
archies, by mistrust of solutions, denouements and completions,

by self-consciousness issuing in tremendous earnestness but also far-reaching mockery . . .', as one critic put it. The paradox was summed up in Ronald Sukenick's appropriately titled *The Death of the Novel and Other Stories* (1969), where he argued that, in 'the world of post-realism', where literature in the conventional sense ceases to exist, the writer is renewed: 'The contemporary writer—the writer who is acutely in touch with the life of which he is a part—is forced to start from scratch: Reality doesn't exist. God was the omniscient author, but he died: now no-one knows the plot . . .'.

What is less certain is whether the various texts and performances that have been gathered under the general name of postmodernism represent a coherent movement, rather than a sequence of very various possibilities afforded by the wish to challenge previous realism and monumental modernism, with its confidence about the authority of narrative. In fact the 'post-' term often seems to have been more useful to critics than writers themselves, a way of perceiving them under the gaze of what one hostile critic calls 'the various fundamentals of the poststructuralist creed, such as the fictional status of the human subject, the dreary obsession with 'absence'—in particular the absence of origins and originals—and the paradoxical view that representation is at once all-powerful and impotent in its main task of referring to the world outside the self'. Much that is called postmodern has been swamped in the critical discourse surrounding it, which has drawn together a wide and disparate variety of innovative American writers of several generations. They include not only Nabokov, Hawkes, Pynchon, Barth, Vonnegut, Brautigan, Gaddis, Gass, Barthelme, Elkin, Kosinski and Coover, but also important successors like Sukenick, Gilbert Sorrentino, Federman, Major, Steve Katz, Stephen Dixon, Max Apple, Don DeLillo, Rudolph Wurlitzer, and Paul Auster. Some are chiefly formalists, concerned with the possibilities of open story and the creation of complex meta-texts; others are writers of political and social satire; some are minimalists like Barthelme ('fragments are the only forms I trust'), and others like Pynchon are writers of epic glut and excess. Inevitably the critical definitions vary. For some the works of such writers express the language crisis of the age, the loss of exterior referent and the human subject, for others they represent the playful age of story in a time of parodic discovery. To some these are writers struggling in the prison-house of language and trapped in the city of words, to others they are the voices of a new 'surfiction' where, as Raymond Federman claims, 'all distinctions between the real and the imaginary, the conscious and the subconscious, between the past and the present, between truth and untruth, will be abolished.' All that is clear is that the postmodern episode represented an attempt to break free of many of the established conventions of genre and narrative, representation and characterization, and that it has been a form of writing highly alert to the late twentieth-century cultural situation and its more open world of styles. Its chief achievement is surely that, in returning to some of the fundamental questions of narrative, representation, fictionality, literariness, surface, and depth, it has opened the doors of literary convention and brought a new era of radical enquiry not just to American fiction but the novel internationally.

3.

Though postmodernism is often seen as a break with representation and referentiality, it is clearly a fiction of the post-war world and its crises and anxieties. There is no doubt that the Second World War and the crises of representation and responsibility it posed had a crucial impact on Sixties fiction, and fed its preoccupation with the modern unreality. This is evident in the work of John Hawkes, a contemporary surrealist who during the war served as ambulance driver in Italy and Germany. In 1949 he published his novel *The Cannibal*, which, set over a complicated time-scale from 1914 to 1945, deals with the psychotic rise of totalitarianism in Nazi Germany, and its impact on the escapees from the great European 'Asylum', who wander its derelict wastes in the cannibal world of post-war disorder. Hawkes has named among his influences the French surrealists (especially Lautréamont and Celine) as well as the tradition of American Gothic. He has seen the constant element in surreal fiction as 'a quality of coldness, detachment, ruthless determination to face up to the enormities of ugliness and potential failure within ourselves and in the world around us, and to bring to this exposure a savage or saving comic spirit and the saving beauties of language'. He has also insisted that his world should be seen as an historical one, his economy of the grotesque having its origin in the 'spiritless, degraded landscape of the modern world'. Hawkes set two novellas, *The Goose on the Grave* and *The Owl* (both 1954), in Italy and war-torn Europe, showing the impact that the Fascist inheritance and the collapsed post-war landscape had on his writing. Though *The Beetle Leg* (1951) is an American Western, it too shares the same sterile landscape, and in *The Lime Twig* (1961) Hawkes returned to another devastated European setting, a wartime and post-war England he had never visited, but, drawing on British detective stories and Graham Greene, was able to populate with bombed-out buildings, race-gangs, and random violence.

But, though Hawkes's landscapes are historical, they are also imaginary—Gothic worlds removed from familiarity and revealing their fictional or invented nature. They begin, indeed, in consciousness and fantasy, born of the psyche of a writer consciously exploring violence and desire, a psyche shared out among his characters themselves. Hawkes has explained the novel as a form attempting to explore 'the terrifying similarity between the unconscious desires of the solitary man and the disruptive desires of the world', and explained his own work as committed to 'nightmare, violence, meaningful distortion, to the whole panorama of dislocation and desolation in human relationships'. His novels attempt to break the border where the clear distinction between external reality and inner consciousness is presumed to lie. As he says, the task of his work is to generate a vision of psychic intensity which can be shaped into an aesthetic wholeness, as 'materials of the unconscious are beaten, transformed into the fictional landscape itself.' Here, as in much Gothic, the ego is dissolved into landscapes that are both strange and metaphoric, and social images that reflect his most central themes—force and victimization, authority and submission, the world of ego and the world of undifferentiated erotic consciousness. His novels and stories form a dreamscape of war and conflict, death and detritus, asylums and prisons, islands and deserts—places where inner terror and outward anxiety or horror can coalesce.

Hawkes's is a highly subjective vision, drawing its intensity from the desires and dreams of the author as well as from perceptions of the real historical world. His stories are, as he puts it, 'an exclamation of psychic materials which come to the writer already distorted, prefigured in the inner schism between the rational and the absurd'. Far from being, like the work of John Barth or Donald Barthelme, highly controlled verbal constructs, his novels are open-ended, semi-formless, and dream-like, a visionary exploration of the imagination. His characters often live in a totalitarian or a rigidly controlled world, but are released by other forces into eroticism and death. In *The Cannibal*, a central figure is the Nazi Zizendorf, whose fantasies are central to the book. Hawkes's novels of the Sixties, when his work won greater recognition, become ever more like psychoanalytic texts. *Second Skin* (1964), is told by an ex-naval lieutenant, Skipper, who, marooned on a mythic Caribbean island, tells a tale about his daughter's suicide which is filled with references to Greek myths. Hawkes described his next three books—*Blood Oranges* (1971), *Death, Sleep and the Traveler* (1974), and *Travesty* (1976)—as 'a triad of novels concerned with sex, myth, the imagination, and the absurd'. They have a strong erotic content and are also concerned with the encounter with death, or the designification of the self. In 1980 Hawkes published *The Passion Artist*, the story of Conrad Vost, his most compelling recent hero, a self-imprisoned male living an Eastern European city of iron and prisons, who is released into flesh and death by the violence of the women around him. More recent books—*Virginie* (1982), *Adventures in the Alaskan Skin Trade* (1985), and *Whistlejacket* (1988)—have been more directly concerned with erotic extremes and the issue of gender. Hawkes is important for his modern surrealism, but it is significant that he now lives partly in France, where his fiction has been particularly honoured, though less for its postmodern characteristics than for its contribution to the surrealist tradition.

If Hawkes's fiction began with a response to the Second World War, so did the fiction of Joseph Heller, whose *Catch-22* was one of the most powerful, mood-catching novels from the start of the Sixties. Heller started the book in 1953, but his portrait of a group of American flyers in a corrupt, benighted, wartime Italy, carrying out an unending series of bombing missions for no apparent reason, caught the critical mood of the Kennedy years when it came out in 1961. Ironic nihilism was not new to American fiction—it is present in Melville, the late Twain, and Nathanael West—but Heller's voice is a direct response to a world dominated by military institutions and systems, which cold war America had become. Modern warfare is a form of corporate capitalism, run on the principle of 'catch-22', an institutional perversion of all logic in the interests of running a system. Under the US Air Force 'catch-22', if you want to get out of combat duty, you must first be certified insane; but, as anyone who wants to get out of combat duty must be sane, you cannot get out of combat duty. This is a world where sanity is madness, madness sanity, where the human is mechanical and the mechanical human, and such absurd formulae provide both the black humour and the structure of the book. In a world where man is bound to the machine of war organization, where a corrupt technological system battles unideologically against another such system, the only response can be pain, wry anarchy, the humour of absurdity. There are no just causes; war is fought for technology and organization, not morality or culture. Enemies are death-dealing forces which are either evaded or not; death is pervasive and purposeless; the army is staffed by freaks programmed to perform senseless acts. All intelligence goes into evasion and escape, since 'the spirit gone, man is garbage.' Survival is the art pursued by the book's hero, Captain Yossarian. 'There are now fifty or sixty countries fighting in this war,' he thinks, 'Surely so many countries can't *all* be worth dying for.'

Like many Sixties novels, *Catch-22* is a book about systematic denaturing, by society, military organization, capitalism, and death. It requires a similarly denatured or detached tone from the story-telling itself, for this dark comedy creates a world where things and men are depersonalized, where surreality exceeds reality, and where the human being is no more than a function of his absurd role. Comedy, however, also provides the means of relief, because the absurdity is seen and reacted to, with a sense of resigned suffering also familiar in Jewish humour, to which Heller owes much. The novel provides a brilliant role-call of comic figures: Milo Minderbender, the confidence man and entrepreneur who services the needs of both sides and sells weapons to either; Major Major, who runs his office by seeing people in it only when he's out, and is promoted to Major Major Major; Lieutenant Scheisskopf, whose dream is to create the perfect military parade, and attaches prostheses to his men to do it; the mail clerk ex-Pfc Wintergreen, who really runs the war. This is a world where insanity is contagious, pain and tragedy pervasive. When Yossarian visits Rome, the Eternal City, he finds it eternal only in its continuous and chaotic agonies, for God too has created a universe of catch-22, a lousy world filled with unnecessary suffering. Survival therefore calls for an equal degree of absurdity, a personal manipulation of manipulated language. Yossarian decides to live forever, or die in the attempt. People are trying to murder him, he complains, and he can prove it, because 'strangers he didn't know shot at him with cannons every time he flew into the air to drop bombs on them.' A paranoid with reasons, he finally decides to pursue survival by desertion, but even that remains an absurd possibility.

Heller's book is also implicitly a portrait of cold war America and its Dr Strangelove atmosphere. In his next novel, *Something Happened* (1974), he turns to the subject directly. Its anti-hero Bob Slocum is a corporation man working for a modern institution where everyone is afraid of someone else, to maintain his suburban middle-class family in which everyone—apart from a brain-damaged son—is also afraid of everyone else. Like Yossarian, Slocum longs for innocence ('When I grow up, I want to be a little boy') but even more than Yossarian he lacks the power to claim freedom. Living in a world of 'logical universal schizoid formation', he shares the general corruption and its mood of anesthetized morality and guilty complicity. So does Bruce Gold, in *Good as Gold* (1979), a book which is both homage to and parody of the Jewish-American novel Heller had been accused of failing to write. Gold, a second-generation academic who has largely lost touch with his ethnic past, answers the invitation to deal with 'the Jewish experience in America', even though, as his father points out, he knows nothing about it, wasn't born in Europe where it started, and spends his time in a Seventies Gentile world of joggers, swingers, and adulterers. It is however still a world of catch-22. Anti-Semitism has ceased, but no one has much time for Jews; old liberals have anxious new conservative thoughts; Gold himself is abrim with 'fiery caution and crusading inertia'. While his attempts to recover his Jewish past are unaided by membership of one of the more appalling families in Jewish-American literature, his ambitions, as a doctor of nothing, to succeed in contemporary America are no less troubled. Called in as a specialist in public relations by the US President, Gold has the chance to do 'anything you want, as long as it's everything we tell you to do in support of our policies, whether you agree with them or not. You'll have complete freedom.' Both novels display a social and historical decline that leads to entrapped complicity in a world of eternal paradox, a world created by a God of particularly teasing Jewish disposition, as portrayed in *God Knows* (1984).

Heller's black humour is of course also absurdist Jewish humour, which plays a large part in the fiction of the Sixties—in the novels of Bruce Jay Friedman, the stories of Woody Allen, or the splendidly comic and verbally playful fiction of Stanley Elkin, another bitter comic novelist of the age of rampant commercialism and cosmic compromise (*A Bad Man*, 1967; *The Living End*, 1979; *George Mills*, 1982). But Heller's view of the individual denatured in a world where everything is material and mechanical and all innocence is lost links his work with that of another writer of contemporary pain, comic absurdity, and resigned passivity, Kurt Vonnegut. Vonnegut began writing in the popular form of science fiction, which allowed him to explore scientific and technological systems, space–time relativity, and apocalyptic situations. But behind his work lies a lost Middle American innocence, under threat from technology, waste, and decay, and again the dark experience of the Second World War. His first two books are wry dystopian satires. *Player Piano* (1952) is set in his imaginary upstate New York city of Ilium, where the citizens of the future revolt against its technological perfection, though by the end they seem about to recreate what they have destroyed. *The Sirens of Titan* (1959) introduces another major setting, the imaginary planet of Tralfamadore, and turns on the wry paradox that the great human achievements—the Pyramids, Stonehenge, the Great Wall of China—are merely signals created by space societies to transmit their technical messages through the galaxies. However, in *Mother Night*, Vonnegut turns to Europe under Fascism, and concerns the ambiguous double agent Howard Campbell, who acts both as an American spy and a Nazi propagandist. Once again the theme is the absurdity of human endeavour, which is explored again in *Cat's Cradle* (1963), where technological ambitions lead to a nuclear apocalypse. Here humankind search for consolation in religions like Bokononism, which is founded on 'harmless untruths'—just, you might say, like novels themselves. Vonnegut's fiction was now writing about the world of careless modern technologies and the institutions and systems that serve them, and whether there was any means of reforming or amending them; this is the subject of his *God Bless You, Mr. Rosewater* (1965), which ironically looks at how the problem might be solved through philanthropy. By now Vonnegut's books were clearly recognizable for their distinctive tone: hard to characterize, easy to catch. Naïve *and* sophisticated, it is the tone of bitter-sweet satire, seeking reform of the human spirit, yet resigned before the powers of history and system. If the world functions as a vile joke, there a desire for consolation through stories and fantasies. Absurdist because it suggests the only response to such a world is an agonized laughter or a saving myth, it leads the characters towards a state of resigned passivity but also harmless innocence.

The resigned, anxious voice of Vonnegut's fiction was the author's own, as he showed in his next, most remarkable book *Siaughterhouse-Five or, The Children's Crusade* (1969). The novel was written, he notes folksily on the title page, by 'a fourth-generation German-American now living in easy circumstances on Cape Cod (and smoking too much), who, as an American infantry scout *hors de combat*, as a prisoner of war, witnessed the firebombing of Dresden, Germany, "the Florence of the Elbe," a long time ago, and survived to tell the tale'. It is his most direct encounter with the most terrible event of his life, which over twenty-three years he had been seeking to treat in fiction, searching for the right form, tone, and voice, and meanwhile displacing the theme into other stories. In a sense this book displaces it too, showing us through a series of clever steps out of reality and realism how we use the fantastic to make sense of the senseless. The book is partly a monologue of the author's own ironic resignation; so it goes, he tells us, with detached Tralfamadorian wisdom, as he sees the horrors of holocaust. There is really nothing to tell about a massacre. But he also finds another self in Billy Pilgrim, the childlike, good-natured optometrist from Ilium, New York, whose job in life is making 'corrective lenses', until he is captured in war and imprisoned in the Dresden abattoir, to become witness to the hideous fireball that destroyed the city and 135,000 civilians. But displacement goes further: Billy is kidnapped and taken to Tralfamadore, both a pathological location for a disturbed mind and a place of alternative knowledge, and alternative fiction-making. For on Tralfamadore novels are fragments, not based on earthly cause and effect. They see men as machines, experience life in instants, often reversing it, so that bullets can go back into guns and bombs back into bomb-bays, and accept fatalism ('So it goes'). In Tralfamadorian novels there is 'no beginning, no middle, no end, no suspense, no moral, no causes, no effects', and so all messages are synchronic, but, 'seen all at once, they produce an image of life that is beautiful and surprising and deep.' This could be read as Vonnegut's manifesto for postmodern fiction, or black humour itself. It certainly describes Vonnegut's own methods for both representing and deconstructing the world of the actual, in order to create new 'harmless untruths' that attempt to produce an image of life that is surprising and deep.

It is Vonnegut's complex mixture of tones, techniques, genres, and cultural levels that makes *Slaughterhouse-Five* both a great work of popular science fiction and a 'postmodern' novel. His later fiction has also blended innocent folksiness with bitter satire, crossing fictional self-consciousness with popular forms and comic effects—one of his later books is suitably called *Slapstick* (1976). Thus in *Breakfast of Champions* (1973), perhaps his clearest vision of raped, polluted, junk-dominated contemporary America, he considers whether his characters are victims of their society or of their author's own imagination, just his 'listless playthings'. Several of his books contain a surrogate author, Kilgore Trout; here he makes him responsible for the madness of one of the characters, Dwayne Hoover, and then explains in his own voice 'It's a big temptation for me, when I create a character for a novel, to say that he is what he is because of faulty wiring, or because of the microscopic amounts of chemicals which he ate or failed to eat on a particular day.' He reacts to this guilty literary self-consciousness by 'freeing' his own characters at the book's end, just like Jefferson freeing his slaves. Since they are, however, fictions, there is nowhere else for them to go—except on into Vonnegut's later novels, where quite a few of them reappear. So do Vonnegut's own quirks and values, folksy and sophisticated at once. He has described his later books—like *Galapagos* (1985), a Darwinian fable set a million years in the future; *Bluebeard* (1987), depicting an abstract expressionist painter who shares many artistic qualities with his author; and *Hocus Pocus* (1991), about a Vietnam veteran still persecuted in the repressive America of 2001—as less literary experiments than attempts to express his critical ideas in the form of a contemporary or futuristic moral fable. Indeed more recent works have been more in tune with the 'green' themes of the Nineties than with the postmodern experimentalism of the Sixties.

Vonnegut's kind of vision has been described by the critic Ihab Hassan as 'radical innocence', and the term also suits the work of Richard Brautigan, another central figure of the Sixties. Dying young in 1984, he has often been seen as the John Lennon of the hippie novel. His first novel, *A Confederate General from Big Sur* (1964), contrasts the solid America of the past with the pastiche and mockery of the provisional hippie age. Its central figure is Lee Mellon, a latter-day 'confederate general' who battles against the military-industrial complex, trying to recover a pastoral American innocence in the age of high technology and vast military power. His weapon of recovery is his playful and random imagination; so it is Brautigan's. Historical actuality—such as old Civil War battles—can be transformed by the playful imagination into fantasy and indeterminacy, the revenge of the imagination on fact. The book ends on wistful sadness, but also on a frenzy of the creative imagination, as the author's mind generates, he tells us, 'more endings, faster and faster until this book is having 186,000 endings per second'. Similarly in Brautigan's next 'writing', *Trout Fishing in America* (1967), he plays with the old pastoral form of the angler's notebook to confront the mechanical world of the present. In these forty-seven brief chapter-essays, the title phrase 'Trout Fishing in America' goes through strange transformations. It becomes a place, a person ('Trout Fishing in America Shorty'), a proof of the way language can playfully upturn its denotative function. By fantasy and imaginative play we can restore the animate to the inanimate—as when, in a marvellous comic passage, the narrator visits the Cleveland Wrecking Yard to buy not junk but a 'used' trout stream.

Brautigan's later work mixes hippie provisionality with a continued exploration of the signs and generic inversions of postmodern writing. With *In Watermelon Sugar* (1968), he constructs a fantasy fable, set in a peaceable community, iDEATH, where among the fragments of technological America the inhabitants make a new world out of watermelon sugar. The book is a benign fantasy of peace and gentleness, consciousness fading and finding new meanings, objects losing their fixity and becoming icons, the death of the egotistical self. It is also slightly too sweet, like its title. But Brautigan, who was also a serious poet, went on to show he was a serious explorer of language, image, and literary genre. *The Abortion* (1971), subtitled 'An Historical Romance', mocks the literary library, which limits our view of experience. *The Hawkline Monster* (1974), subtitled 'A Gothic Western', merges two seemingly incompatible forms, the adventure Western and the Gothic novel of displacement, estrangement, and horror. *The Tokyo–Montana Express* (1980) emphasized the meditative, poetic, and epistemological concerns of Brautigan's writing—the stress on the instant of experience, the dissolution of classic identity, the severance of the present from the past. Here we see the postmodern aspects of his work—the belief that old writing is exhausted, but that the image in its playfulness offers new forms of expression and identity. Like many of his contemporaries, Brautigan was seeking to break out of the linear and generic conventions of traditional writing, a key aim of the postmodern endeavour.

4.

One way to explore the aggressive, denaturing, cybernetic landscape that had become the face of Sixties America was to seek, through the imagination, the spirit of some essential innocence. But there were other writers for whom the task of exploring the history of the times demanded a more complex and radical vision. There seems little doubt that of these the most remarkable was Thomas Pynchon, the most outstanding and ambitious novelist to emerge from the decade. Pynchon has deliberately been a disappearing author, keeping his personal history obscure. But we know he studied at Cornell, worked for the Boeing Corporation on the West Coast, and has a scientific education. These are facts of importance for understanding the vast neo-technological universe of his novels, which are large-scale experimental fictions deeply injected not only with the cultural but the scientific knowledge of cold war, hi-tech, space-age America. His books are science fiction in the largest sense, a fiction in which the science and technology are themselves a central part of modern dislocating history. That theme starts early in Pynchon's work, in a short story 'Entropy' (1960), which takes up Henry Adams's sombre, turn-of-the-century reflections on the dislocation of mind and meaning in a modern multiverse which renders intelligence helpless in the face of the very powers it has released. Adams, we recall, was convinced that the history of the world is a history of energy, and that energy was now running loose towards entropy—moving from differentiation towards sameness and the heat-death of culture. Callisto, one of the two key characters in 'Entropy', shares this knowledge, reflecting on the heat-death of the age in his hermetically sealed room. Meanwhile, downstairs the other central character Meatball Mulligan, one of the directionless, body-centred figures who will recur in Pynchon's work, is holding a very physical party. Evidently neither Callisto's hermetic vision nor Meatball's chaotic one is itself enough to contain Pynchon's own inclusive sense of the world, for beyond both of them lies an apocalyptic late modern universe of non-human systems which outrun all consciousness. In this as in Pynchon's later works, the story is a text which is the interface between both their systems—the world of hermetic containment, the world of undifferentiation: complete meaning, and pure randomness. This binary combination and the encyclopaedic text that tries to capture it would become the mode of much of Pynchon's fiction.

It returns again in Pynchon's remarkable first novel *V.*, published in 1963. Here again are two opposed central characters, and two almost discrete stories, brought together in a double narrative motion. One is the story of Benny Profane, who, as his name suggests, is the random modern hero, sailor, street-man, and clown-comedian (or *schlemiel*) who simply 'yoyos' his way through the urban, wasteful, mechanical, underground world of this very populous book. Often in the company of his friends ('the Whole Sick Crew') he is a tourist through—even a sewer-traveller under—the loveless streets of the present. The other is the story of his opposite, the scholarly Herbert Stencil. Described as a 'century's child' (he is born in 1901 and therefore into Henry Adams's multiverse, and like Adams he often refers to himself in the third person), he still seeks the Virgin in the Dynamo world. His father, a former British diplomat, has left a series of gnomic clues pointing towards a great conspiracy or cabal behind modern history. Profane lives in a world of sign-lessness, or lost signification; Stencil lives in a world of signs and symbols, which point the way towards the hidden importance of a lady, V. She has somehow been involved in many central historical events, from the Fashoda crisis to the siege of Malta in the Second World War; she may even be Stencil's mother. His quest is thus a quest for personal identity or parenthood as well as for the pattern or sense of modern history. It proves centreless, for V.'s identities are elusive and plural: the problem is not just who she is, but what. Using his oblique approach of 'attack and avoid', Stencil seeks meaning, and his attempts at discovering history and identity lead him back to many major events in which the letter V. has an apparent significance. But its meaning extends and slips: it is the Virgin, Venus, the spread thighs of sexuality; it is Valetta, capital of Malta, the strange land of Vheissu; it is Void. In historical logic, it seems to signify the emptying out of human history and its sacrifice to mass and technology, a transfer turning on the Second World War, when, as Pynchon will elaborate in a later book, that technology was concentrated in the rockets called V1 and V2.

The paradox of *V.*, a work of monumental ambitiousness, is that its massive research, historical mass and bulk, and intellectual vastness is constructed so that it can be dismantled, disordered, denatured, and doubted. This deconstruction occurs, of course, with V. herself, 'a remarkably scattered concept', a human figure moving through a variety of identities, stages of decadent narcissism and sexual perversion, ageing and de-animation, down to Stencil's final dream of her as a plastic technological object. But as Stencil comes back personless from the past, Profane is there to wander the present, the empty street of the modern world in which 'tourism' prevails and everything drifts towards the inanimate. The book's basic paradox goes deeper: Stencil and Profane essentially represent the two narrative components of the book—one is the pattern-maker and constructor, the other the man of contingency and the deconstructor. Each of them hunts the lettered sign and seeks to discover something of the word and the world, but the quest yields no meaning, since signs exist in disorderly excess, as the book proliferates ever more data beyond the scope of any system, according to the principle of redundancy. Pynchon himself both creates and de-creates his own characters (not the least of them V. herself). As their half-allegoric names suggest, here and in later books, he gives them both personality and personlessness, name and namelessness. What is reduced in one area is compensated for by excess in another: the book is not only remarkably dense (and learned) in its historical content, but socially and geographically amazingly elaborate, a work of vast wanderings in space and time. If the book is about randomness and indeterminacy, it is not a random and indeterminate book; in fact it functions at a high level of referentiality, massing historical, social, and technical facts given great weight by a seemingly 'objective' author.

Pynchon followed it in 1966 with a very different and much briefer novel, *The Crying of Lot 49*, set in California and told in a mode of tragic farce. It is the story of Oedipa Maas, a suburban Californian wife who, as her first name suggests, is also faced with a quest for meaning and identity. Oedipa lives in the disintegrating landscape of the American dream, which may be the American nightmare, on the lapping edge of the inanimate Pacific, in a hyper-technological society filled with multiple systems of communication, a noise-filled, random, plural, and hyper-therapeutic culture. (Pynchon's California owes much to a long line of surreal California fiction, from Nathanael West to Terry Southern, author of *Flash and Filigree*, 1958, and the screenplay of *Dr. Strangelove*.) She has to decipher and execute the will of a former lover, Pierce Inverarity, whose name suggests both truths and lies, and goes to the town of San Narciso, which looks 'like a printed circuit', and where 'a revelation trembled, just past the threshold of meaning.' It seems Inverarity has been mysteriously implicated in the affairs of a complex underground conspiracy and private postal system by which truths deeper than the obvious have been communicated; it is variously known as WASTE and the Trystero, and its deeper meaning may be the meaning of America itself. We never quite know whether Oedipa's search for meaning and revelation is self-induced paranoia or a movement towards deepened understanding—whether we construct from our narcissistic imprisonment the tapestries of the world, or move towards a sense of its significance. Her quest to connect the apparently random tissue of signs and symbols before her is filled with a promise that may be hers alone. It takes her into investigating children's songs, hermetic learning, the story of Thurn und Taxis, and a Jacobean play, *The Courier's Tragedy*, finely parodied by Pynchon. It has been noted that Oedipa's role in the book is very much that of the decoder of a fiction, trying to construct and order its meaning. Finally she attends a stamp auction, where the mystery may be revealed by 'the crying of lot 49'. At this moment the book ends, its enigma unsolved; the hidden and possibly pentecostal mystery remains a mystery, 'another mode of meaning behind the obvious, or none'. Language, sign, and cipher work in the book rather as America does itself, pointing to the possibility, but never the certainty, of securing some 'underground' meaning from its vast space and inanimate sea, its chaotic technological noise, and its internal quests for signification, through the obscure frequencies that populate the world and, certainly, his own book.

Like the later *Vineland* (1990), which returns to California to look at the hippie counter-culture and *its* quest for underground meaning, *The Crying of Lot 49* is a relatively short novel. But there is no doubting the scale of Pynchon's novel of the Seventies, *Gravity's Rainbow* (1973). For some critics this has been the postmodern *Ulysses*; one, Richard Poirier, identifies him as a 'novelist of major historical importance' who, more than any other living writer, 'has caught the inward movements of our time in outward manifestations of art and technology so that in being historical he must also be marvellously exorbitant'. With its massive plot and its compensating plotlessness, its massive list of 'characters' (over 400 of them) and its great sweep of historical and technological data, *Gravity's Rainbow* is certainly 'exorbitant', and defies simple summary. Once again it is a novel where data exceeds the power of interpretation, for those inside the story and those outside it. Again history is overwhelmingly present both as fact and overwhelming process, and incorporated into a map of neurosis and paranoia. The book returns us to what one critic has called 'the crucial, explosive, fecund nightmare of all our psychoses and all our plots', that pervasive reference-point of so much postmodern writing. Here the war is seen as a total modern system. The governing metaphor of the book is the trajectory of the supersonic German rocket, the V2, and its gravity-guided curve of aspiration and destruction. The rocket, with its complex physics as well as its modern metaphysics, with its human scientific input and its grand and annihilating technological indifference, is once again that mixture of the plotted and the apparently plotless that has always given Pynchon his theme. The key narrative plot is that Lieutenant Tyrone Slothrop has been given childhood programming at Harvard by a German scientist, Lazlo Jamf, and is then attached in wartime to the British forces. When the German V2 rockets start falling on London they descend exactly on the site of his sexual conquests, linking not only phallus and rocket but randomness and plot. The presumption is that Slothrop has somehow been programmed much as the rockets have, for Jamf has also designed the erectile targeting plastic for the V2. From this point, innumerable international plots and conspiracies interweave, taking the story through from the war into the post-war occupation 'Zone' in Germany after the collapse of the Third Reich—a place of defeat and disorder that points the story on towards the conflicts and apocalyptic technologies of peacetime. If rocketry invokes paranoia, the random chaos of the world invokes anti-paranoia. The book suggests that the late scientific universe is a vast contemporary construct, with pattern on one side and raw chaos on the other, in which everyone is implicated. We are all part of the circuits of rocketry, our sex interlocked with death, our energy with annihilation. Amid all this, some of the characters seek, like Herbert Stencil, for a 'Real Text', and others experience the chaos of the world.

The reader is in somewhat the same position. *Gravity's Rainbow* is a seamless epic for postmodern and apocalyptic times, less a conventional literary text than an all-encompassing attempt to write a novel of our late modern chaos, from a considerable historical and scientific knowledge, and with an anxious political intelligence. Again, the book produces that excess of reference—an ever-spawning multiplication of its story, a massing of historical and technological data, an encylopaedic incorporation of military science—that marks Pynchon's distinctive method. This has been called the 'paranoid style' of writing, in which the world's random and inhuman energies stimulate textual excess and a redundancy beyond decoding. The book is a foray into contemporary history, but also a revolt against it ('Secular history is a diversionary tactic', it tells us). The method incorporates many tones and devices: comic strip, filmic techniques, music-hall songs, extended scientific exposition. It refuses direct linear narrative, and if the characters constantly multiply in exotic growth, they as suddenly disintegrate, and disappear from the action, as Slothrop himself does midway through the story: 'There ought to be a punchline, but there isn't,' we are told, 'The plans went wrong. He is being broken down instead, and scattered.' Characters and reader share a common bafflement in the face of incomprehensible cosmic processes and unstructured boundaries, with, once again, too much meaning, or none. As one critic has it, this is 'a work of low message value at the zero degree of interpretation', but it also evidently has a gnostic aim, a desire to produce a sense of sacred mystery. Indeed it is plainly an endeavour at the global novel, a contemporary work of summation.

Pynchon's most recent novel, *Vineland* (1990), is set in 1984 in the California of the Reagan years, and is about the conflict between political survivors from the radical times of the Sixties and the forces of modern government power. Closer than its predecessor to the contemporary political thriller, it can also be classed with his earlier work as what has been called the 'cybernetic novel', the novel of modern systems and technologies, and has parallels in the work of other writers, in some of John Barth's fiction or the experimental novels of William Gaddis (*The Recognitions*, 1955; *JR*, 1976; *Carpenter's Gothic*, 1985), for example. Historically alert and historically conditioned, Pynchon's cybernetic novels generate, like the contemporary world and its technologies, information in excess of mastery, and signals in excess of our capacity to receive and order them. As the twentieth century turned, Theodore Dreiser conceived of a world in which inhuman or inanimate energy was greater than human, so that the human becomes itself an object and the object takes on the character of a person or a mechanistic hero. Pynchon, who might be called a reluctant determinist with a dream of reforming the inanimate mass in which we live, the history in which we sink, has made himself central to modern fiction by taking that problem on into the chaotic science of the postmodern world, hunting through its codes and technologies for his own obscure and uncertain revelation.

5.

In 1967 John Barth, who began writing fiction in the climate of 1950s existential absurdity and produced significant experimental fiction in the 1960s, wrote his famous essay 'The Literature of Exhaustion', about the situation of the serious writer in a time overwhelmed by previous literary forms and glutted with new and random styles. Often read as an exemplary statement of the postmodern spirit (though the notion of postmodernism is something Barth has sometimes affirmed and at other times mocked), the essay actually takes as its example of the contemporary writer the Argentinian modernist Jorge Luis Borges. Of Borges it can be said that he is both a highly modern and a peculiarly timeless writer, setting his stories in many ages and places and writing symbolist fables about the task of writing itself. For Barth he is the example of the one who comes *after*, the writer of baroque exhaustion who, faced with an age of ultimacy, responds by writing brilliant footnotes to the existing literary corpus. Twelve years after, Barth countered his essay with a second, 'The Literature of Replenishment', which virtually upturns his case. He explained that his first essay had not been so much about an age of literary exhaustion but the principles of literary recovery, which came from the ability to mock and undermine inherited convention and restore the fictional essences of story-telling and narrative. He also defined the situation of the postmodern writer as one where the writer is conscious that the age of realism and that of high modernism have both passed. If it is no longer possible to write realistically—'What the hell, reality is a nice place to visit but you wouldn't want to live there, and literature never did, very long,' Barth once said—or with the élite monumentality of the moderns, it is possible, as contemporaries like Gabriel García Márquez and Italo Calvino showed, to find the essence of story-telling and produce a new synthesis of forms.

Barth's two essays can profitably be read as commentaries on the stages of his own work. As he says in 'The Literature of Exhaustion', you might, in a time when literary forms and structures seem 'used up', find yourself writing books like his own *The Sot-Weed Factor* or *Giles Goat-Boy*, 'novels which imitate the form of the Novel, by an author who imitates the role of Author'. Barth's early work was in fact created in the postwar climate of existentialism, but it developed into an endeavour to reconstruct fiction again from its beginnings, and he duly became a leading figure in the 'fictionalist' movement of the Sixties. His first two novels from the Fifties, *The Floating Opera* (1956) and *The End of the Road* (1958), are black comic—or as he called them 'nihilistic'—fables about feelings of loss of essence and modern inauthenticity, though both are very much concerned with the necessary human hunger for stories. The first of these tells the retrospective story of the middle-aged lawyer Todd Andrews from his decision to commit suicide—life being plotless and pointless—to his equally absurdist decision not to, since 'There is, then, no "reason" for living (or suicide).' The ending depends on which version you read; Barth was to become an endless reviser of his own texts. *The End of the Road* is the tale of an even more weatherless hero—he introduces himself by declaring, 'In a sense, I am Jacob Horner'—who has been trying to recover from the condition of modern absurdity, plotlessness, or 'cosmopsis', and has been having rehabilitation in Mythotherapy and Scriptotherapy. He takes a job teaching English at Wicomico State Teachers' College, where he cannot decide between 'descriptive' or 'prescriptive' grammar—language that is simply the case or language with rule and order—and has an affair with the wife of his colleague Joe Morgan. This ends with a bungled abortion and the death of Rennie Morgan, and with Jacob Horner waiting, as weatherless as before, at the railroad terminal, once again at 'the end of the road'.

Perhaps Barth's origins in absurdist existentialism, where the world seems only a parody of itself, explain the kind of mythotherapy he himself takes on in his novels of the early Sixties, when he became an exemplary dweller in the great literary labyrinth, a Borgesian weaver of tales within tales. In *The Sot-Weed Factor* (1960) he showed himself as a brilliant maker of pastiche, writing in the manner of the earliest English novelists of the eighteenth century (and particularly Smollett). The result is a long picaresque tale, with digression, tales within tales, and parodic language, about the life, adventures, and 'swivings' of one Ebenezer Cook and his tutor Henry Burlingame as they make their way to the new colony of Maryland. Cook (1672–1732) actually existed, and was the author of the long comic poem that provides the novel with its title, a 'sot-weed factor' being the eighteenth-century term for a tobacco merchant. Cook had also been the 'laureate of Maryland', a title Barth has coveted for himself, and plainly vies for in his later novels. But *The Sot-Weed Factor* is less an historical novel than a fiction about eighteenth-century fiction, freely claiming every indulgence in fantasy. Barth then departed historical picaresque for modern myth, and wrote *Giles Goat-Boy* (1966), where he made his hero the child of a virgin somehow impregnated by a computer, and then reared among the goats as half-man and half-animal. The story is told by the computer-father, in 'reels' and 'tapes', and this is clearly another example of the 'cybernetic novel' in its fascinated use of the modern technologies. The book is a parodic allegory, set on a university campus which is also the universe or the cosmos (this is, you could say, the ultimate campus novel). The campus is divided into East Campus and West Campus, run by two computers EASAC and WESAC, which compete with each other in an obvious allusion to the cold war. Appropriately the novel is constantly dividing into binary pairs (Barth was always fond of twins)—East/West, man/animal, mind/body, male/female—which Giles attempts to resolve by becoming Grand Tutor. Giles himself is a modernized version of the questing hero common to all myths, though what he has to achieve is not the traditional victory over adversaries but nothing less than 'the revised new syllabus'. It is indeed a work of meta-myth, endeavouring to recycle all the mythic stories, with the author replaced in that task by a well-stored or storied computer. This is indeed a novel that imitates the form of the Novel, by an author who imitates the role of Author.

In 1968 the French critic Roland Barthes published his influential essay 'The Death of the Author', in which he argues that the author does not write; he is written, by language and discourse. In the same year his near-namesake John Barth came out with a book that seemed to confirm the proposal that in the world of modern technologies and discourses the author is constructed or written from elsewhere. *Lost in the Funhouse: Fiction for Print, Tape, Live Voice* (1968) is a series of linked stories based, he tells us, on the endless circle of the Möbius strip ('Once upon a time there was a story that began once upon a time . . .'). The volume is a bravura performance for post-authorial times, playing with all the essential materials, modes of narrative, and strategies of discourse that are used in making fictions. The author is presented as adrift in the funhouse of his own imaginative creations; here he fragments, sub-divides, attempts to rediscover himself, changing the relations of author to protagonist to action to reader. These are brilliant improvisations on the postmodern theme, and they remind us of what we should never forget, that Barth is frequently a very funny writer. In one story, 'Night-Sea Journey', the author becomes a spermatozoon, narrating his way from initial conception to consciousness. Other stories deal with the struggle of fictions, or their narrators, to come into existence, while the story 'Glossolalia' reminds us that all art is a speaking in strange tongues: 'The laurelled clairvoyants tell our doom in riddles.'

Several of these stories return to the world of classic myth—a task renewed in the admirable volume *Chimera* (1972), three stories of return to narrative origins. In them Barth self-consciously revisits, reconstructs, and interrogates three founding tales: *The 1001 (or Arabian) Nights*, and the myths of Perseus and Bellerophon. In the opening tale, 'Dunyazadiad', he appears himself to contemplate in admiration the world's most successful story-teller, Scheherazade of *The 1001 Nights*: by spinning a labyrinthine web of tales within ever more tales, she saves her own life, proves the dictum that we publish or perish, and succeeds in avoiding the death of the author. Barth appears in his tale as a genie, ready to confess his own bewilderment in fiction's labyrinth: 'I've quit reading and writing; I've lost track of who I am; my name's just a bundle of letters; so's the whole body of literature; strings of letters and empty spaces, like a code I've lost the key to.' The chimera of *Chimera* is the elusive reality that must always lie at the heart of fiction—justifying its bewildering array of stories, devices, multiple narrators, its ciphers, hieroglyphs, alphabets, languages, its mazes and labyrinths, its suspenses, deferrals, climaxes and consummations, its erotic seductions and sexualities, which surely must point the way toward some narrative womb or heartland. But Barth is assured in the tale that 'the key to the treasure *is* the treasure'—the telling of the story is itself the meaning of the story, and the reality of fiction lies in its very fictionality, its wonderful *as if*.

In *Chimera* Barth gestures at the many more stories he wishes to tell, and the many more authors he wishes to be. We might take this as the beginning of his literature of replenishment. In the book, he mentions a blocked novel called *Numbers*, another called *Letters*. In 1979 came the volume *Letters*, written by (or to and from) John Barth, for it consists of letters sent between several of the central characters of his earlier novels and their author. If *Letters*—which Barth describes as 'an old time epistolary novel'—is yet another mocking monument by a very self-referential author, it also makes it plain that there was now a substantial monument of past work by Barth himself there to be mocked. Barth was now in a position not only to parody but revise and reconstruct, in fact replenish, the substantial body of fiction he had made. So the book can be read as an interrogation both of the novel in general and Barth's own fictional invention in particular. At the same time it invokes a new muse, Lady Germaine Amherst, elderly, British, the former mistress of many of the great British writers, though also evidently a determined post-Leavisite: 'I am *not* the Great Tradition!' she pronounces, 'I am *not* the ageing Muse of the British Novel!' Now teaching in America at Marshyhope State University, she writes to offer Barth the honorary degree of Doctor of Letters, though other contending candidates and academic politicians prove to be Barth's own fictional characters. The book thus introduces his characters into a postmodern world where they can imagine themselves factual, and argue their fate with their creator. Though, as the book says, it may be 'back to Letters, to history, to realism', Great Traditions are clearly not needed; this is a world where canons are in dispute, and one of the canons Barth is disputing is the one he created himself. This *is* a literature of replenishment, a type of proof that out of the postmodern paradox can come plenitude; his own objects of invention come 'alive' to dispute, to multiply, to recreate the stories in which they were created, and be recruited into Barth's latest fictional project. In turn they help recreate their creator, who is at last able to become a successor to the successors of Ebenezer Cook, a laureate of Maryland, and a true doctor of letters who has every right to doctor his own letters.

The books that followed thereafter—*Sabbatical: A Romance* (1982), *Tidewater Tales: A Novel* (1987), and *The Last Voyage of Somebody the Sailor* (1991)—are also evident works of self-replenishment, most of them set around Chesapeake Bay in Maryland and making it the playground of his fiction. *Sabbatical*, which I discuss in more detail in the next chapter, is a tale of sea-voyaging designed to show the sea-origins of much (and especially American) myth and legend. *Tidewater Tales* links contemporary characters to the world of the great fictional narrators and myth-makers, including Don Quixote and Barth's beloved Scheherazade, who returns again in *The Last Voyage*, an enormous story-telling marathon that journeys back to the Arabian world of Sinbad the Sailor, and takes the action to a contemporary but very mythical Baghdad, untouched by recent disasters. These novels connect his work with the inventive, sophisticated, often half-parodic revival of oral narratives and multicultural myths that has fed the writing of authors like Salman Rushdie, displaying the same love of fantasy and pure delight in story. Barth, an academic as well as a writer, has always been something of an author's author, learned in the history of his medium, the problems of narrative theory, the anxieties of modern writing, and the self-doubts of the contemporary creator. His works have become increasingly interwoven, sometimes to the point of self-parody, but his fiction is as fine a study-course in the universe of story as one could find, and it constructs a strong record of the significant directions and deviations of contemporary fiction. Barth has become the postmodernist as pure story-teller, and if his work sometimes seems like a great narrative Beaubourg—a latter-day monument of exposed piping and service-ducts, a contemporary museum of forms in which the past can only be recovered and stored in the form of pastiche and parody—the enterprise is redeemed by his very sense of plenitude, his faith that fiction is indeed a form of human replenishment.

But this has certainly not been the case for all his postmodern contemporaries, and certainly not for Donald Barthelme, a very pure minimalist who, in a famous phrase in his anti-novel *Snow White* (1967), once declared, 'Fragments are the only forms I trust.' Barthelme, who died in 1989, produced four novels— *Snow White*, *The Dead Father* (1975), *Paradise* (1986), and *The King* (1991)—all concerned with the dismantling of established legend and the parodic and fragmentary nature of the world after the death of patriarchal authorship. Appropriately his finest work is to be found in the shorter form of the short story, this work being largely collected together in the two anthology volumes *Sixty Stories* (1985) and *Forty Stories* (1987). These bring together much of the work of his splendid (and often illustrated) volumes of three decades, including *Come Back, Dr. Caligari* (1964), *Unspeakable Practices, Unnatural Acts* (1968), *City Life* (1970), *Sadness* (1972), *Amateurs* (1976), and *Great Days* (1979). Barthelme trained as an art historian, edited an art magazine, and wrote many of his pieces for the *New Yorker*, an appropriate home for these highly sophisticated tales of brain-damaged city life. He was one of the great purists and minimalists of the late modern movement, and his often extremely brief stories justify their chosen brevity. Where the early tales largely emphasize a sense of historical dismay, the feeling of living in an anonymous, programmed and language-crazed modern urban society, the later ones frequently explore and justify their author's aesthetic intentions, and with far more clarity and humour than is found in most of his experimentalist contemporaries. On the one hand they depict a world that seems always under nameless and formless threat, a world where the solidity of reality dissolves and chaos takes over; on the other, they work on the contemporary condition of language itself, and its relative failure of signification, its intrinsic detachment from reality. The result is that all his work is emphatically parodic. He once observed that parody is 'a disreputable activity, ranking only a little higher on the scale of literary activity than plagiarism', but Barthelme's work converts the parodic into a literary necessity. As Morris Dickstein has said of his writing, 'the trash of inert language is his meat and drink,' and this allows for an elaborate process of conversion, his writing being 'a collage of styles bleached and truncated into one pure and rigorous style of its own'.

In Barthelme's fiction, writing is inexorably beyond the world of realism, and language has suffered a fundamental loss of reference. In the clearly allegorical story 'At the Tolstoy Museum', in *City Life*, all that is left of the work of the great realists are the sad remnants. 'At the Tolstoy Museum we sat and wept. Paper streamers came out of our eyes,' the story begins, in a familiar Barthelme tone (this is a 'serious' parody of the Psalms). The great realists are admired but dead fathers who can no longer serve us, and can only be replaced by the 'paper streamers' of the present (the paper streamers Barthelme uses actually include visual illustrations). This departure is evidently painful, and leads to a condition that Barthelme calls 'sadness', 'Sadness' being the title of one of his best stories as well as his dominant literary tone. This sadness, an ironic but emotional self-awareness, is the general modern condition, though at times in his work it is fed by direct political dismay. And sadness is the product of his awareness of loss of signification, of narrative order and the sense of reality that once marked the writing of literature and the making of art. It is thus the reason for the substitution of realistic methods by a world, or a language, made up of junk, *dreck*, random fragments, ironic and improbable juxtapositions, shift of subject, foregrounding of text over content. His fiction is hence built of random and collage-like items, constructing a universe that seems to be made entirely of quotes drawn from the vast variety of utterance that surrounds us—the language of newspaper reports, artbooks, science, philosophical treatises, old novels, even paintings and drawings. In 'Robert Kennedy Saved from Drowning' (*Unspeakable Practices*), Robert Kennedy is presented through the multiple quotations that made up his public image, but then 'saved from drowning', represented to us as a feeling human being through the clarity of collage. 'Views of My Father Weeping' (*City Life*) begins with two teasingly painful sentences ('An aristocrat was riding down the street in his carriage. He ran over my father.') but then undermines them ('Yet it is possible that it is not my father who sits there in the centre of the bed weeping. It may be some-one else, the mailman, the man who delivers the groceries...'). These can seem like random variations, but they are a form of irony, leaving us with the feeling that this story that seems to lead nowhere (it ends with the word 'etc.') is in fact a story about pain.

Where Barth's stories show the endless hunger to narrate, Barthelme's seem largely concerned with the collapse of effective narration. Because statements of ostensible fact jostle with each other without an apparent relation, Barthelme's tales become primarily a text. At times they directly parody the work of other writers; more usually they take the form of what has been called 'meta-parody', which is to say they use parody as a tone of voice to create an independent world. It is a world made up of fundamental absences—hence the condition of 'sadness', which is actually a vision of irony as it confronts a vacant, storyless, and self-negating world. Appropriately, in one of his most explicit stories, 'Kierkegaard Unfair to Schlegel', Barthelme considers two of the great philosophers who have concerned themselves with the nature of irony. Schlegel sees irony as something that 'deprives the object of its reality in order that the subject may feel free'; Kierkegaard holds that the ironist deprives the object of its reality because he says something about it which is not what he means. Barthelme looks ironically at both, but his own attitude is closer to Schlegel's, seeing irony as a way of depriving objects of their reality in order to express their and our condition. He thus comes to see parody and irony as two of the necessary forms of contemporary writing— or any writing that sees the world adrift from the essences once believed in and considered real. The result is a literature of collage, about which he said: 'The point of collage is that unlike things are stuck together to make, in the best case, a new reality. The new reality, in the best case, may be or imply a comment on the other reality from which it came and may also be much else. It's an *itself*, if it's successful.' Barthelme's work, when it is most successful and poised, is indeed a witty and very modern 'itself'.

6.

The exploration of the relationship between fictionality and reality can be seen as one of the essential projects of some of the most interesting writing of the Sixties. 'Reality is not a matter of fact, it is an achievement,' wrote William H. Gass (himself a professional philosopher as well as a writer of fiction) in *Fiction and the Figures of Life* (1970), adding that the good novelist must keep us 'kindly imprisoned in his language, there is literally nothing beyond'. Gass's own brilliant, self-examining fiction includes the novel *Omensetter's Luck* (1966); an erotic novella, *Willie Masters' Lonesome Wife* (1968), partly based on the analogy between fictional and sexual seduction; the story collection *In the Heart of the Heart of the Country* (1968); and a long-term and still-awaited fictional project, *The Tunnel*, concerned with war-time Germany, parts of which have appeared in magazines. Gass also wrote an important 'philosophical inquiry', *On Being Blue* (1976), and both his fiction and his theoretical writings display him as a nominalist deeply preoccupied by the devious relation between language and reality.

Similar preoccupations are to be found in the work of Robert Coover, who addresses Cervantes in his story collection *Pricksongs & Descants* (1969), which consists of what he calls 'seven exemplary fictions'. 'The novelist uses familiar myths or historical forms to combat the content of those forms and to conduct the reader . . . to the real, away from mystification to clarification, away from magic to maturity,' he tells the master, adding 'And it is above all to the need for new modes of perception and fictional forms able to encompass them that I, barber's basin on my head, address these stories.' The stories are, again, stories visibly in the process of construction, and we watch them parody other forms or change direction as they attempt the pursuit of 'the new reality'. The reconstitution of forms for reality's sake is the theme of a number of Coover's very inventive novels—*The Origin of the Brunists* (1965), *The Universal Baseball Association, Inc., J.*

Henry Waugh, Prop. (1968), *Gerald's Party* (1986), and *A Night at the Movies* (1987), a large-scale film parody—all dealing with the way our public myths become versions of our public realities.

Others of Coover's books remind us that the story-teller does possess some moral and political responsibility to explore the relation between fictional creation and public history. His *A Political Fable* (1968, 1980), originally published as 'The Cat in the Hat for President' mocks the presidential election in the year when Richard M. Nixon was elected to that office. Nixon becomes one of the narrators of *The Public Burning* (1977), which deals with a crucial moment in post-war American history: the arrest, trial for espionage, and execution of Ethel and Julius Rosenberg in 1953, at a peak of the cold war. Coover heavily fictionalizes this episode, making the actual execution into a public spectacle (presented by Cecil B. DeMille) in Times Square. Times Square is not only a central New York location; it is also the source of contemporary annal, since it is here that the *New York Times*, the American paper of record, is published. Looking back through, and then transfiguring, the newspaper files, Coover explores both the fictionality of the actual fact, and then the way facts become mythologies. Against official myth-making, Coover sets his own, bringing in American popular myths and folk-heroes, above all Uncle Sam, to explore and explain the occasion. By giving Nixon, who took part in the trial, a cruel and self-exposing soliloquy, Coover is able to display that fiction does not simply make a record of history. Public history is already a fiction; its events can thus be explored freely within the fictional universe and, through play and fantasy, be reconstructed to give a sense of the national reality.

Coover's highly elaborate transaction between fictional play and public events represents one of the ways in which the fictionalists of the Sixties found their way back to the treatment of social realities. There were, however, other methods, as in the work of E. L. Doctorow, a writer who indeed drew on the same subject of the Rosenberg case for his novel *The Book of Daniel* (1971). Rather like some recent historians—Hayden White, for example, who in his book *Metahistory* (1973) argues that history-writing is subject to the same narrative laws and practices as the writing of fiction—Doctorow has held that it is the writer's task to build the bridge between fiction and history, because 'there is no fiction or non-fiction as we commonly understand the distinction, there is only narrative.' Thus, in *The Book of Daniel*, Doctorow fictionalizes the Rosenberg family (he calls them the Isaacsons) and makes the story partly an attempt on the part of the son, Daniel, to write the story in order to understand the radical history of the Fifties and Sixties, and indeed the Jewish political tradition. Doctorow also deals with the intermingled world of American fact and fiction in other works, including *Welcome to Hard Times* (1960), *Ragtime* (1975), and *World's Fair* (1985). In the highly playful *Ragtime*, set in the early years of the century, real figures like Sigmund Freud and J. P. Morgan are brought together with imaginary ones to produce a seemingly plausible yet entirely fictional record of American life. Doctorow was once asked if Morgan and Henry Ford had ever really met; 'They have now,' he said. His work can equally be read as a contribution to the postmodern and the Jewish-American political novel, to meta-fiction and to the New Journalism. Doctorow seems to suggest that the postmodern experiment has helped us to understand the conditions of a late twentieth-century realism, that, in a world where most realities we experience are already mediated—filtered through media technologies, shaped according to political mythologies, drawn into the imagery of popular culture—the new novel provides a necessary scepticism, and a way of understanding the mechanisms at work.

7.

About the nature and interest of the phenomenon of postmodernism, the critics can and will continue to argue. For, just as there never was any one and single modernism, so there will never be one and single version of the shadowy experimental phase that succeeded it. For some, postmodernism will represent a large theoretical generalization about the entire late twentieth-century condition; others will see it as a way of providing a convenient arch over a time of experimental variety and great artistic liveliness. In some eyes, the episode will be seen as essentially American, Gertrude Stein's prophecy that the modern would ultimately find its home in America come to roost; in others it is part of a much larger episode that has shaped contemporary writing internationally. Postmodernism in the novel sometimes means essentially the fictions of meta-fiction, and sometimes many types of realism as well. And as for the question of whether postmodernism marks the art of a deconstructive age in which signifier has floated free of signified and only the art of provisionality and indeterminacy is possible, that will continue to be disputed with those who think (I do) that there has not been postmodernism but postmodernisms, an eclectic variety of tendencies that found they had some common ground with each other, but which in many cases has led its best practitioners onward to other things.

It helps to remember that terms of this kind do not arise naturally or according to some law of historical inevitability; and also that, increasingly, they do not necessarily represent the devotions of the practising writer but the workings of critical theory, which of course is itself an aspect of contemporary writing, and must construct its own critical fictions. As I said earlier, it is probably most useful and illuminating to acknowledge, first, that this was a general climate to which many writers did not (as we shall see) subscribe. Secondly, its long-term significance will probably lie in the place American experimental writing takes in an era of new profusion and discovery in the international arts, in an era of both technological change and movement towards a global multiculturalism. It is also as well to remember that, in the United States, postmodernism was not an escape into art from the events of post-war American history; it expressed many of the anxieties of the post-war age after the Holocaust, the rise of the cold war, the growth of military technologies, smart weapons and systems, conspiracy theories, confused and often troubled national images, and damaged myths. It was also an expression of the increasing stylistic and generic abundance, and the cultural heterodoxy, of contemporary American life. It belonged to a time when it was harder to express the case for a realistic consensus, a time rich in pastiche, parody, stylistic excess, and pluri-culturalism. If it expressed critical anxieties about the state of the individual and the age (Barthelme's 'sadness'), it also displayed its narrative plenitude. Significantly many of its writers have been multigeneric (Vonnegut is both science fiction writer and experimentalist, and the same could be said of Pynchon) or multicultural. Raymond Federman, author of *Take It Or Leave It* (1976), 'an exaggerated second hand tale to be read aloud either sitting or standing', and an important critic, is Franco-American. The late Jerzy Kosinski, author of *The Painted Bird* (1965), was Polish-American, and Walter Abish, author of *How German Is It* (1980), Jewish-Austrian-American. There was the new black writing of authors like Clarence Major, the new American Indian writing of authors like N. Scott Momaday, author of *House Made of Dawn* (1968). The feminist revolt of the times, discussed in a later chapter, was both an aspect of postmodernism and to a degree a revolt against it. It played a dominant role in the 1960s and 1970s and exercised a continuing and freeing influence on the writing to follow. It may be wisest not to attempt a single definition of anything so obviously varied and plural, but to see it all as part of the quest by the late modern imagination to find discovering forms for presenting life and consciousness in our ever-changing and troubling world.

8

Late Postmoderns: Five Fictional Enquiries of the 1980s

So long as the mind keeps silent in the motionless world of its hopes, everything is reflected and arranged in the unity of its nostalgia. But with its first move this world cracks and tumbles: an infinite number of shimmering fragments is offered to the understanding. We must despair of ever constructing the familiar, calm surface which would give us peace of heart.

Albert Camus, *The Myth of Sisyphus* (1942)

Reality is only a sector of the imaginary field which we have agreed to give up, from which we have agreed to withdraw our fantasies. This sector is surrounded on all sides by the imaginary field where the gratification of desire through fantasy continues to be carried out.

J.-F. Lyotard, *Discours/Figure* (1971)

1.

OVER the Seventies, the revolutionary spirit that had so affected the arts of the Sixties changed greatly, political passions increasingly turned into personal concerns, and newer issues—women's rights, gay rights, the green movement—entered the American public agenda. Around that time the experimental excitement that had been so apparent in fiction began to fade, though it became ever more evident that over recent years the novel internationally had changed greatly, shifting in style and mannerism, departing from the post-war climate of realism, and expressing a late modern spirit more openly favourable to literary experiment. As experiment came nearer to being a general literary convention, some of the large claims made for postmodernism in the high, hopeful days of the Sixties inevitably came in for reassessment. In 1969, in his *The Death of the Novel and Other Stories*, Ronald Sukenick had been able to see it all as the moment of great overturning. The age of realism had been left behind, literature in its conventional and canonical sense no longer existed, and 'the contemporary writer—the writer who is acutely in touch with the life of which he is a part—is forced to start from scratch'. For other writers like John Barth (in 'The Literature of Exhaustion'), the end of literature meant something different. The novelist now lived in the age of ultimacy, so that

If you happened to be Vladimir Nabokov you might address the felt ultimacy by writing *Pale Fire*: a fine novel by a learned pedant, in the form of a pedantic commentary on a poem invented for the purpose. If you were Borges you might write *Labyrinths*: fictions by a learned librarian in the form of footnotes, as he describes them, to imaginary or hypothetical books. And . . . if you were the author of this paper, you'd have written something like *The Sot-Weed Factor* or *Giles Goat-Boy*: novels which imitate the form of the Novel, by an author who imitates the role of Author.

During the Seventies, this sense of bright expectation or else of literary extremity had amended itself towards something more realistic. When Barth reassessed his own position in 1979, he now saw postmodernism as something of an academic industry, a theoretical programme for admitting writers to the club, or else clubbing them into submission. His own heroes changed, to Calvino and Márquez, writers of comic and cosmic play and magical realism. And the task of the writer was, he felt, less to define a clear theoretical position in relation to realism or élite modernism than to set to work to write what he called 'the best next thing'.

It can be said of many of the writers, old and new, who wrote through the Seventies and the Eighties that they were primarily concerned less with grand historical arguments than with writing 'the best next thing'. Some of them continued to work in the spirit of postmodern enquiry, some shifted their energies in other directions, often reassessing their relation to the mode of 'realism' that was once regarded as the enemy. In the era of what Christopher Lasch entitled 'The Culture of Narcissism', where he read in American culture an uneasy and troubled fascination with the nature of self and role, when books like Erving Goffman's *The Presentation of Self in Everyday Life* (1969) or the intense personal speculation of Robert M. Pirsig's *Zen and the Art of Motorcycle Maintenance* (1974) seemed to explore or express the contemporary spirit, it was often works of therapeutic hunger that caught the prevailing mood—Philip Roth's *The Professor of Desire* (1977), which relates sexual fantasy to public themes; Jerzy Kosinski's *Blind Date* (1977); John Hawkes's *The Passion Artist* (1979). Stories frequently took place less in a 'real world' than in some realm of the authorial consciousness where laws of imagination had pre-eminence, often displaying a doubt about the authenticity of relations with others that seemed a mark of the entire culture. About some of these books which showed how fictional experiment both continued and was changing, I wrote as they appeared. It seems worth drawing together and updating some of these observations as one way to suggest the shifting fictional spirit of the late Seventies and early Eighties.

2.

Walter Abish, *How German Is It* (1981)

According to modern literary theory, one of the tasks of serious literature is to defamiliarize—not to reassure us with the established conventions, to present us with the recognizable and the often written, but to lead us towards a new perception of experience, narrative order, and aesthetic wholeness. In the 1970s and 1980s it was often European writers who provided us with this service: writers like the Austrians Peter Handke and Thomas Bernhard, with their works of hard modern landscape and chilly estrangement; the Italian Italo Calvino, playfully writing of the dislocation of objects and perception; the Czech Milan Kundera, or the Israeli Amos Oz. If we are to look for their close equivalent in American fiction, we find it in Walter Abish, a writer who in many respects hardly seems an American novelist at all. He was born in Austria to a family of prosperous Viennese Jews who fled Hitler and eventually settled in Shanghai; he later moved to Tel Aviv, trained in the Israeli army, and learned the profession of town planner. He moved to the USA in 1960 and has lived there chiefly since. It is not surprising therefore that his works of fiction have an international landscape and a polyglot spirit, a persisting interest in the complexities and deviances of language. The short stories of his collections *Minds Meet* (1975) and *In the Future Perfect* (1977) are greatly concerned with language, the process of naming, and the way we come to imagine the world. His 'permutational' novel *Alphabetical Africa* (1974) constructs an imaginary Africa entirely through a system of language, structuring its description in the order of the alphabet, and *How German Is It* (1981), his finest work, is a book that seeks to define a Germany he had never actually visited except through the instrument of language. None the less America is important to him, because there, he once said in an interview, 'I *know* what is familiar.'

The phrase is significant because familiarity and unfamiliarity are the essential themes of Abish's work. He has said that the danger of fiction is that it familiarizes us with the world, and so satisfies the simple perceptions of the self. It is only when we forget the self, when we enter the world of the undomesticated and the atrocious, when we see the exterior world as uncanny, that the novel can innovate. In this Abish's work links him with the work of the more serious and philosophical postmoderns: he resembles Donald Barthelme, for instance, in using language to upset our faith that there are always real depths below linguistic surfaces, in his refusal to name reality as if it were something real and given, or to use the conventions of narrative to shape and order experience back into a familiar design. He has a deep interest in American painting and film, and shares its preoccupations with framing and shaping, fixing and holding, the relation of surfaces to depths, and, a poet himself, he has clear links with the 'New York School' of poets like Kenneth Koch and John Ashbery, whom he frequently quotes. At the same time he writes of a centreless world which might be anywhere, and which he in effect constructs for himself. This involves his writing in a double process. 'This is a familiar world,' begins the story 'This Is Not a Film This Is a Precise Act of Unbelief', in *Minds Meet*, 'It is a world crowded with familiar faces and events. Thanks to language the brain can digest, piece by piece, what has occurred and what may yet occur . . . Three years ago Mrs Ite walked through her familiar world and found that something was missing.' If the task of such a story is to make clear the foreign within the familiar, he is equally concerned—in his two novels—with the opposite: as he said in the same interview, 'I tend to establish or re-establish the familiar in what is foreign,' and it is clear that one of his aims is the composition of place in a seemingly placeless world.

The intention is so plain that Abish avoids the often random playfulness of other American postmoderns. Indeed in his work, style endeavours to achieve authority, attempts in an apparently contingent world to acquire a significant message or recover a sense of the authentic. Several of the stories of *In the Future Perfect* are concerned with building the basic vocabulary out of which narrative might be made; thus 'In So Many Words' begins by declaring the limited word supply out of which the story might achieve sequence, structure, and narrative. Moreover the narratives he does tell are generally stories of crisis or atrocity arising from our linguistic and psychic distortions and deprivations, often represented with a flat but chilling irony. As he explains in one of the stories of *Minds Meet*:

When a word is not understood, the person using it is obliged to spell it aloud . . . In the more rural sections of the US people do not resort to spelling difficult words . . . Instead they plunge a V-shaped knife into the other fella, who moans 'Ohhh.' O also happens to be the fifteenth letter of the alphabet. For some reason it is often used by insecure people.

Most of the stories in this and *In the Future Perfect* are therefore pained attempts at finding the relation of words to things, at discovering a destination to the apparently arbitrary process of listing or naming. The story 'Ardor/Awe/Atrocity' is constructed on three sets of telling and troubling words from each letter of the alphabet. 'I'm not really concerned with language,' Abish told his interviewer, 'As a writer I'm principally concerned with meaning.' He also described himself as a 'writer-to-be', suggesting that such is the condition of language that the meaning must constantly be deferred, though in some stories, like 'Crossing the Great Void', there appears to be a final destination, even if it is somewhere in the desert. Abish has explained that in life we constantly confront situations that defy explanation, 'Yet we interpret and explain. Anything. Everything.' It might be said that Abish's stories frequently defer explanation, but they do not deny it.

The best and fullest story in *In the Future Perfect* is 'In the English Garden', which has the further interest that we now know it to be the original foray into his novel *How German Is It*. It was triggered by a remark by John Ashbery: 'Remnants of the old atrocity persist, but they are converted into ingenious shifts of scenery, a sort of "English Garden" effect to give the required air of naturalness, pathos and hope.' It is not hard to see where, for a Jewish writer who as a child has fled the Holocaust, that sense of 'old atrocity' arises. Kazuo Ishiguro once remarked of the other great modern atrocity—the dropping of atomic weapons on Hiroshima and Nagasaki—that the risk of representing it directly in fiction is exactly that of making it too familiar, too inert, by framing it within the consolations of language and form. Hence we need to write with an art of indirection and reticence, avoiding direct address to the realities in order to approach them from the depths, and undermine them. It is not hard to see the link between Ishiguro's fiction, which is always governed by rules of reticence and codes of social restraint, and the spirit of Abish's writing. 'In the English Garden' thus concerns the visit of an American writer to the town of Brumholdstein, a new German city that has been built on the site of a former concentration camp, where, therefore, the citizens have succeeded in familiarizing and therefore obscuring the past. Brumholdstein is also named after a distinguished German philosopher of things:

The city is named after a German philosopher who, like many of his predecessors, inquired into the nature of a *thing*. He started his philosophical inquiry by simply asking, *What is a thing?* For most of the inhabitants of Brumholdstein the question does not pose a great problem. They are the first to acknowledge that the hot and cold water taps in the bathrooms are things, just as much as the windows in the new shopping center are things. Things pervade every encounter, every action.

Yet the American writer, with his simple maps of Germany, is also compelled to see the world through surfaces, through its prevalence of things.

Abish's extended version of this story, *How German Is It*, is one of the best and most demanding American novels of recent years, though it is also plainly contentious. Again about a writer protagonist, Ulrich Hargenau, visiting the world of Brumholdstein, it confronts the question of what Germany 'is' from the standpoint not only of the protagonist but from that of the actual writer, who had not to that point visited it, though had lived under its threat and within its language. The book depends heavily on filmic techniques, on reading the images of modern Germany as signs: this is a society made of signifying systems, designer clothes and cultural relics, fast cars and clean modern apartments, *things*. This is the story of an attempt to define through gradual recognition, through fitting language to example and map and city-plan to the city itself. But of course this constructs a Germany of realism, and the danger of realism is that it papers over the cracks and fissures, the subterranean systems, the archaeology of the hidden atrocity. Germany is more than a place; it is the expression of a type of philosophy, and Abish writes of 'the unique German way of seeing and appraising an object'. Again the city is the construct of a philosopher, Brumhold, who is indeed based on Martin Heidegger, the German philosopher of things who allied himself with Nazism. On the one hand, then, the book is about the way we use the powers of the mind to develop an historical amnesia; on the other, it is about the fact that all our phenomenologies, especially those of a modern *chosiste* world obsessed by objects, is a map of extraordinary surfaces laid over confusing depths.

. Abish starts *In the Future Perfect* with an epigraph from the Swiss film-maker Alain Tanner (by whom his work seems influenced): 'My country has escaped history for a very long time.' In an important passage in *How German Is It*, the protagonist's brother reflects on the double meaning of 'German' existence. On the one hand, he declares, 'we cannot very well separate our understanding of existence from our understanding of history,' but 'we can comprehend with Brumhold that his search for meaning, his philosophical quest for *Dasein* is not linked to this or that event, to one year or another (after all, we are not more or less German because of the events of 1914 or 1945, to take two years more or less at random), but to a universal history, a history of human awareness.' Abish may seem to be a writer of the postmodern flat surface; he is also concerned with the fact that words and things do have histories, and that a world of synchronic realities is a world of illusion. The critic Jerome Klinkowitz has justly identified this kind of writing as 'experimental realism', and so it is. Like a good deal of the newer writing, Abish is using the anxious, compromised instrument of language, the prime object of modern critical speculation (in deconstructive criticism for example, which has made a paradox out of the idea of rhetorical authenticity), as a means of quest through the interlocking worlds of the familiar and the unfamiliar, of awe and atrocity—in the hope or belief that we can find depths below the surfaces, and so accept moral responsibility for our utterance.

3.

John Barth, *Sabbatical: A Romance* (1982)

When, in his essay 'The Literature of Replenishment' (1979), John Barth argued that the task of the late modern writer was simply to get on with the 'best next thing', without too much theory or proselytizing, he was presumably on the way to his own. His next novel, *Sabbatical: A Romance*, marks a change in the spirit of his writing. It is not that Barth here forgets that fiction can always be seen as an enquiry into fiction. In *Sabbatical*, footnotes dangle from the page bottoms, tales interweave with other tales, and the work is composed, we are told, by an authorial twosome, Fenn and Susan, who are eight years married and on a sailing sabbatical (on their boat *Pokey, Wye I.*) round a favorite Barth seascape, the islands and harbours of Maryland's Chesapeake bay. The book is also a backward voyage to some of the sources of narrative, a notion that is of course not new in Barth's work, but played here in a somewhat different way. It brings back much of the classic stuff of sea-story: travels and mysteries, digressions and episodes, sea-monsters and uncharted islands, the mariner's garrulity. From the sea, stories are supposed to start, and there are Homer parallels, Virgil parallels, and (of course) Joyce parallels. There are also parallels to the parallel narrators; each of the narrators is also a twin, and each twin has a story. Some of the stories are sentimental, some grotesque. A girl is multiply raped and tortured, an abortion performed; but meanwhile families lead family lives, and a later life marriage achieves a kind of peace. If that is a love story, there is also a spy story; after all, Maryland is close to Washington, the place of CIA plots and conspiracies. Fenn himself is an ex-CIA man, but he is also the descendant of Francis Scott Key (who wrote 'The Star-Spangled Banner', and who provided first names on to F. Scott Fitzgerald). Susan teaches literature and descends from Edgar Allan Poe, who wrote *The Narrative of Arthur Gordon Pym*, which helps in the story's unravelling. Poe and Key are both old Chesapeake Bay writers, who both wrote American 'romance', one of terror and the other of sentimental patriotism. And so does Barth, reflecting here on the double American vision, which is given both to good and evil.

Thus there is a tradition, and indeed it is all there in the name of the boat: 'Pokey, Wye I.' (The book certainly has a Poe key.) *Sabbatical* may therefore be experimental, but it is evidently 'about' something: about the splendours of American political life, and equally about the crises of identity and the struggles of gender relationship that make the present so difficult to interpret (hence the two narrators). It draws again on the now-familiar metaphor that narrative is itself a form of sexuality, made of foreplay and climax; but, because the two story-tellers are both independent beings and lovers sexually intertwined, the familiar metaphor can become the basis for a new allegory. Thus beyond all the fictional play—the parodies and literary references, the twins and doubles, the plots and counter-plots—there lies what is clearly meant as a more abiding principle of generation, as the male seed and the female ova come to embody (like the sea) the deepest principles of creativity. Barth's experiment here is to find the story that lies behind or beyond story: generation or creativity itself. That view of things has evidently proved fecund, or procreative; it has spawned already at least two successors, *Tidewater Tales* (1987) and *The Last Voyage of Somebody the Sailor* (1991), which once more draw on the idea of the sea-story as the true source of narrative. By allegorical voyaging Barth has, it seems, indeed found the literature of replenishment; and in a far larger and more oceanic sense than his essay on the topic could give us to expect.

4.

William Gaddis, *Carpenter's Gothic* (1985)

In 1955, thirty years before publishing *Carpenter's Gothic*, William Gaddis produced a vast, perplexing, anagrammatic, encyclopaedic tale about the world as fiction and forgery, and called *The Recognitions*. The book explored a universe of dark and complex plots where what is faked and forged seem the staples of nature and human existence, raising the question of whether there is anything any longer which is true, or genuine. The book was very textual or lexical, given to complex inner ciphering and elaborate learning, and it developed through characters who do not so much experience as suffer a plot that seems to evolve for its own independent sake. Recognition was, in fact, what the book was slow to get; it came out in a time when the spirit of experiment was not strong, and its refusal to concede anything to the reader won it no praise. However, for a number of critics (including myself) it gradually came to appear as one of the main starting-places of a new direction in contemporary American experiment in fiction, and can have clear claim to have influenced the development of the post-psychological and technological novel as it evolved over the following decades, opening the pathway toward writers like Thomas Pynchon and the fiction of our latter-day historical labyrinth.

There followed a long wait for Gaddis's second novel, which might have appropriately come out in the 1960s, when his kind of writing began to win a more general acceptance. In the event it was not until twenty years later, in 1975, that his next book, *JR*, appeared. It was equally encyclopaedic, and equally extraordinary, the 726-page-long tale of an 11-year-old sixth-grader who masters and manipulates the great plots and systems of conglomerate capitalism, and becomes an insider trader in the world of the great fiction called money. 'Money' is the first word of the novel, spoken in 'a voice that rustled', and money—interconnecting, spawning, multiplying and mastering—dominates the book. In its vast world of mechanisms, master-plots, and vast international manipulations, it is Wall Street that commands, provoking company failures, financial chicaneries, even the collapse of entire African republics. But the system, being a modern system, is open to leakage, and when a sneakered, diamond-sweatered schoolboy, JR, invades it, speaking to brokers and Wall Street on the school telephone through a clotted handkerchief ('No but I haven't talked overtime . . . But I don't have sixty cents . . .') he soon builds up a vast commercial enterprise covering the entire country. The story also takes us into the world of art, of encyclopaedias, the mysteries of wills and testaments. Codes dominate the novel, which is a seamless, unchaptered text presented almost entirely through dialogue; the characters have names like diCephalis and Vogel, Bast and Joubert, and minimal identity, for the method allows no psychological detail. All are speakers rather than agents, part of endless talk show unwinding in conference rooms, bedrooms, toilets, cafeterias, museums, and over telephones, intercoms, radios and TV sets. Apart from Wall Street itself, a main setting is an allegorical Long Island high school of the post-Gütenberg age. It is dominated by audio-visual systems, the principal doubles as the president of the local bank, and the down-at-heel faculty maintain a secondary existence in the world of Wall Street. Here JR learns his lessons in selfhood through investment, and comes to see business as the world of modern art displaced.

It was hard to find critical words to describe Gaddis's distinctive style, with its learning, its elaborate ciphering, its proliferation of text for its own sake, its awareness of producing writing in a world that has tipped over into science, technological consciousness, entropic decline. However, by comparing his work with Pynchon's, it became useful to talk about the 'cybernetic' or the 'technetronic' novel, evidently fed by modern information theory, and committed to almost mechanical, or certainly non-psychological, styles and techniques that could capture the noise and redundancy, the endless chatter and clatter, the buzz and blip, of the computer-led age. And just like Pynchon's, Gaddis's style could be called the 'paranoid' style: a way of writing of a world so made up of plots, conspiracies, codes, and systems that the individual character within it is necessarily swamped by overwhelming exterior discourses and even the literary language itself becomes part of it. Both terms are useful in catching at Gaddis's complex, baroque, and sometimes puzzling manner, and his perception of a shaping world of systems. What they do not catch is one of his strongest qualities: his sense of fiction as itself a worthy forgery, and along with that his marvellous satiric vitality.

These two novels made it clear that Gaddis is one of the remarkable figures of the recent American novel, though, unlike Pynchon's, his work seems largely to have remained the interest of a narrow readership, perhaps even a cult. *Carpenter's Gothic*, his third novel in thirty years, is a briefer book than its predecessors and might, at a mere 262 pages, be considered in Gaddis terms a novella. It lacks the overwhelming mass of the earlier two novels, and indeed some of the superb structuring that goes with that kind of scale. But it shows no lack at all of his striking and baroque technique, nor of his talent for constructing labyrinthine plots and large conspiracies. The direct action of the book is brief and tightly held in one place: the story takes place over a few days and is set in one single rented house on the Hudson river. Here lives Liz, the book's passive 'heroine', or perhaps its still centre, injured after a plane crash, and the heiress to a corporation fortune which, as in Dickens's equally Gothic *Bleak House*, is subject to endless litigation. Here comes and goes her husband, Paul, another scarred protagonist, a Vietnam veteran and opportunistic media consultant who is, like JR, wheeling and dealing in the big world beyond, the world of international corporations, corporate law, Washington politics, fundamentalist religion. Here too, in a locked room, are the papers of the owner of the house, a geologist, McCandless. Liz consoles herself in the McCandless house with Gothic fantasies, and especially with images from Orson Welles's film of *Jane Eyre*, one of the great novels of what has been called 'domestic gothic', but also a distorting mirror on her own condition. Meanwhile the world enters unremittingly, through the ceaseless ringing of the telephone, the mail in the mailbox, the intrusion of newspaper headlines (TEARFUL MOM), through the television set and the unstoppable, incomprehensible penetration of the corrupt commercial, political, and religious practices of contemporary America, hyped up, drugged up, born again, and increasingly fundamentalist.

This house is very appropriately built in 'carpenter's gothic', the American domestic style that adapted more aristocratic European Gothic forms by using the materials and skills that were locally to hand. 'All they had were the simple dependable old materials, the wood and their hammers and saws and their own clumsy ingenuity bringing those grandiose visions the masters had left them down to a human scale with their own little inventions . . . a patchwork of conceits, borrowings, deceptions,' recalls McCandless when he too returns to the house. These houses are both facts and forgeries, actually built from the outside as façades, so that their insides could be filled in randomly later. This provides an unmistakable parallel to those who live their lives there now. They too are trying to sustain their own 'conceits, borrowings, deceptions' despite the pressure of the world. But, just like Pynchon's Oedipa Maas in *The Crying of Lot 49*, Liz can only struggle to find an imperfect sense of the random interruptions, the disorders, the leaking signs, the vast outward systems. She picks up loose connections from words in dictionaries, images in books and, of course, films, and she has a brief love affair with the decent but defeated McCandless, who is also lost amid the disorder of his own accumulated papers.

The Gothic novel, imported to America largely by Charles Brockden Brown at the turn into the nineteenth century, soon became a way of dealing with American sentiments and perhaps above all with the national weaving of myth and history, in a land that seemed spared most external historical pressures. In one sense Gothic was the European presence in America itself, and Brown made much of various European conspiracies and cabals, like the Illuminati—just as Pynchon does with the Trystero system in *The Crying of Lot 49*. Brown himself believed in a kind of carpenter's gothic: the American Gothic novel would not need, he said, European castles or feudal manners, and indeed it could be based on American materials and 'a series of adventures growing out of the conditions of our own country'. Or, as his inheritor Edgar Allan Poe put it, its terror would not be that of Germany, but of the soul. The intimacy between the development of this Gothic tradition and the American novel itself has since then come to be recognized in criticism, most notably by Leslie Fiedler's brilliant *Love and Death in the American Novel*, which makes an entire tradition out of this displacement of Gothic to the land and landscape of historical displacement, America itself. It has also been persistently recognized in recent fiction, in the work of writers from Richard Brautigan to Joyce Carol Oates. This history all clearly bears on Gaddis and his conception for the novel. His 'carpenter's gothic', the book itself, is concerned with the 'conditions of our country', which are generally dark and destructive and, as in good Gothic, they impose terrible pressures on mind, logic, and human sensitivity. Beyond McCandless's house lies an America of dark imperialism, which is also shrouded in the ignorance of raging and self-righteous fundamentalist faiths. Liz's husband Paul is thus promoting the cause and reputation of a media evangelist, the Reverend Ude, who conducts a benighted attack on science and evolution, abortion and Marxism, on behalf of a mission which is in fact a cover for the exploitation of mineral resources in Africa. This is a time of hearts of darkness, mindless revelations, holy wars, and hunger for apocalypse.

As in Gaddis's earlier novels, with which there are obvious connections (false faiths, controlling systems, pervasive and destructive absurdity), his characters are ritual talkers: they make tales and interpretations which, competing together, structure a sense of the cumulative conspiracy of life. In all the stories there is concealed some falsehood. Liz herself seeks 'some hope of order restored, even that of a past itself in tatters, revised, amended, fabricated in fact from its very outset to reorder its unlikelihoods, what it all might have been . . .'. Liz and McCandless both write fictions, and both are powerless before the larger fictions of life, the conspiracies that do actually have power and access. And, as in the earlier books, Gaddis shows his great stylistic precision and satirical bite. If Gothic fiction has always been about the struggle of reason and extremity, it has also been about the power of fiction, and the value to the writer of just those same 'conceits, borrowings, deceptions'. With them, the book implies (and not for the first time in the history of the American novel), we can rebuild the form itself, carpenter together our new Gothic to write the novel of our own dark, disordered, irrational, and fundamentalist age. *Carpenter's Gothic* is, like the previous books, wonderfully concerned with the materials of its own making. But it is the seriousness and complexity of his home-made structure, his power of play with borrowings and deceptions, that makes him still one of the best of contemporary American novelists.

5.

Robert Coover, *Gerald's Party* (1986)

When the American edition of this book appeared, the invitation to attend Gerald's party had already been signed by some very striking names. Various writers in the forefront of the contemporary experimental novel, including William Gass, John Calvin Batchelor, and Walter Abish, declared the significance of the occasion, while the dedication of the book was to John Hawkes. But then Coover himself belonged among those striking names, having by this date set his wide and flamboyant talents to a variety of themes and fictional adventures that made him a central figure in this new writing—ever since his first powerful collection *Pricksongs & Descants* (1969) had shown him to be an adventurous explorer of the nature, the magic, and the erotics of story-telling. His subjects had spread from baseball (or rather a false myth about it, which becomes true) to the Rosenberg executions, and his range from erotic fantasy to political satire. *The Public Burning* (1977) involved him in exploring the inner life of Richard Nixon, and his *A Political Fable* (1968; 1980) mocked the national need for a magical and transforming figure who could recover the whole modern spirit of America in, of course, short media bytes. Like Hawkes and some other of the writers who have sometimes been called magical realists, Coover has been part of an inventive mood in fiction that has at times seemed to link the aesthetic and Gothic obsessions of Poe, the erotic rage of Sade or Genet, and the surrealism of Céline with the contemporary taste for pastiche and parody.

Parody has been seen as a persistent feature of postmodern writing. At Gerald's party, where everything is talked about, one of the guests, Tania (who will however later be found dead in Gerald's much-used bathroom), tells us what parody is: 'the intrusion of form, or death (she equated them), into life'. Gerald's being a smart but variegated party, many of the guests have strong aesthetic thoughts: one offers Gerald his wife in exchange for a lesson on the nature of theatre, a fair swap. This is perhaps not surprising, since the guests are the product of some complex aesthetic thoughts themselves. They also, however, have most of the other preoccupations of partygoers, including food, drink, spectacular clothing, sex, urination, the blockage of the upstairs toilet, spilled dishes, lost drinks, mistaken identities, and, as it turns out, murder. In fact what Tania calls 'the intrusion of form, or death . . . into life' occurs early, on page 12, when the body of Ros, actress, artist's model, pornographic filmstar, and whore (and so the focus of a thousand motives), is found dead on the living room carpet. If parody is important, it is well to have a genre to parody, and now we have the detective story. Inspector Pardew, a philosophical detective who believes in the simultaneity of time (an obvious problem in his task of elucidating cause and effect), turns up to deduce that the murder occurred half an hour after he himself arrived. Other new arrivals include some heavy cops, various photographers and TV camera crews, and more and more reporters, actors, and film-makers, determined to report or rather to fictionalize the event. Meanwhile, around this corpse, and then the several more that will appear before this Agatha Christie occasion is done, Gerald's party goes on. This is a novel of chatter (even more chatter than in Gaddis's *JR*): a chatter of voices, names, faces, faeces, drinks, dishes, overheard gags, endless gossip, and story-telling, set in a mounting curve of extreme events and accelerating and overstimulated desires.

It must be said that out of it all Coover constructs a brilliant novel. *Gerald's Party* has been called a mock murder-mystery, but the drawing-room detective story is only one of several forms he chooses to parody and play with, in a novel of remarkably sustained invention and impersonation. The party here becomes a theatre, a fairy-tale, a filmscript, and of course an ever-accelerating trade in the space between the ostensibly real and the evidently fantastic. Like, I suppose, a party, it is a field of desire and dream ever dissolving and reforming, filled with pratfalls and interrupted fornications, sudden redirections of group activity and weird rituals. Thus 'Butcherblock Blues', 'The Host's Hang-Up', and 'Candid Coppers' are some of the many games and dramas staged for the reader's delight. Stories—the overall story itself, and then the stories inside the stories—are, after all, cunning deceptions people play on each other, and here they develop into many kinds of tease, according to various aesthetic and erotic laws: estrangement, reversal, deception, false culmination. In perfunctory fashion the mystery is actually solved, but it clearly does not matter. The sexual pursuit of Gerald by Alison, the girl he is attracted by, starts in pratfall and turns to disaster. But what is there to detain the reader is the overall manipulation—of a massive cast of extraordinary and ever-shifting figures, along with the constant multiplying and then dissolving of styles and situations—all displayed through the noise of party itself: the unremitting and antiphonal babble of human voices.

Gerald's Party is both an aesthetic and erotic novel, a flamboyant and indeed brilliant display of a busy and inventive author's repertoire, in other words a great and teasing performance. The book has many postmodern habits: the characters are voices and so virtually characterless, and voices and bodies change into other clothes or even other bodies in a continuous metamorphosis. There is a great deal of redundancy, or excess of noise, which could be annoying to some of the neighbours. There is a declared philosophical dimension, in that the question of the relation of form to reality frequently recurs, as does the familiar question of that between the story-teller's and the lover's ways of pursuing foreplay and achieving culmination. There are also many deaths, a variety of urinary and faecal disasters, and a good many Gothic brutalities and tortures; there is no doubt that the Gothic has indeed returned to American fiction, if it ever left. The guests, or those of them who manage to survive through 312 pages in the same house on the same evening, confess that they have finally had a great time. It must be said that if the reader was out of town that night and missed it in the flesh, that could only have been a good thing. As parties go, however, it remains an infinitely memorable evening, perhaps even the party to end parties. In fiction, at least, one is glad not to have missed it. It is the party of postmodernism, though there is something conclusive about it, and one wonders if anything like it ever need be held again.

6.

Paul Auster, *The New York Trilogy* (1985–6)

In the 1980s, postmodern writing did not disappear from American fiction. It did, however, take on somewhat graver and less flamboyant tones in its maturity, and it also began to look with greater care at its relations to reality, which also did not disappear. If 'reality' was, as Nabokov had said, a word that meant nothing except in quotes, and if once 'realism' and 'experiment' had been flags raised by camps at war, they now increasingly engaged in peaceful intercourse and profitable trade, and therefore Jerome Klinkowitz came up with his useful formulation 'experimental realism'. A good example of this trend is Paul Auster, a writer who, along with Walter Abish and Leonard Michaels, can be seen as a distinguished late contributor to what could now well be called 'the postmodern tradition'. Auster's *New York Trilogy*—which consists of three interlinked novels, *City of Glass* (1985), *Ghosts* (1986), and *The Locked Room* (1986), later collected into one—appears to be founded on the subversion of a phrase of Tzetevan Todorov in a famous essay on detective fiction: 'no author of detective fiction can permit himself to indicate the imaginary character of the story, as happens in "literature." '

Like Todorov and other modern critics, Auster takes the detective story as fiction's prototype, as Coover did in *Gerald's Party* at around the same date. Here writer, detective, and reader appear to be interchangeable, and the reader, seeing through the eyes of the detective, shares his work of seeing significance everywhere—but is unable to give the offered world a plot or circumference, until certain orders have been discovered and certain deductions drawn. So the *New York Trilogy* is a sequence in which nothing can be overlooked: not just the action and the powerful sense of an overwhelming urban reality it discloses, but the nature of language and the always-interlocking roles of writer, character, reader. In *City of Glass* the detective-story writer Quinn is called late at night by a client seeking the services not of Quinn himself but of the author, Paul Auster. In *Ghosts* a detective called Blue is hired by White to watch Black, and so discovers himself in a world of bizarre doubles. In *The Locked Room* the narrator finds himself pursued by and pursuing an old friend, Fanshawe, who is another author who disappeared, leaving behind to the narrator not only his manuscripts but also his wife and child.

The New York Trilogy tells its stories with considerable dramatic suspense, but they also break their frame to make fiction into a true 'investigation'. This simultaneously includes investigation within the world of present urban social reality, and investigation into language, writing, and literary history. Quinn is an author who writes about a detective hero, Max Work. Turned himself into a detective, he becomes the protagonist for a further author, Paul Auster—who then in turn becomes a character within the story. The mystery he investigates he creates rather than solves. In the same way, Blue does not know whether he has been hired to watch or be watched, and whether the reports he writes are reports on his quarry or are reports that are designed to reveal and expose himself. The disappeared friend Fanshawe dominates and begins to construct the life of the narrator, who is presumably Paul Auster. Indeed he provides an explanation for this and also the two previous books, suggesting that in some sense Auster did not actually write them but was written by and into them. Each new book therefore adds a fresh frame to what has already been written, and reveals the increasing complexity and the growing theoretical confidence of a writer who is investigating, amongst other things, himself. At the same time he is investigating the nature and origins of the genre he is using. Thus the stories all have concealed literary sources, as do many contemporary American stories, where each writer seems to show a canonical hunger to construct a justifying tradition. In *City of Glass* there is, again, Edgar Allan Poe, a source of American Gothic and the first cerebral detective-story writer (he too regarded the detective story as a tale of 'ratiocination'). In *Ghosts* the fictional ghosts in the book include the great American Transcendentalists, Melville, Thoreau, and Whitman. Nathaniel Hawthorne wrote an early fantastic novel called *Fanshawe*, which he then suppressed, and also a story called 'Wakefield' in which a man disappears in order to understand and observe his own life.

Auster's books are postmodern in the sense that they are clearly reflexive fictions about fiction. But that is not quite the end of the story, or the close of the investigation. Auster, a teacher of creative writing at New York University, and a poet, critic, and translator, has always written close to his own personal, Jewish, experience. He had earlier written a remarkable memoir, *The Invention of Solitude* (1982), which reveals troubled domestic origins (a murder in the family) and explores his own discovery of language as the expression of a fundamental human solitude. Like Abish, though with a different conclusion, he reflects on the relation between language and the self, on both the necessity and the solipsism of our naming of things: 'each thing leads a double life, at once in the world and in our minds, and . . . to deny either one of these lives is to kill the thing in both its lives at once.' The book is an attempt to construct the power of memory in a world that eludes us forever. He thus shares with Abish and many recent writers who have clearly been aware of contemporary and historical philosophical arguments about language (as I say, especially those of deconstruction) a concern with the way the writer must reconstitute it as the instrument both of autobiographical and phenomenological expression. Auster's works of fiction already show an almost puzzling variety. His *In the Country of Last Things* (1987) is set in an imaginary devastated city, and is an apocalyptic novel with a deep historical concern. His *Moon Palace* (1989) is a fascinating work of complicated fantasy built on the images of the moon-shot age. *The Music of Chance* (1991) deals with a random space—filled with travel and chance—between the moment a father dies and leaves a legacy and the time, a year later, it arrives. Like Abish's, Auster's is a fiction of displacement, a displacement that once again has something to do with Jewish origins but also with the dislocating texture of contemporary life, in which the familiar is also the alien. Like Abish, he sees that to explore the world as a labyrinthine and confused text is still to explore it in some fashion; to reconstruct memory, to master solitude, to find good fortune in the random, to discover the living reflection of things, is to engage in the true act of detection for which the writer is responsible, the detection, out of chaos, of story itself, and ultimately perhaps of reality.

9

After the Post: American Fiction from the 1970s to the 1990s

The words can sound so precise that they even sound flat, but they can still carry, if used right, all the notes.

Raymond Carver, 'On Writing' (1981)

'These are days of secular optimism, of self-celebration. We will improve, prosper, perfect ourselves. Watch any car crash in any American movie. It's a high-spirited moment like old-fashioned stunt flying, walking on wings. The people who stage these crashes are able to capture a light-heartedness, a carefree enjoyment that car crashes in foreign movies can never approach.'
'Look past the violence.'
'Exactly. Look past the violence, Jack. There's a wonderful brimming spirit of innocence and fun.'

Don DeLillo, *White Noise* (1984)

1.

IN 1989, the old New Journalist Tom Wolfe, fresh from best-selling success with his New York novel *The Bonfire of the Vanities* (1988), published in *Harper's* a highly controversial article, 'Stalking the Billion-Footed Beast: A Literary Manifesto for the New Social Novel'. Chiefly an account of the methods he had used to conceive, prospect, research, and write his block-busting book, it described how a New Journalist who had once dismissed the 'boring' novel as an irrelevant modern form, and proposed that novelists should step aside and leave the literary task to journalists, had come to write one himself. It also contained a rapid-fire attack on the American novelists of the previous two decades, who had, he said, neglected the true business of fiction by attempting 'to establish an avant-garde position way out beyond realism'. The result had been a series of self-regarding experiments, which he named as absurdist novels, magical realist novels, puppet-masters' novels, neo-fabulist novels, minimalist novels, even K-mart novels, which had 'Rustic Septic Tank Rural settings'. An entire generation of novelists, he suggested, probably misled by Philip Roth's famous essay of 1961, 'Writing American Fiction'—which noted that the American actuality was continually outdoing the American writers' talents, and that contemporary absurdity was the envy of any novelist—had simply allowed the great, real subject of the age, the energetic, Byzantine material growth and the multiethnic change of American urban society, to slip away from their attention—until, fortunately, Wolfe himself had time to set journalism aside for a while and plug the gap.

What the age needed, Wolfe said, was nothing less than a massive social novel firmly in the tradition of Balzac, Dickens, Thackeray, and Zola, a documentary novel of modern American urban life, and of manners, mores, money, and process. He had always believed, he said, that 'the future of the fictional novel would be in a highly detailed realism based on reporting, a realism more thorough than any currently being attempted . . .', and that the novelists' task 'is not to leave the rude beast, the material, also known as life around us, but to do what journalists do, or are supposed to do, which is wrestle the beast and bring it to terms'. Wolfe's own formula for wrestling with the beast in *The Bonfire of the Vanities* (his first novel, though built up out of decades of lively and stylish journalism), was simple and, as he said, 'head-on'. The book owes a good deal to the tradition of the European social novel, though rather more to the lineage of the American city novel, the tradition that goes back to Dreiser's *Sister Carrie* and *An American Tragedy* (with which it has some similarities of plot), Dos Passos's *Manhattan Transfer*, James T. Farrell's *Studs Lonigan*, and *Of Time and the River*, by another, earlier, equally ambitious Tom Wolfe. But it is not exactly a work of urban naturalism; nor does it concede much to expressionist techniques or modern experimental techniques, despite occasional stylistic flourishes. Wolfe says that he aimed to do for contemporary New York City what Thackeray's *Vanity Fair* did for mid-nineteenth-century Britain, creating a novel of metropolitan styles, manners, hypocrisies, and vanities. The allusion to Thackeray is repeated in the novel's title, and in its urbane and detached tone. But it finally owes most to two conventions largely derived from contemporary American journalism: the objective, naturalistic, exploratory method of researching and documenting social processes and practices by going out and reporting the detailed workings of the criminal justice system and the politics of the Bronx; and the stylish, subjective method of capturing and displaying the smart news of the tastes, fashions, poses, and trends of the times.

With these resources, along with a virtuoso satirical flair, Wolfe sets out to confront the new New York City of rampant capitalism, money- and style-fever, plutography (the graphic following and recording of the deeds of the rich and the famous), along with the ethnic, class, and gender hostilities, the racial muggings and murders, the political, financial, and legal corruption, and the fundamental contrasts of the Eighties, when New York became something like a Third World city, divided between the Park Avenue apartment and the skyscrapered yuppie world of Manhattan on the one hand, and the underclass world of half-burned out, drug-heavy Harlem and the crime-ridden Bronx on the other. In this world of contrasting sophistication and barbarism, where a subway ride is a ride into danger, Wolfe sets his story of Sherman McCoy, a yuppie bond trader and 'master of the universe' who is suddenly thrown into the lawless, or law-corrupted, jungle of the second city. Wolfe's novel is itself a walk on the wild side by a novelist whose own social and cultural identity lies in the world of style, wealth, and manners. Sharp as is the book's satirical cultural observation, Wolfe is a novelist of smart surfaces, bound up in many of the vanities he satirizes. So the work could reasonably read as a novel of the New Conservatism of the leaner, keener, meaner Reagan years, when liberalism became a dirty word. And, ironically enough, Wolfe himself was to admit that contemporary actuality can indeed outdo the novelists' talents; some of the absurdities he explores, in the legal system and among the black leadership, were not simply to be mirrored but exceeded after the book appeared.

As for Wolfe's attack on his contemporaries, this possesses

many of the qualities of the novel itself. It is spirited, satirically sharp, and a lively piece of self-advertisement, by a former American Studies graduate from Yale, informative, interesting, and questionable at once in its account of the directions taken by recent American fiction. The American novelists of the Sixties and Seventies may indeed have been highly preoccupied with textual experiment and fictionalist aesthetics, but they were also very concerned with the nature of contemporary American history and the feel of the American super-reality. Wolfe describes his own approach as 'head-on'; they usually preferred the tactics that Thomas Pynchon's Herbert Stencil calls 'approach and avoid'. But what has made Wolfe's attack so relevant is not simply that it serves as a manifesto for his own writing, but that it uses his populist influence to tip the scales even further in a direction in which they had tilted already. In fact they had been tilting this way—in the direction of a re-emergence of realism— ever since the mid-Seventies, in the work of such writers as Coover, Doctorow, Mailer, and Abish, and indeed in the work of writers internationally. For, after the experimental excitements of the later Sixties, many western writers were turning towards forms of neo-realism, or towards means and themes that would allow them to approach the changing world of power and politics; cultural and technological development; shifting ethnic, gender, and religious relations; and the need for expression among many groups and nationalities who had begun to seek a new sense of historical identity and a significant narrative of their lives.

In fact 'realism' had never truly gone away. It is sometimes convenient to write twentieth-century literary history in two large strokes: there was modernism and then, in due time, there was postmodernism. The history misleads and abbreviates, for throughout the century there has been, in the line of the novel, a sustaining and powerful history of realism, along with a sequence of recurrent disputes about its veracity, philosophical plausibility, or relevance. Virtually no work that sees itself as antithetical to realism does not contain it as a main constituent, and most major movements considered anti-realist have seen themselves as in the end a new form of realism. One reason for the apparent decline of realism in the Sixties was a decline in critical arguments on its behalf, as criticism itself saw fiction in the light of post-modern interpretations. Yet, when the smoke of battle had cleared, and the cloud of tear-gas around the Pentagon dispersed, when the Sixties counter-culture declined in the early Seventies, the 'me decade' (Wolfe himself is credited with the phrase) came along, and disaster in Vietnam and a more sober economic realism began to prevail, it was apparent that a good part of the old army was still left standing. Saul Bellow, John Updike, and Philip Roth had not ceased to be the major American writers. Bellow continued to publish significantly (*More Die of Heartbreak*, 1987), Updike continued his key American story of 'Rabbit' Angstrom to the point of mortality (*Rabbit at Rest*, 1990), and Philip Roth's recent writing pressed ever closer to the real world that lay behind his own fictional enterprise (*The Counterlife*, 1986; *The Facts*, 1988, semi-fictional autobiography; and *Patrimony*, 1991, a powerful personal memoir about the death of his father). Bellow in particular remained the most vivid and imaginative explorer of the late American Byzantium, with its rising glut of commodities and its decline of inner spirit. Nor did he neglect to make the case for the novel of realism, seizing the day of his acceptance speech for the Nobel Prize for Literature in 1976 to criticize the influence of the *nouveau roman* and its speculations in reality, and reminding the writer that, in an age of crisis, the task to hand remained largely the same: to pursue 'a broader, more flexible, fuller, more coherent, more comprehensive account of what we human beings are, who we are, and what this life is for'. Gore Vidal was now no longer the raunchy author of the sexually explicit, morally ambiguous *Myra Breckenridge* (1968) but the grand chronicler of the march of the American Presidents through the national history (*Lincoln*, 1984, *Empire*, 1987). He devoted several of the essays of his *Matters of Fact and of Fiction* (1977) to the follies he saw induced by the explorations of the *nouveau roman* and the faults of an academicized American fiction written in one seminar room to be studied in the next. John Gardner, who died young in 1982, was a writer of serious fantasy with postmodern credentials, the author of *Grendel* (1971), *The Sunlight Dialogues* (1972), and the fine novel of West Virginia *Mickelsson's Ghosts* (1982). Yet he argued in his

On Moral Fiction in 1978 that 'the theory of fiction as mere language' had caused writers to avoid the central question, that of literature's representative moral power and influence.

It was true that, during the Sixties and early Seventies, many of the now well-established sub-genres of American fiction—Southern fiction, Gothic fiction, Jewish-American fiction, black fiction, regional realism, or for that matter science fiction—seemed to exist less for their own sake than as yet another field for experimental pastiche and parody. Yet they had retained their broader meanings into the next decade: Gothic fiction in Joyce Carol Oates and science fiction in Ursula Le Guin became important means for exploring the issues of feminism and female representation in modern narrative. Black fiction, in the work of Toni Morrison and Alice Walker, became a means for the mythic recovery of the hidden, un-narrated history of black suppression. Regional fiction acquired new and strong realistic voice in the work of writers like Raymond Carver, Bobbie Ann Mason, Garrison Keillor, Carolyn Chute, Robert Love Taylor, and Jayne Anne Phillips. Jewish-American fiction was reinvigorated by the fiction of Stanley Elkin, Walter Abish, Paul Auster, and Cynthia Ozick. The great American city that Wolfe called the modern subject was not neglected: there were the novels of Paul Auster (*New York Trilogy*), Madison Smartt Bell and of Jay McInerney, whose *Bright Lights, Big City* (1984) and *Story of My Life* (1988) cover with a harder irony some of the world Wolfe was calling into fiction. The inflation of events by the modern media that concerns Wolfe had been explored by Robert Coover and Don DeLillo, whose *White Noise* (1984) is one of the most vivid novels of the Eighties. Various dimensions of modern multiculturalism had been developed by writers like Ishmael Reed (*Reckless Eyeballing*, 1986), Toni Cade Bambara (*The Salt Eaters*, 1980), Louise Erdrich, and Maxine Hong Kington.

Certainly 'postmodernism' had established an aesthetic self-examining climate in American fiction, asking what it means in the contemporary world to create a narrative, construct a history, name the world, bring a fiction into being. It was part of a larger intellectual enquiry into the nature of modern naming and narrative, matched in the philosophy of Richard Rorty, the history writing of Hayden White or Simon Schama, or indeed contemporary science with its new notions of indeterminacy and chaos theory. It encouraged a view of the novel as a changing, discovering mode of imaginative and narrative enquiry, responsive to altering structures of human understanding and the shifting shapes of contemporary historical and existence in a pluralized, mobile, and highly modern culture. By the end of the Seventies it was apparent that this late modern experimental spirit was more than an American event, that the novel was drawing on ever-widening cultural and narrative sources, in Eastern Europe, Latin America, Africa, India, and the Arab world, and that its character was never less easy to define. If the spirit of late twentieth-century fiction included the cybernetic novels of Thomas Pynchon or William Gaddis, the minimalist fragmentation of Donald Barthelme, the self-parody of John Barth, the resigned science fiction of Vonnegut, it also included the combinatorial games of Italo Calvino, the prolix abundance of Umberto Eco, the inter-galactic gnosticism of Doris Lessing, the Victorian pastiche of John Fowles. Even in the American marketplace a wider map of possibilities opened in the Seventies and Eighties. Many of the most widely read authors in the United States came, like Milan Kundera, Gabriel García Márquez, and Italo Calvino, from outside it, while Umberto Eco's pastiche medieval detective story *The Name of the Rose* (1983) was an American bestseller.

The handy Sixties distinction between 'realism' and 'experiment' grew ever less credible. New fiction from Latin America (Márquez, Julio Cortazar, Manuel Puig, Mario Vargas Lhosa, Alejo Carpentier, Miguel Ángel Asturias) and a more multicultural Europe (Salman Rushdie, Kazuo Ishiguro, Timothy Mo) displayed both a widening range of narrative sources and a growing sense of the fantastic and unreal as themselves powers within history. It became convenient to talk of 'magic realism', which is generally traced back to Jorge Luis Borges's *Universal History of Infamy* first published in 1935, and is usually used to mean the realism born of a fantastic, disordered, or simply an oral history. Thus it could also be applied to work coming from Germany, like Günter Grass, or especially from Eastern Europe, books by

Milan Kundera, Josef Skvorechy, or Vladimir Voinovich, which subverted conventions of realism but were still fundamentally concerned with history, power, and politics. As Kundera said, undermining realism was one means in which we might break free of political and aesthetic constraint into 'laughter and forgetting'; the testing of realism was no escape from reality, but 'an investigation of human life in the trap the world has become', which was based on 'our special humour: a humour capable of seeing history as grotesque.' Through the Seventies it was clear that the argument for realism—albeit an elusive and ironic realism—was being renewed. And increasingly critical terminology about the novel began to speak in apparent paradoxes: of neo-realism, experimental realism, photo-realism, hyper-realism, ironic realism, critical realism, fantastic realism, magic realism, and dirty realism.

2.

The term 'dirty realism', which seems to have been invented by Bill Buford in the magazine *Granta*, is the kind of writing to which Wolfe gave the name 'K-mart realism'. It refers to a flat form of writing, hyper-detailed and socially specific, that did much to provide the tone for American fictional writing during the Eighties. It was particularly associated with a group of writers— Raymond Carver, Richard Ford, Tobias Wolff, Jayne Anne Phillips (*Machine Dreams*, 1984), Ann Beattie, Bobbie Ann Mason (*In Country*, 1985; *Love Life* (stories), 1989), and Frederick Barthelme—whose work is in practice extremely varied, but is generally highly regional to particular parts of the United States and detailed in its attention to its ordinary life. The best known is Raymond Carver, also a distinguished poet, who concentrated on the short story form, and never published a novel. His first story collection, *Put Yourself in My Shoes*, appeared in 1974, and was followed by several influential volumes, including *What We Talk About When We Talk About Love* (1981) and *Cathedral* (1983). A collected *The Stories of Raymond Carver* came out in 1985, only three years before his early death. Carver's stories are realistic in a highly mannered and distinctly sharp-focus way, written with tight precision of a Hemingway, but having the vivid reportorial clarity of an Edward Hopper painting. Many are set in the Pacific North-West or the Midwest, and most deal with working-class or lower-middle-class lives, the lives of mechanics, secretaries, farmers, bankrupts, or alcoholics. They use highly familiar settings—the mall, the fast-food counter, the trailer park, the bowling alley—and usually turn on small and often seemingly insignificant incidents. Heavy with social and domestic detail, much concerned with objects and goods, presented through vernacular dialogue, they depend on the plain surprise of the banal.

Carver's strength, and his influential place in recent fiction, lies in the fact that, though his stories can be read as pure observed experience, they acquire a metaphoric clarity because of their flavour of pervasive unease. The characters are taciturn and unexpressive, but also vulnerable and exposed; something in their lives or situation appears to be unspoken. There is an implied further meaning in each relationship, or some emotional disclosure yet to be supplied. Carver is in fact a highly self-conscious minimalist, creating a sense of a surface awaiting its own depth; this links his work to that of more obviously experimental writers like Thomas Pynchon, Walter Abish, or Donald Barthelme. Like Barthelme, Carver works predominantly within the contained short-story form and is concerned with the apparently random and contingent details of the ordinary, the items of what Barthelme called *la vie quotidienne*. But Carver's works never overtly subvert or mock the realistic convention, and his *vie quotidienne* seems less a mannered textual construct than a report from the real world itself, which is therefore made familiar and unfamiliar at once. If these stories have Barthelme's air of absence, sadness, disconnection, and negativity, they also remain devoted in a very literal way to the precise, vernacular detail of the most ordinary of lives. The same half-banal qualities are found in other work of the Eighties: for example, in the fiction of Carver's good friend Richard Ford, author of *The Sportswriter* (1986) and the stories of *Rock Springs* (1987). Like Carver, Ford is a writer of the American vernacular—'I just want that good old American flat-vowel language in my head,' he has said—and a vivid and precise recorder of what he calls in *The Sportswriter* 'the normal applauseless life of us all'.

Similarly, Bobbie Ann Mason speaks of writing for those beyond the normal world of fictional report, concerning herself with 'the culture shock one can experience because of geographic and economic isolation'. In her novel *In Country*, she portrays remote and rural lives that have lost virtually all their meaning and real history in an age of modern technologies and mass-media images, though what above all administers the shock to these lives is the experience of the Vietnam War. Likewise in Jayne Anne Phillips's more experimental *Machine Dreams* (1984) technological and military fantasies from Vietnam replace older and more organic relations in her deprived rural West Virginia world. It could be said, indeed, that the Vietnam War did much to shake Americans into a sobered realism and a sense of human impotence in a mechanical and military age. It provided images of random, machine-made violence and feelings of historical senselessness; it also generated awareness of the late modern technologies and extraordinary space-age gadgetry which had become a part of normal life. Where some American writers treated the war with great directness—Michael Herr in *Despatches* (1977), Tim O'Brien in *Going After Cacciato* (1978), Robert Mason in *Chickenhawk* (1984)—others traced its place in the heart and soul of American life. One of these was Robert Stone, who in his fine *Dog Soldiers* (1974) follows through the corruptions and exploitations practised in South Vietnam into American culture through the link of drug trafficking to the United States. Stone was one of several important novelists who had trained, like Wolfe, as a journalist, and used his experience as a foreign correspondent to explore the nature of American military power and its imperial ambitions. Another was Joan Didion, author of *Play It As It Lays* (1970) and *Democracy* (1984). Both Didion and Stone explore further American adventurism in Latin America, Stone in *A Flag for Sunrise* (1981), which links the Vietnam experience to intervention in Central America. At the end of the novel a central character concludes ironically: 'A man has nothing to fear, he thought to himself, who understands history'. What is clear is that understanding

American history means understanding it has lost its power as dream.

Understanding American history, whether in political adventures abroad or in the era of rising urban violence and drug abuse at home, was clearly an approach that fitted the sobered, unutopian political mood of the Seventies. It equally fitted the following mood of entrepreneurial endeavour, growing commercialism, commodity culture, and the sense of mass hypnosis that seemed to be the tone of life in the Reaganite Eighties. Even among more affluent lives, it seemed, were lived in a world where randomized commodities had replaced real experience. In the more urban, bourgeois personal experience of the characters of writers like Lois Gould (*Not Responsible for Personal Articles*, 1978), Ann Beattie (*The Burning House* (stories), 1982; *Love Always*, 1985), or Alice Adams (*Superior Women*, 1984), the same sense of banality and emptiness prevails. Even life in the Los Angeles or Manhattan fast lane was no relief, according to the 'bratpack' novels of Bret Ellis (*Less Than Zero*, 1985); Michael Chabon (*The Mysteries of Pittsburgh*, 1988); or Jay McInerney (*Bright Lights, Big City*, 1984; *The Story of My Life*, 1988). McInerney's *Bright Lights, Big City* looks at an aspirant publisher trying to escape from the department of Literary Verification into the Fiction Department ('In fact you don't want to be in fact, you want to be in fiction'). In the fiction of the Eighties, it grew ever harder to distinguish between the two.

There is little wonder that that ever-observant critic Jerome Klinkowitz was soon finding in the drift of some of this writing—particularly in the writing of Thomas McGuane (*Nobody's Angel*, 1982; *Something to Be Desired*, 1984; the film-script *The Missouri Breaks*, 1975); Dan Wakefield (*Selling Out*, 1984); and Richard Yates (*Young Hearts Crying*, 1984)—what he chose to call the new American 'novel of manners', a fiction of a world of ritual life-styles, forms, and conventions, in which, however, the forms are often the imprisoning patterns of a life pre-plotted and fictionalized by social powers elsewhere. What was notable was that much of this newer writing, though often more realistic than the work of the previous generation, was also far more acerbic. Its prevailing note is often that of bitter irony, an expression of a dismay about the emptiness, random violence, mechanism, and delusion of many American lives. This sharp and edgy tone is particularly caught in the fiction of Don DeLillo, the author of *Americana* (1971), *Ratner's Star* (1976), *Running Dog* (1978), and *White Noise* (1984) and *Mao II* (1991). DeLillo, who is often brilliantly funny, writes on the edge of science fiction, writing of the banality, boredom, and then finally the violence of an American culture entirely pervaded by objects, images, and media systems, a world where 'everything we need that is not food or love is here in the tabloid racks'. In *Ratner's Star* he observes that in contemporary America 'existence is nourished from below, from the fear level, the place of obsession, the starkest tract of awareness,' and this is the note of his novels. In *White Noise* a teacher in the department of Hitler Studies is faced with the new, abstract, ahistorical threat of a chemical cloud in a world where disaster is part of the American way of life. For much of this late modern realism, reality itself is a decadent and absurd fantasy in the midst of plenitude. It is reality itself that has the quality of a fictional paradigm, allowing the world inside the novel to be depicted neutrally as simply real.

It is often the way of a time of realism that it displays not so much a clear aesthetic tendency or programme as a spirit of general versatility, a formal pragmatism that is freely used to engender new content. This more recent writing has won the name 'neo-realism' because it has tended towards an ironic or ostensibly neutral report on contemporary or even future American life. It is rarely a realism of felt authenticity, nor of moral humanism; some of it is marked by an extreme violence. For this reason Tom Wolfe's view—that the late twentieth-century American writer should behave as a secretary to the times and as a journalist (reporting is, he says, 'the most valuable and least understood resource available to any writer with exalted ambitions'), going out into life to observe manners, experience, and social processes—simplifies the task many contemporary writers have attempted, with more or less success. What is particularly striking about Wolfe's argument, and the 'downpouring of literary republicanism' of which it is part, is that it does return us to many of the debates of the 1880s and 1890s with which this book began.

That was another time when the world seemed in fundamental change and motion, old ideas and values seemed to crumble, the human being was exposed to powerful external forces, and the energies and directions of American history seemed to be running out of control. Then, too, the writer wanted above all to be *there*, in the factories, streets, ghettos, and skyscrapers, at the imperial wars and social battlefields, exploring the points of conflict and the new modes of daily life. That too resulted in a period of many realisms, a literature of pluralized voices and over-accumulated content, until it was duly followed by the more ordered and aesthetic shapings of the modern movement. That earlier realism also reflected the sense of lost or changing convictions, exposure to new processes, lives lived under ironic circumstances, and was born of a time when one phase of history seemed to come towards its end and another took on its millennial and uncertain shape. Over recent years superpower America has lost some of its historical confidence, and has begun to find its way through the shoals of a rapidly changing world order. And as its abundance has come to dismay as well as satisfy, its cities become more terrifying and ungovernable, its wealth insufficient to solve its problems, its problems of drugs, disease and poverty apparently insuperable, then perhaps the very plural realism that has grown over the Eighties is an understandable response to the times.

3.

But though the American novel as it developed from the Seventies and into the Nineties may have grown less dominated by a clear aesthetic attitude, it has certainly been dominated by clear tendencies, these mostly arising from the deep changes that have been reordering an American society which has been more conservative in its mood and less certain than before in its direction and future. Of these the most important has been the rise of the women's movement, which has had a powerful impact on recent fictional expression. American fiction, especially since the Second World War, has never been short of major female writers. Besides the familiar figures of Eudora Welty, Katherine Anne Porter, Carson McCullers, Harper Lee, Flannery O'Connor (many of these central to the Southern revival of the 1940s), there were exploring writers like Tillie Olsen, author of *Yonnondio* (written mostly in the Thirties but published in 1974), and Hortense Calisher, whose writing over several decades includes the volumes *Extreme Magic* (1964) and *On Keeping Women* (1977), and whose work captures both female sexuality and androgyny with poetry and complexity. One of the strongest voices of American social fiction was the urban, urbane, and highly ironic Mary McCarthy, whose fiction gave, from a sharp and vivid female viewpoint, a modern history of the world of radical modern ideas—utopian emancipation in *The Oasis* (1949), Marxism and feminism in *The Group* (1963)—in their various forms, from the bohemian Twenties, through the Marxist Thirties, to the liberal Fifties and the counter-cultural Sixties. Her educated female protagonists enter these societies with optimistic hopes and reforming zeal, only to find, in McCarthy's world—which spares nothing and no one—that they pay a considerable price for their contradictory dreams.

McCarthy has found her natural successor in Alison Lurie, another writer of sharp ironic intelligence and Jane Austen-like moral vigour, whose novels give us a devastating contemporary chronicle of social and sexual change. Her *The Nowhere City* (1965) explores the story of an academic couple who go from the American East Coast to the much more provisional world of Los Angeles, the 'nowhere city', and find themselves among the psychological and sexual confusions of 'an eternal dizzying present'. *Imaginary Friends* (1967) deals with modern utopianism; a sociologist goes to investigate the radical dreams of a minor Christian sect in upper New York State, and finally decides to reveal himself as their Messiah. With *The War Between the Tates* (1974) Lurie looked, with her usual sharp bite, at the ever-changing American battleground, the family, in the generational, cultural, and gender wars of the dying Sixties. Her novel *Foreign Affairs* (1984) is a transatlantic novel, set in the United States and Britain, and reminds us that her work contains Jamesian qualities, a power to stand apart and observe the manners of the social preoccupations, political dreams, and sexual aspirations of her age. Her most direct treatment of feminism is *The Truth*

About Lorin Jones (1988), where a young woman art historian in sexual revolt against the conditions of her own life tries a lesbian relationship and seeks to reclaim and mother back into public respect an older artist, only to find that she is not quite what she had seemed. The plot is appropriate—a similar if slightly less ironic story is told in Mary Gordon's *Men and Angels* (1985)— because the book reflects the feminist need to reconstruct a significant tradition of women's art in America. Lurie retains her distance, her ironic gift for detachment and scepticism, while acknowledging the power of a fundamental myth of the times.

Already during the Seventies, the new women's fiction was becoming a counterpoint to postmodernism, which was largely a male affair. Some important works of experiment by women writers appeared at the time, most notably those of two authors whose main work lay in other genres. Susan Sontag, essayist and cultural critic, produced two experimental novels, *The Benefactor* (1963) and *Death-Kit* (1967), and the poet Sylvia Plath her novel of self-enclosure and schizophrenia, *The Bell Jar* (1963). But it was with the rise of the Women's Liberation movement following the appearance of Betty Friedan's influential *The Feminine Mystique* (1963) and Kate Millett's *Sexual Politics* (1970), which criticized the portrayal both of women and gender in fiction, that women's writing began acquiring a character of collective consciousness and a committed political, moral, and aesthetic purpose it had not shown since the 1890s. By the early Seventies a group of striking novels by women positively explored the female experience in a world of male domination, and declared an independence—and often a sexual freedom and frankness— largely new to mainstream American fiction, changing general attitudes to sexual representation. These included Erica Jong's vigorous sexual comedy *Fear of Flying* (1973), Judith Rossner's *Looking for Mr. Goodbar* (1975), Lisa Alther's wild and surreal comedy of American life, *Kinflicks* (1976), Marge Piercy's fantasy *Woman on the Edge of Time* (1976), Sarah Davidson's *Loose Change* (1977) and Marilyn French's novel about gender exclusion *The Women's Room* (1977). And though many of these were works of realism portraying contemporary life from the female perspective, they also opened out into a variety of other genres—

parody, as in Erica Jong's *Fanny* (1980); science fiction, in Piercy's novel and Ursula Le Guin's inventive *A Wizard of Earthsea* (1968) and *The Left Hand of Darkness* (1969); Gothic romance in the work of Rachel Ingalls and especially Joyce Carol Oates.

Oates, who is already the author of more than fifty books (fiction, drama, poetry, literary criticism), proved to be one of the most prolific, multitalented writers in recent fiction, and the range of her literary antecedents as well as her literary gifts makes her clearly one of the authors of John Barth's 'literature of replenishment'. Her first novel, aptly called *With Shuddering Fall*, appeared in 1964; since then she has written fiction which mixes Gothic estrangement with high social observation. Her work has used a variety of genres and covered a variety of eras and settings. She has set her novels in her Faulkner-like 'region' of Eden County, New York State, as well as in academia, the Detroit slums, the Pennsylvania backwoods, and the historical past or the shadowy spaces of the land of Gothic. Her first and most essential debt is in fact to the American Gothic tradition, and she has all the fascination usual in that genre with unconscious forces, seduction, incest, violence, rape, and murder, sometimes to the point of sensationalism. But she has spread beyond this into a parodic variety of forms—academic comedy in *Unholy Loves* (1979) and a number of short stories, dynastic American epic in *Bellefleur* (1980), pure Gothic myth and horror in *A Bloodsmoor Romance* (1982), detective fiction in *The Mysteries of Winterthurn* (1984), and the thriller in *Kindred Passions* (1987). She has thus constructed an enormously varied fictional world, at times highly literary and allusive, but also distinctively hers—marked by her preoccupation with estrangement and horror, with the dynastic relation between past American secrets and the disorders of the contemporary success-driven and violent American present. Her work, especially more recently, has strong feminist overtones, using its Gothic tradition to explore the ambiguities of gender and the sexual bases of fantasy. More recent books have turned back to the more familiar social world, of which she is a strong portraitist. Though various in quality, and apt to use sensation for its own sake, she is at best a writer of great importance.

If stylistic abundance is a quality of Oates's own work, it is also a characteristic quality of contemporary women's writing in general. Women writers have increasingly claimed the freedom to explore or experiment with the literary conventions, languages, and archetypes of an American tradition that historically was heavily dominated by male images. Like other writers who, feeling overwhelmed by the dominant canon, have attempted to establish a new heritage of their own (blacks, Hispanics, native Americans), they have been concerned to re-explore the past and establish predecessors from Harriet Beecher Stowe to Kate Chopin to Djuna Barnes and Anaïs Nin. One task of this writing has thus been what the Canadian feminist writer Margaret Atwood (*The Edible Woman*, 1969; *Surfacing*, 1972; *The Handmaid's Tale*, 1985) calls 'surfacing', or seeking a place beyond 'writing' to escape from familiar forms and repetitions. If postmodern writers complained of the 'used-upnedness' of writing, many women writers, not surprisingly, have considered their problem the opposite—to construct and develop a tradition and a discourse that, far from being exhausted, seemed scarcely to have begun. But where the feminist fiction of the Seventies was highly concerned to lay the path, the abundance and variety of recent women's fictions suggests it is there to use. Women writers now have a substantial part in all the familiar genres, while at the same time their writing has been an attempt at creating new forms and languages for representing a novel and contemporary experience.

Thus the contemporary repertory has become one of widely various and multidirectional voices. It includes the reflexive and fragmentary world of Renata Adler's *Speedboat* (1976) and *Pitch Dark* (1983); the tale of the mixed and confusing choices of female identity in Marilynne Robinson's *Housekeeping* (1980); the fragile evocations of the spoiled rich in Ellen Gilchrist's *In the Land of Dreamy Dreams* (1981); the deep family pain of Anne Tyler's *Dinner at the Homesick Restaurant* (1982) and the mordant humour of *The Accidental Tourist* (1985); the agonized tale of marriage breakup in Nora Ephron's also very funny *Heartburn* (1983); the punk fiction of Kathy Acker in *Blood and Guts in High School* (1984) and then her more complex *Don Quixote*

(1986); and the technical experiment and political observation of
Joan Didion's novel of California politics, *Democracy* (1984). It
also includes the lesbian celebration of Lisa Alther's *Other
Women* (1984), the feminist romance of Marge Piercy's *Fly
Away Home* (1984), the sensitive and critical exploration of
adolescent self-discovery of Gail Godwin's *The Finishing School*
(1985), and the bitterly anti-male fiction of Andrea Dworkin in
Ice and Fire (1986).

Of these very various developments, probably the most important of all has been the role of women's writing in the development
of ethnic or what is sometimes called 'minority' literature. Both
Grace Paley and Cynthia Ozick have, for example, contributed
powerfully to the tradition of Jewish-American as well as that of
women's fiction. Paley's 'stories of men and women at love', *The
Little Disturbances of Man* (1959) and *Later the Same Day*
(1985), show her as a writer of poetic dialogue and radical
imagination. Ozick is a novelist and story-writer deeply committed
to the Jewish heritage and the memory of the Holocaust, evocat-
ively summoned up in the two fine stories of *The Shawl* (1989).
Her novel *The Cannibal Galaxy* (1983) is an attempt to build a
literary bridge between the Yiddish and Anglo-Saxon traditions
of metaphor and mysticism, and *The Messiah of Stockholm*
(1987) is a subtle story of fictions and realities, about a Swede
who thinks he is the son of the Polish writer Bruno Schulz, but is
suddenly reminded of the dark facts of Schulz's extermination,
which are far more terrible than those of his books. Ozick's work
resists the replacement of reality by fiction, while using the
metaphoric powers of fiction to establish its own powerful voice.

Not surprisingly though, the fiction that has had the strongest
right to claim it was speaking from a doubly repressed but real
tradition is that from the several important black women writers
who played so big a role in the development of the American
novel in the Seventies and Eighties. The most important is surely
Toni Morrison, a writer of high ambitions, strong mythic powers,
and epic sweep. To date her novels are *The Bluest Eye* (1970),
Sula (1973), *Song of Solomon* (1977), *Tar Baby* (1981), and
Beloved (1987); she has also written some important criticism.
Her work could well be identified as a form of magic realism; she

draws on oral narratives, African folk-tales, remembered ghost stories, all part of an urgent sense of the powers of myth and a desire to recover the hidden fables that might guide black culture. At the same time she is influenced by Melville, Hawthorne, and Faulkner in her belief in the power of literary myth and legend, and its expression of the paradoxes and ambiguities of human identity. *Sula* is a poetic fable about a promiscuous girl whose immorality transforms and releases an entire community. *Song of Solomon*, which is likewise full of magical elements, takes its black characters journeying backwards into the myths of their own psychic and racial past. *Tar Baby* draws on the Brer Rabbit legends to tell the story of a woman struggling towards independent identity. *Beloved*, her finest novel so far, deals with the dying days of slavery and the period of Reconstruction, telling of a black mother who kills her young daughter when the slave owner comes to return her to slavery. The daughter, Beloved, returns as a ghost, and Morrison uses the book to create life out of death, motherhood out of cruelty, and forgotten history out of silence. Like her other books, it uses allegory, fantasy, free invention, oral legend, literary myth, and poetic and song-like methods to construct a memorable narrative that can banish the darkness that enfolds so much of black life. Morrison, who has not only taught in universities but worked as a publisher's editor, was able to encourage, and influence, the work of several other black women writers—perhaps especially Gayle Jones, author of *Corregidora* (1975) and *White Rat* (1977), novels which also share Morrison's concern with oral history and legend, and the poetry and song of black vernacular speech.

Morrison and Jones were two of several significant black women writers who emerged over the Seventies and Eighties. Others included Toni Cade Bambara, Maya Angelou, and Nikki Giovanni, but the other undoubtedly major figure is Alice Walker. Walker shares with Morrison an epic range, a strong and redeeming vision of life, and a concern to construct an imaginative past. Walker, born of a black sharecropper family, managed to gain herself a university education, and her fiction links the poverty of Southern black life with the expanding horizons of life in changing, more urban and more open America. She has written in a wide variety of forms, including poetry and essays, argued the case for 'womanist' prose, and produced recuperative biographies of the earlier black writers Langston Hughes and Zora Neale Hurston. Her novels to date are *The Third Life of Grange Copeland* (1970), *Meridian* (1976), and *The Color Purple* (1982). Important and vital histories of modern black experience and of double oppression—of blacks by whites and women by men—her books reflect the growing freedoms opened by the Civil Rights movement, but also the need not just for blacks but for all human beings to pass beyond the struggle for personal and collective independence into a timeless vision of life. *The Color Purple*, which won a Pulitzer Prize for its author, and was made into a fine film, is the most ambitious, powerful, and moving of her novels, which express both political passion and a strong and deeply personal religious emotion. Told in the form of letters, *The Color Purple* is the story of a group of black women who struggle from a world of poverty and social backwardness, of racial suppression and sexual abuse from their own menfolk, towards a vivid female identity. But the quest is not only political but spiritual, a movement towards the transcendent image of creation in its spiritual beauty that is symbolized in the book's title.

It is not only in the black tradition that women writers have been leading figures in the construction of a cultural identity, and have assumed the task of retrieving historical myth and legend. Maxine Hong Kingston has written of the history, the stories, and fate of Chinese-American women in *The Woman Warrior* (1976). Louise Erdrich, who is part Chippewa Indian, has—following in the tradition of N. Scott Momaday—explored Native American life on and off the reservation in her fiction, which she writes in close collaboration with her husband, Michael Dorris, also a novelist (they are the jointly credited authors of the novel *The Crown of Columbus*, 1988). Her *Love Medicine* (1984) consists of fourteen thematically interlinked stories about reservation life in North Dakota, in a world where Indians are reduced to poverty, alcoholism, and suicide, and yet retain a tribal wisdom, a tradition of shamanism, and a veneration of all life, which give them dignity. *The Beet Queen* (1986) moves off the reservation to explore Midwest small-town life and its contemporary ethnic variety, while *Tracks* (1989) deals with an earlier Native American history of suppression and extermination. These three books interrelate as part of a Northern plains series, with a fourth volume planned. Again, Erdrich's work is notable for its mixture of contemporary social realism on the one hand and a commitment to legend and native oral myth on the other. It typifies a decade when fiction has turned away from the purely aesthetic to the ethnic, from abstract myth towards the myths of various American peoples, when national issues have become personal and regional issues, and when formal revolution has been replaced by 'speaking out'.

And, in the age of 'speaking out', it was not surprising that gay writing found a strong, though—as the AIDS epidemic spread—an increasingly troubled, voice. The lesbian novel developed in the work of Marge Piercy and Joanna Russ, author of *The Female Man* (1975), and Patricia Highsmith, best known, of course, as a powerful crime novelist. Male gay fiction had already established a tradition of sorts in the work of Tennessee Williams, James Baldwin, Gore Vidal, Truman Capote, and above all the free-form, experimental gay fantasy of William S. Burroughs. He clearly influenced the work of John Rechy, whose *City of Night* (1963), *This Day's Death* (1970), and *Bodies and Souls* (1983) owe much to Burroughs's sense of the fantastic and Gothic. Coleman Dowell produced works of frank gay eroticism in *One of the Children Is Crying* (1968) and *Too Much Flesh and Jabez* (1977), while David Leavitt has finely recorded the impact of gay self-discovery on modern American family life in the stories of *Family Dancing* (1984). In *A Boy's Own Story* (1982), Edmund White wrote equally delicately of growing up into gay experience; his more recent work, like the tellingly titled *The Beautiful Room Is Empty* (1988), has been a coming to terms with the bleaker world of loss and suffering that devastated gay lives after the appearance of AIDS.

The importance of much of this writing lies less in its aesthetic invention, which is often considerable, but in the fact that it constructs through the power of fiction an American world that has grown ever more plural and various, more multiple not just in its sources of expression but in the sources of the very claim to expression. It depicts a society vastly more aware of its mixture of racial identities, much more open to the variety of human life-styles, and often much more divided—between sex and sex, wealthy and underclass, one ethnic group and another. It also depicts the abundance of ethnic and regional myths and fables, the multiplicity of human stories and fantasies, of Gothic tensions and shaken lives, in the contemporary bonfire of the vanities. It thus represents a realism of a new kind, less concerned with the social detail of traditional realism, and certainly less able to draw on realism's general moral community or on shared and established certainties about the self and history. It is in general an anxious realism, the product of complex and chaotic times when, as Morris Dickstein has observed, the lapel badges read 'Desperately Clinging to Utopian Illusions', and writers seemed to possess either an individualized or a chaotic sense of the national history. Nor is this writing a conscious revolt of realism against experiment, and in fact it incorporates a good many of its elements—its merging of the true and the false, its feeling for the incredible as much as the familiar in American life, its sense of the Gothic, the strange, the outrageous, and the legendary, all of which takes its place within the compass of the real. This may be the world of Wolfe's billion-footed beast, contemporary society itself, but the beast remains open to many individual interpretations.

By the beginning of the Nineties, when the cold war appeared to be at an end and a new millennium came into view, the United States as it was depicted in its fiction had come to be a less than buoyant and comfortable inheritor of the modern technological energies and high American hopes that had flourished at the beginning of the century. The world as mapped by contemporary American novelists looks, in fact, very different from that explored by the writers of even twenty years earlier, when in a surge of experimental excitements mixed with historical trauma new writers seemed ready to transform the entire nature and direction of American fiction. The new writing of the present may have moved closer to realism and to some degree away from radical innovation of form. But it still displays many of those innovations, just as does for that matter the architectural, social,

and psychological landscape of contemporary America itself.
But today the experimental novel, perhaps in part thanks to the
digestive practices of commercial publishing, seems to be simply
one more genre in an era of plural and multiplying genres. And
some of the best work now being produced is being done through
the formal and imaginative extension of the various generic
literary types. The Gothic exoticism never far from the American
novel seems to be riding high. Science fiction, the form opened
by Kurt Vonnegut, is being richly developed by writers like
Ursula Le Guin and Samuel Delany. The crime novel, the novel
noir, has such performers as Elmore Leonard (*Glitz*, 1985) and
George V. Higgins, the Boston writer of law, crime-, and street-
talk, whose *The Friends of Eddie Coyle* (1972) and *Trust* (1989)
are works of precise and careful vernacular notation, which add
to the rich tradition left by Raymond Chandler and Dashiell
Hammett. Children's fiction has been enlarged in the work of
Rachel Ingalls and Russell Hoban, whose *Riddley Walker* (1980)
is also a contribution to the experimental novel. It may well be
that the variety, formal multiplicity, and cultural multi-ethnicity
of recent fiction represents the ultimate triumph of postmodernism, displaying the Byzantine variety of style and cultural source,
the endless search for new styles and roles, the hungry hyper-
modernity and melting-pot variety that marks the spirit of
contemporary American life.

4.

A hundred years previously, at the start of the 1890s, Henry
Adams sat down in 'helpless reflection' at the Columbian Exhibition in Chicago, and wondered what the twentieth century would
become. He had an intimation of an imploding energy that would
take the mind into the twentieth century multiverse, while giving
it no clear guide, direction, or ordered education. He saw a world
that was looking, not backward towards the guiding agrarian
past, but anxiously forward, into the age of great cities and new
technologies, a world that was not post-something but pre-
something. The passage through the turn of a century was at
hand; there were imperial wars, signs of social chaos and class

division, a confusion of sexual roles, a sense of dangerous outside threats and epidemics. The signals from the future were energetic, but obscure. Adams was perceiving and interpreting that turbulence which has marked the turn of most of the recent centuries, from the revolutions of the eighteenth century onward, and which suggests the breakdown of orderly and familiar structures, the loss of habitual signposts and established canons in life and art. The task was to look forward and onward, to see how the coming change might best be ordered and expressed. It already seems very likely, if the fiction around us is any guide, that this might also be the mark of our own passage through the Nineties and beyond them, into the mysterious next century.

The American Novel Since 1890:
A List of Major Works

The following list is selective and extends beyond the authors covered in the text. Not all works by authors mentioned are included; dates are of American publication.

WALTER ABISH (1931–)
Alphabetical Africa (1974); *Minds Meet* (stories, 1975); *In the Future Perfect* (stories, 1977); *How German Is It* (1981).

KATHY ACKER (1947–)
Blood and Guts in High School (1984); *Don Quixote* (1986); *Empire of the Senseless* (1988).

ALICE ADAMS (1926–)
Careless Love (1966); *Superior Women* (1984).

RENATA ADLER (1938–)
Speedboat (1976); *Pitch Dark* (1983).

JAMES AGEE (1909–55)
A Death in the Family (1957).

CONRAD AIKEN (1888–1973)
Blue Voyage (1927).

LISA ALTHER (1944–)
Kinflicks (1976); *Other Women* (1984).

SHERWOOD ANDERSON (1876–1941)
Windy McPherson's Son (1916); *Marching Men* (1917); *Winesburg, Ohio* (stories, 1919); *Dark Laughter* (1925).

MAX APPLE (1942–)
Zip (1978); *Free Agents* (1984).

MARGARET ATWOOD (1939–)
The Edible Woman (1969); *Surfacing* (1972); *Life Before Man* (1982); *The Handmaid's Tale* (1985).

PAUL AUSTER (1946–)
The Invention of Solitude (memoir, 1982); *The New York Trilogy* (*City of Glass*, 1985; *Ghosts*, 1986; *The Locked Room*, 1986); *In the Country of Last Things* (1987); *Moon Palace* (1989); *The Music of Chance* (1991).

NICHOLSON BAKER (1957–)
The Mezzanine (1988); *Room Temperature* (1990); *U and I* (1991).

JAMES BALDWIN (1924–87)
Go Tell It On the Mountain (1953); *Giovanni's Room* (1956); *Another Country* (1962); *Tell Me How Long the Train's Been Gone* (1968); *If Beale Street Could Talk* (1974).

TONI CADE BAMBARA (1939–)
Gorilla, My Love (1972); *The Salt Eaters* (1980).

RUSSELL BANKS (1940–)
Continental Drift (1985); *Success Stories* (1986); *Affliction* (1989).

DJUNA BARNES (1892–1982)
Nightwood (1936).

JOHN BARTH (1930–)
The Floating Opera (1956); *The Sot-Weed Factor* (1960); *Giles Goat-Boy* (1966); *Lost in the Funhouse: Fiction for Print, Tape, Live Voice* (1968); *Chimera* (stories, 1972); *Letters* (1979); *Sabbatical: A Romance* (1982); *The Last Voyage of Somebody the Sailor* (1991); *The Friday Book* (essays, 1984).

DONALD BARTHELME (1933–89)
Come Back, Dr. Caligari (stories, 1964); *Snow White* (1967); *Unspeakable Practices, Unnatural Acts* (stories, 1968); *City Life* (stories, 1970); *Sadness* (stories, 1972); *The Dead Father* (1975); *Sixty Stories* (1985); *Paradise* (1986); *Forty Stories* (1987); *The King* (post., 1991).

FREDERICK BARTHELME (1943–)
Second Marriage (1984); *Tracer* (1985).

JOHN CALVIN BATCHELOR (1943–)
The Birth of the People's Republic of Antarctica (1983); *The Further Adventures of Haley's Comet* (1984); *American Falls* (1985).

JONATHAN BAUMBACH (1931–   )
Reruns (1974); *My Father More or Less* (1982); *The Life and Times of Major Fiction* (1987).

ANN BEATTIE (1947–   )
The Burning House (1982); *Love Always* (1985); *Picturing Will* (1989).

MADISON SMARTT BELL (1957–   )
Straight Cut (1987); *Year of Silence* (1987); *Soldier's Joy* (1989).

SAUL BELLOW (1915–   )
Dangling Man (1944); *The Victim* (1947); *Henderson the Rain King* (1959); *Herzog* (1964); *Mr. Sammler's Planet* (1970); *Humboldt's Gift* (1975); *The Dean's December* (1982); *More Die of Heartbreak* (1987).

THOMAS BERGER (1924–   )
Reinhart in Love (1961); *Little Big Man* (1964); *Vital Parts* (1970); *Regiment of Women* (1973); *Nowhere* (1985).

PAUL BOWLES (1910–   )
The Sheltering Sky (1949); *Let It Come Down* (1952); *Collected Stories* (1979).

T. CORAGHESSAN BOYLE (1948–   )
The Descent of Man (1979); *Greasy Lake* (1985); *World's End* (1987).

RAY BRADBURY (1920–   )
Farenheit 451 (1953); *Something Wicked This Way Comes* (1962).

RICHARD BRAUTIGAN (1935–84)
A Confederate General from Big Sur (1964); *Trout Fishing in America* (1967); *In Watermelon Sugar* (1968); *The Hawkline Monster: A Gothic Western* (1974); *Dreaming of Babylon* (1977); *The Tokyo–Montana Express* (1980); *So the Wind Won't Blow It All Away* (1982).

CHARLES BUKOWSKI (1920–   )
Tales of Ordinary Madness (1967); *Ham on Rye* (1982).

JOHN HORNE BURNS (1916–53)
The Gallery (1947).

WILLIAM S. BURROUGHS, JR. (1914–   )
The Naked Lunch (Paris, 1959; New York, 1962); *The Ticket That*

Exploded (1962); *Nova Express* (1964); *The Wild Boys* (1971); *Cities of the Red Night* (1981).

JAMES BRANCH CABELL (1879–1958)
The Eagle's Shadow (1904); *Jurgen* (1919).

ABRAHAM CAHAN (1860–1951)
Yekl: A Tale of the New York Ghetto (1896); *The Rise of David Levinsky* (1917).

ERSKINE CALDWELL (1903–87)
Tobacco Road (1932); *God's Little Acre* (1933).

HORTENSE CALISHER (1911–)
Extreme Magic (1964); *On Keeping Women* (1977).

TRUMAN CAPOTE (1924–74)
Other Voices, Other Rooms (1948); *Breakfast at Tiffany's* (1958); *In Cold Blood* (1966); *Music for Chameleons* (1981).

RAYMOND CARVER (1939–88)
Put Yourself in My Shoes (1974); *Will You Please Be Quiet, Please* (1976); *What We Talk About When We Talk About Love* (1981); *Cathedral* (1983); *The Stories of Raymond Carver* (1985).

WILLA CATHER (1873–1947)
Alexandra's Bridge (1912); *O Pioneers!* (1913); *My Ántonia* (1918); *A Lost Lady* (1923); *The Professor's House* (1925); *Death Comes for the Archbishop* (1927); *Not Under Forty* (essays, 1936).

MICHAEL CHABON (1963–)
The Mysteries of Pittsburgh (1988); *A Model World and Other Stories* (1991).

JEROME CHARYN (1937–)
Going to Jerusalem (1967); *War Cries Over Avenue C* (1985); *Metropolis* (1986).

RAYMOND CHANDLER (1888–1959)
The Big Sleep (1939); *Farewell, My Lovely* (1940); *The Lady in the Lake* (1943); *The Long Goodbye* (1953).

JOHN CHEEVER (1912–82)
The Wapshot Chronicle (1957); *Bullet Park* (1969); *Falconer* (1977); *The Short Stories of John Cheever* (1979).

SUSAN CHEEVER (1943–)
A Handsome Man (1981); *Doctors and Women* (1987).

CHARLES W. CHESNUTT (1858–1932)
The Conjure Woman (stories, 1899); *The House Behind the Cedars* (1900); *The Marrow of Tradition* (1901).

KATE CHOPIN (1851–1904)
At Fault (1891); *Bayou Folk* (stories, 1894); *The Awakening* (1899).

CAROLYN CHUTE (1947–)
The Beans of Egypt, Maine (1985); *Letourneau's Used Auto Parts* (1988).

EVAN S. CONNELL, JR. (1924–)
The Anatomy Lesson (1957); *Mrs. Bridge* (1959); *Mr. Bridge* (1969).

ROBERT COOVER (1932–)
The Origin of the Brunists (1965); *The Universal Baseball Association, J. Henry Waugh, Prop.* (1968); *A Political Fable* (1968; reissued 1980); *Pricksongs & Descants* (stories, 1969); *The Public Burning* (1977); *Gerald's Party* (1986); *A Night at the Movies* (1987); *Pinocchio in Venice* (1991).

JAMES GOULD COZZENS (1903–78)
Guard of Honor (1948); *By Love Possessed* (1957).

STEPHEN CRANE (1870–1900)
Maggie: A Girl of the Streets (1893); *The Red Badge of Courage* (1895); *George's Mother* (1896); *The Open Boat* (stories, 1898).

E. E. CUMMINGS (1894–1962)
The Enormous Room (1922).

GUY DAVENPORT (1927–)
Tatlin! (1974); *The Jules Verne Steam Balloon* (1987).

SARA DAVIDSON (1943–)
Loose Change (1977); *Friends of the Opposite Sex* (1984).

SAMUEL R. DELANY (1942–   )
Babel—17 (1966); *Empire Star* (1966); *Empire: A Visual Novel* (1973).

DON DELILLO (1936–   )
Americana (1971); *Great Jones Street* (1973); *Ratner's Star* (1976); *Running Dog* (1978); *White Noise* (1984); *Libra* (1988); *Mao II* (1991).

JAMES DICKEY (1923–   )
Deliverance (1970).

JOAN DIDION (1934–   )
Slouching Towards Bethlehem (1968); *Play It As It Lays* (1970); *A Book of Common Prayer* (1977); *Democracy* (1984).

ANNIE DILLARD (1945–   )
Pilgrim at Tinker Creek (1974); *Teaching a Stone to Talk* (1982).

STEPHEN DIXON (1936–   )
Fall & Rise (1984); *Garbage* (1988); *Love and Will* (stories, 1989).

E. L. DOCTOROW (1931–   )
Welcome to Hard Times (1960); *The Book of Daniel* (1971); *Ragtime* (1975); *Loon Lake* (1980); *Lives of the Poets* (1984); *World's Fair* (1985).

J. P. DONLEAVY (1926–   )
The Ginger Man (Paris, 1955; New York, 1958); *A Singular Man* (1963); *The Beastly Beatitudes of Balthazar B.* (1968), *The Onion Eaters* (1971).

MICHAEL DORRIS (1945–   )
A Yellow Raft on Blue Water (1988).

JOHN DOS PASSOS (1896–1970)
One Man's Initiation—1917 (1920); *Three Soldiers* (1921); *Manhattan Transfer* (1925); *U.S.A.* (*The 42nd Parallel, 1919, The Big Money*, 1930–6); *Mid-Century* (1961).

COLEMAN DOWELL (1925–85)
One of the Children Is Crying (1963); *Too Much Flesh and Jabez* (1977); *White on Black on White* (1983).

THEODORE DREISER (1871–1945)
Sister Carrie (1900); *Jennie Gerhardt* (1911); *The Financier* (1912); *The Titan* (1914); *The 'Genius'* (1915); *An American Tragedy* (1925).

ANDREA DWORKIN (1946–)
Ice and Fire (1986).

STANLEY ELKIN (1930–)
Boswell (1964); *A Bad Man* (1967); *The Living End* (1979); *George Mills* (1982); *The Magic Kingdom* (1985); *The Rabbi of Lud* (1987).

BRET EASTON ELLIS (1964–)
Less Than Zero (1985); *American Psycho* (1991).

RALPH ELLISON (1914–)
Invisible Man (1952); *Shadow and Act* (essays, 1964).

NORA EPHRON (1941–)
Heartburn (1983); *Crazy Salad Plus Nine* (1984).

LOUISE ERDRICH (1954–)
Love Medicine (1984); *The Beet Queen* (1986); *Tracks* (1989).

JOHN FANTE (1909–33)
Wait Till the Spring, Bandini (1938).

JAMES T. FARRELL (1904–78)
Young Lonigan (1932); *The Young Manhood of Studs Lonigan* (1934); *Selected Essays* (1964).

WILLIAM FAULKNER (1897–1962)
Soldiers' Pay (1926); *Mosquitoes* (1927); *Sartoris* (1929); *The Sound and the Fury* (1929); *As I Lay Dying* (1930); *Light in August* (1932); *Absalom, Absalom!* (1936); *Go Down, Moses* (stories, 1942); *Collected Stories* (1950); *A Fable* (1954); *Essays* (ed. J. Meriwether, 1966).

RAYMOND FEDERMAN (1928–)
Double or Nothing (1972); *Take It or Leave It* (1976); *The Voice in the Closet* (1979); *The Twofold Vibration* (1982).

F. SCOTT FITZGERALD (1896–1940)
This Side of Paradise (1920); *Flappers and Philosophers* (stories, 1920);

The Beautiful and Damned (1922); *The Great Gatsby* (1925); *All the Sad Young Men* (stories, 1926); *Tender Is the Night* (1934); *The Last Tycoon* (1941); *The Crack-Up* (essays, post., 1945).

RICHARD FORD (1944–   )
A Piece of My Heart (1976); *The Sportswriter* (1986); *Rock Springs* (stories, 1987).

HAROLD FREDERIC (1856–98)
The Lawton Girl (1890); *The Damnation of Theron Ware* (1896).

MARILYN FRENCH (1929–   )
The Women's Room (1977).

BRUCE JAY FRIEDMAN (1930–   )
Stern (1962); *A Mother's Kisses* (1964); *The Dick* (1970); *Tokyo Woes* (1985).

HENRY BLAKE FULLER (1857–1929)
The Cliff-Dwellers (1893); *With the Procession* (1895).

WILLIAM GADDIS (1922–   )
The Recognitions (1955); *JR* (1975); *Carpenter's Gothic* (1985).

JOHN GARDNER (1933–82)
Grendel (1971); *The Sunlight Dialogues* (1972); *October Light* (1976); *Mickelsson's Ghosts* (1982); *On Moral Fiction* (essays, 1978).

HAMLIN GARLAND (1860–1940)
Main-Travelled Roads: Six Mississippi Valley Stories (1891); *Jason Edwards* (1892); *Prairie Folks* (stories, 1893); *Rose of Dutcher's Coolly* (1895); *Crumbling Idols* (essays, 1894).

WILLIAM H. GASS (1924–   )
Omensetter's Luck (1966); *In the Heart of the Heart of the Country* (stories, 1968); *Willie Master's Lonesome Wife* (1968); *The First Winter of My Married Life* (stories, 1979); *Fiction and the Figures of Life* (essays, 1970).

KAYE GIBBONS (1960–   )
Ellen Foster (1987); *A Virtuous Woman* (1989); *A Cure for Dreams* (1991).

ELLEN GILCHRIST (1935–   )
In the Land of Dreamy Dreams (1981); *Victory Over Japan* (1984); *Second Chances* (1986).

ELLEN GLASGOW (1874–1945)
The Descendant (1897); *The Battle-Ground* (1902); *The Deliverance* (1904); *Barren Ground* (1925); *Vein of Iron* (1935).

GAIL GODWIN (1937–   )
Glass People (1972); *Dream Children* (1976); *A Mother and Two Daughters* (1982); *The Finishing School* (1985); *A Southern Family* (1987); *Father Melancholy's Daughter* (1991).

MICHAEL GOLD (1892–1967)
Jews Without Money (1930).

MARY GORDON (1949–   )
Final Payments (1978); *Men and Angels* (1985); *Temporary Shelter* (1987).

LOIS GOULD (1938–   )
Such Good Friends (1970); *Not Responsible for Personal Articles* (1978).

SHIRLEY ANN GRAU (1929–   )
Keepers of the House (1964); *Nine Women* (1985).

ALFRED GROSSMAN (1927–   )
Acrobat Admits (1959).

ALLAN GURGANUS (1947–   )
Oldest Living Confederate Widow Tells All (1989).

DASHIELL HAMMETT (1894–1961)
The Maltese Falcon (1930); *The Glass Key* (1931); *The Thin Man* (1934).

JOHN HAWKES (1925–   )
The Cannibal (1949); *The Lime Twig* (1961); *Second Skin* (1964); *Death, Sleep and the Traveler* (1974); *The Passion Artist* (1979); *Virginie: Her Two Lives* (1982); *Whistlejacket* (1988).

JOSEPH HELLER (1923–   )
Catch-22 (1961); *Something Happened* (1974); *Good as Gold* (1979); *God Knows* (1984); *Picture This* (1988).

ERNEST HEMINGWAY (1898–1961)
In Our Time (1925); *The Sun Also Rises* (in England *Fiesta*) (1926); *Men Without Women* (1927); *A Farewell to Arms* (1929); *For Whom the Bell Tolls* (1940); *The Old Man and the Sea* (1952); *The Garden of Eden* (post., 1987).

MICHAEL HERR (1940–   )
Dispatches (1977).

GEORGE V. HIGGINS (1939–   )
The Friends of Eddie Coyle (1972); *Trust* (1989).

PATRICIA HIGHSMITH (1921–   )
Strangers on a Train (1950); *The Talented Mr Ripley* (1955); *Found in the Street* (1986).

RUSSELL HOBAN (1925–   )
Turtle Diary (1975); *Riddley Walker* (1980).

WILLIAM DEAN HOWELLS (1843–1916)
The Rise of Silas Lapham (1885); *A Hazard of New Fortunes* (1890); *A Traveler from Altruria* (1894); *The Kentons* (1902); *Criticism and Fiction* (essays, 1892).

JOSEPHINE HUMPHREYS (1945–   )
Dreams of Sleep (1984).

ZORA NEALE HURSTON (1903–60)
Jonah's Gourd Vine (1934); *Their Eyes Were Watching God* (1937).

RACHEL INGALLS (1940–   )
Mrs. Caliban (1982); *The End of Tragedy* (stories, 1987).

JOHN IRVING (1942–   )
Setting Free the Bears (1969); *The World According to Garp* (1978); *Hotel New Hampshire* (1981); *The Cider House Rules* (1985); *A Prayer for Owen Meany* (1988).

HENRY JAMES (1843–1916)
The Portrait of a Lady (1881); *The Tragic Muse* (1890); *The Spoils of*

Poynton (1897); *What Maisie Knew* (1897); *The Awkward Age* (1899); *The Sacred Fount* (1901); *The Wings of the Dove* (1902); *The Ambassadors* (1903); *The Golden Bowl* (1904); *The Ivory Tower* (post., 1917); *The Art of the Novel* (prefaces, ed. R. P. Blackmur, 1934); *The Future of the Novel* (essays, 1956).

SARAH ORNE JEWETT (1849–1909)
A Country Doctor (1884); *Tales of New England* (1890); *The Country of the Pointed Firs* (1896).

GAYL JONES (1949–   )
Corregidora (1975); *White Rat* (1977).

JAMES JONES (1921–77)
From Here to Eternity (1951); *The Thin Red Line* (1962); *Go to the Widow-Maker* (1967).

ERICA JONG (1942–   )
Fear of Flying (1973); *Fanny* (1980); *Parachutes and Kisses* (1984); *Serenissima* (1987).

STEVE KATZ (1935–   )
The Exaggerations of Peter Prince (1968); *Moving Parts* (1977); *Wier and Pouce* (1984).

GARRISON KEILLOR (1942–   )
Lake Wobegon Days (1985); *Leaving Home* (1987); *We Are Still Married* (1989).

WILLIAM MELVIN KELLEY (1937–   )
A Different Drummer (1962); *Dem* (1969); *Dancers on the Shore* (1970).

WILLIAM KENNEDY (1928–   )
Legs (1975); *Ironweed* (1983).

JACK KEROUAC (1922–69)
On the Road (1957); *The Dharma Bums* (1958); *Doctor Sax* (1959).

KEN KESEY (1935–   )
One Flew Over the Cuckoo's Nest (1962); *Sometimes a Great Notion* (1964); *Demon Box* (1986).

JOHN OLIVER KILLENS (1916–   )
And Then We Heard the Thunder (1963); *'Sippi* (1967); *Great Gittin' Up Morning* (1972).

MAXINE HONG KINGSTON (1940–   )
The Woman Warrior (1976); *China Men* (1980).

JERZY KOSINSKI (1933–91)
The Painted Bird (1965); *Steps* (1969); *Being There* (1971); *Blind Date* (1977); *Pinball* (1982); *The Hermit of 69th Street* (1987).

RING LARDNER (1885–1933)
The Love Nest (stories, 1926); *Collected Short Stories* (1941).

DAVID LEAVITT (1961–   )
Family Dancing (stories, 1984); *The Lost Language of Cranes* (1988).

HARPER LEE (1926–   )
To Kill a Mockingbird (1960).

URSULA LE GUIN (1929–   )
A Wizard of Earthsea (1968); *The Left Hand of Darkness* (1969).

ELMORE LEONARD (1925–   )
Glitz (1985); *Bandits* (1988).

SINCLAIR LEWIS (1885–1951)
Our Mr Wrenn (1914); *Main Street* (1920); *Babbitt* (1922); *Elmer Gantry* (1927); *The Man Who Knew Coolidge* (1928).

JACK LONDON (1876–1916)
The Call of the Wild (1903); *The Sea-Wolf* (1904); *The Iron Heel* (1907); *Martin Eden* (1909).

ALISON LURIE (1926–   )
The Nowhere City (1965); *Imaginary Friends* (1967); *The War Between the Tates* (1974); *Foreign Affairs* (1984); *The Truth About Lorin Jones* (1988).

MARY McCARTHY (1912–89)
The Groves of Academe (1952); *A Charmed Life* (1955); *The Group* (1963); *Cannibals and Missionaries* (1979).

CARSON MCCULLERS (1917–67)
The Heart Is a Lonely Hunter (1940); *Reflections in a Golden Eye* (1941);
The Member of the Wedding (1946); *Clock Without Hands* (1962).

KATHERINE MACDOWELL (1849–83)
Like Unto Like (1878); *Dialect Tales* (1883); *Suanee River Tales* (1884).

CYRA MCFADDEN (1935–   )
The Serial (1977).

THOMAS MCGUANE (1939–   )
The Sporting Club (1969); *Nobody's Angel* (1982); *Something to Be Desired* (1984).

JAY MCINERNEY (1955–   )
Bright Lights, Big City (1984); *Ransom* (1985); *Story of My Life* (1988).

NORMAN MAILER (1923–   )
The Naked and the Dead (1948); *The Deer Park* (1955); *An American Dream* (1965); *Why Are We in Vietnam?* (1967); *The Armies of the Night* (reportage, 1968); *Ancient Evenings* (1983); *Tough Guys Don't Dance* (1984).

CLARENCE MAJOR (1936–   )
All-Night Visitors (1969); *No* (1973); *Emergency Exit* (1979); *Such Was the Season* (1987).

BERNARD MALAMUD (1914–86)
The Natural (1952); *The Assistant* (1957); *The Magic Barrel* (stories, 1958); *The Fixer* (1966); *The Tenants* (1971); *Dubin's Lives* (1979); *God's Grace* (1982).

J. P. MARQUAND (1893–1960)
The Unspeakable Gentleman (1922); *The Late George Apley* (1937); *H. M. Pulham, Esq.* (1941).

BOBBIE ANN MASON (1941–   )
In Country (1985); *Spence + Lila* (1988); *Love Life* (stories, 1989).

ARMISTEAD MAUPIN (1944–   )
More Tales of the City (1980); *Baby Cakes* (1984); *Significant Others* (1988).

LEONARD MICHAELS (1933–   )
Going Places (stories, 1969); *The Men's Club* (1981).

PAUL MICOU (1959–   )
The Music Programme (1989); *The Cover Artist* (1990).

ARTHUR MILLER (1915–   )
Focus (1945).

HENRY MILLER (1891–1980)
Tropic of Cancer (1934); *Black Spring* (1936); *Tropic of Capricorn* (1939); *The Rosy Crucifixion* (*Sexus, Plexus, Nexus*, 1945–60); *Quiet Days in Clichy* (1956).

N. SCOTT MOMADAY (1934–   )
House Made of Dawn (1968); *The Way to Rainy Mountain* (1969); *The Names* (1976).

WRIGHT MORRIS (1910–   )
The Field of Vision (1956); *Ceremony in Lone Tree* (1960); *Plains Song* (1980).

TONI MORRISON (1931–   )
The Bluest Eye (1970); *Sula* (1973); *Song of Solomon* (1977); *Tar Baby* (1981); *Beloved* (1987).

VLADIMIR NABOKOV (1899–1977)
The Real Life of Sebastian Knight (1941); *Bend Sinister* (1947); *Lolita* (Paris, 1955; USA, 1958); *Pale Fire* (1962); *Ada or Ardor* (1969); *Transparent Things* (1972); *Look at the Harlequins* (1974).

FRANK NORRIS (1870–1902)
McTeague: A Story of San Francisco (1899); *The Octopus* (1901); *The Pit* (1903); *Responsibilities of the Novelist* (essays, 1903).

JOYCE CAROL OATES (1938–   )
With Shuddering Fall (1964); *Them* (1969); *Wonderland* (1971); *Marriages and Infidelities* (stories, 1973); *Unholy Loves* (1979); *Bellefleur* (1980); *A Bloodsmoor Romance* (1982); *The Mysteries of Winterthurn* (1984); *Kindred Passions* (1987); *American Appetites* (1989); *Because It Is Bitter and Because It Is My Heart* (1990).

TIM O'BRIEN (1946–   )
Going After Ciaccato (1978); *Nuclear Age* (1986).

FLANNERY O'CONNOR (1925–64)
Wise Blood (1952); *A Good Man Is Hard to Find* (stories, 1955); *Everything that Rises Must Converge* (stories, 1965).

JOHN O'HARA (1905–70)
Appointment in Samarra (1934); *BUtterfield 8* (1935); *Ourselves to Know* (1960).

TILLIE OLSEN (1913–   )
Tell Me a Riddle (1961); *Yonnondio* (1974).

TOBY OLSON (1937–   )
The Woman Who Escaped from Shame (1986).

CYNTHIA OZICK (1928–   )
The Cannibal Galaxy (1983); *The Messiah of Stockholm* (1987); *The Shawl* (1989).

GRACE PALEY (1922–   )
The Little Disturbances of Man (stories, 1959); *Later the Same Day* (1985).

WALKER PERCY (1916–   )
The Moviegoer (1961); *Love in the Ruins* (1971); *The Second Coming* (1980).

JAYNE ANNE PHILLIPS (1952–   )
Machine Dreams (1984); *Fast Lanes* (stories, 1987).

MARGE PIERCY (1936–   )
Woman on the Edge of Time (1976); *Fly Away Home* (1984).

DAVID PLANTE (1940–   )
The Foreigner (1984); *The Native* (1987).

SYLVIA PLATH (1932–63)
The Bell Jar (1963).

KATHERINE ANNE PORTER (1890–1980)
Flowering Judas (1930); *Pale Horse, Pale Rider* (1939); *The Leaning Tower* (1944); *Ship of Fools* (1962).

CHAIM POTOK (1929–   )
The Chosen (1967); *My Name is Asher Lev* (1972).

J. F. POWERS (1917–   )
The Presence of Grace (stories, 1956); *Morte d'Urban* (1962); *Look How the Fish Live* (stories, 1975).

REYNOLDS PRICE (1933–   )
A Long and Happy Life (1962); *Permanent Errors* (1970); *The Source of Light* (1981); *Kate Vaiden* (1986); *Good Hearts* (1988).

JAMES PURDY (1923–   )
63, Dream Palace (1956); *The Color of Darkness* (stories, 1957); *Malcolm* (1959); *Cabot Wright Begins* (1964); *On Glory's Course* (1984).

MARIO PUZO (1920–   )
The Godfather (1969).

THOMAS PYNCHON (1937–   )
V. (1963); *The Crying of Lot 49* (1966); *Gravity's Rainbow* (1973); *Slow Learner* (stories, 1984); *Vineland* (1990).

JOHN RECHY (1934–   )
City of Night (1963); *This Day's Death* (1970); *Bodies and Souls* (1983).

ISHMAEL REED (1938–   )
The Free-Lance Pallbearers (1967); *Yellow Back Radio Broke Down* (1969); *Mumbo Jumbo* (1972); *Flight to Canada* (1976); *Reckless Eye-balling* (1986); *Cab Calloway Stands In for the Moon* (1987).

MARILYNNE ROBINSON (1944–   )
Housekeeping (1980).

JUDITH ROSSNER (1935–   )
Looking for Mr. Goodbar (1975); *Attachments* (1977); *August* (1983).

HENRY ROTH (1907–   )
Call It Sleep (1934).

PHILIP ROTH (1933–   )
Goodbye, Columbus (stories, 1959); *Letting Go* (1962); *When She Was Good* (1967); *Portnoy's Complaint* (1969); *The Professor of Desire* (1977); *Zuckerman Bound: A Trilogy and Epilogue* (1985); *The Counterlife* (1986); *Reading Myself and Others* (essays, 1975); *The Facts* (autobiography, 1988).

DAMON RUNYON (1884–1946)
Guys and Dolls (1932); *The Best of Runyon* (1938).

JOANNA RUSS (1937–   )
The Female Man (1975).

J. D. SALINGER (1919–   )
The Catcher in the Rye (1951); *Nine Stories* (in Britain *For Esmé—With Love and Squalor*)(1953); *Franny and Zooey* (1961); *Raise High the Roofbeam, Carpenters and Seymour* (1963).

HUBERT SELBY, JR. (1926–   )
Last Exit to Brooklyn (1964); *The Room* (1971).

LESLIE MARMON SILKO (1948–   )
Ceremony (1977); *Storyteller* (1981).

UPTON SINCLAIR (1878–1968)
The Jungle (1906); *The Metropolis* (1908).

ISAAC BASHEVIS SINGER (1904–91)
Gimpel the Fool (stories, 1957); *The Magician of Lublin* (1960); *The Slave* (1962); *The Manor* (1967); *Shosha* (1978); *The Collected Stories* (1982); *The King of the Fields* (1988).

LEE SMITH (1944–   )
Family Linen (1985); *Fair and Tender Ladies* (1988).

SUSAN SONTAG (1933–   )
The Benefactor (1963); *Death-Kit* (1967); *Against Interpretation* (essays, 1966).

GILBERT SORRENTINO (1929–   )
Imaginary Qualities of Actual Things (1971); *Mulligan Stew* (1979); *Odd Number* (1985).

TERRY SOUTHERN (1924–)
Candy (1958); *The Magic Christian* (1959); *Blue Movie* (1970).

WALLACE STEGNER (1909–)
Big Rock Candy Mountain (1943); *A Shooting Star* (1961); *Angle of Repose* (1971); *The Spectator Bird* (1976); *Crossing to Safety* (1987).

GERTRUDE STEIN (1874–1946)
Three Lives (1909); *Tender Buttons* (prose poetry, 1914); *The Making of Americans* (1925); *Things As They Are* (1950); *Lectures in America* (essays, 1935).

JOHN STEINBECK (1902–68)
In Dubious Battle (1936); *Of Mice and Men* (1937); *The Grapes of Wrath* (1939); *East of Eden* (1952).

ROBERT STONE (1937–)
Dog Soldiers (1974); *A Flag for Sunrise* (1981); *Children of Light* (1986).

WILLIAM STYRON (1925–)
Lie Down in Darkness (1951); *The Confessions of Nat Turner* (1967); *Sophie's Choice* (1979).

RONALD SUKENICK (1932–)
Up (1968); *The Death of the Novel and Other Stories* (stories, 1969); *Out* (1973); *Long Talking Bad Conditions Blues* (1979); *Blown Away* (1986); *In Form* (essays, 1985).

PETER TAYLOR (1917–)
Collected Stories (1969); *In the Miro District* (stories, 1977); *Summoned to Memphis* (1986).

ROBERT LOVE TAYLOR (1941–)
Loving Belle Starr (1984); *Fiddle and Bow* (1985); *The Lost Sister* (1989).

PAUL THEROUX (1944–)
Picture Palace (1978); *The Mosquito Coast* (1982); *The London Embassy* (stories, 1982); *Chicago Loop* (1990).

JOHN KENNEDY TOOLE (1937–69)
A Confederacy of Dunces (1980).

JEAN TOOMER (1894–1967)
Cane (fiction/poetry, 1923).

MARK TWAIN (1835–1910)
The Adventures of Huckleberry Finn (1884); *A Connecticut Yankee in King Arthur's Court* (1889); *Pudd'nhead Wilson* (1894); *The Man That Corrupted Hadleyburg* (1900); *The Mysterious Stranger* (post., 1916).

ANNE TYLER (1941–)
If Morning Ever Comes (1964); *The Tin Can Tree* (1965); *Dinner at the Homesick Restaurant* (1982); *The Accidental Tourist* (1985); *Breathing Lessons* (1988).

JOHN UPDIKE (1932–)
The Poorhouse Fair (1959); *Rabbit, Run* (1960); *Couples* (1968); *Rabbit Redux* (1971); *The Coup* (1979); *Rabbit Is Rich* (1981); *Hugging the Shore* (essays, 1983); *The Witches of Eastwick* (1984); *Roger's Version* (1986); *Rabbit at Rest* (1990).

CARL VAN VECHTEN (1880–1966)
Nigger Heaven (1926); *Spider Boy* (1928).

GORE VIDAL (1925–)
Julian (1964); *Washington, D.C.* (1967); *Myra Breckinridge* (1968); *Burr* (1974); *1876* (1976); *Creation* (1981); *Lincoln* (1984); *Empire* (1987); *Matters of Fact and of Fiction* (essays, 1977).

KURT VONNEGUT, JR. (1922–)
Player Piano (1952); *The Sirens of Titan* (1959); *Mother Night* (1961); *Cat's Cradle* (1963); *Slaughterhouse-Five* (1969); *Breakfast of Champions* (1973); *Deadeye Dick* (1982); *Galapagos* (1985); *Bluebeard* (1987).

DAN WAKEFIELD (1932–)
Starting Over (1973); *Selling Out* (1984); *Returning* (1988).

ALICE WALKER (1944–)
Meridian (1976); *The Third Life of Grange Copeland* (1970); *You Can't Keep a Good Woman Down* (stories, 1981); *The Color Purple* (1983).

ROBERT PENN WARREN (1905–)
All the King's Men (1946); *The Circus in the Attic* (stories, 1947); *World Enough and Time* (1950); *Meet Me in the Green Glen* (1971).

EUDORA WELTY (1909–   )
A Curtain of Green (stories, 1941); *Delta Wedding* (1946); *Losing Battles* (1970); *The Optimist's Daughter* (1972); *Collected Stories* (1980); *The Eye of the Story* (essays, 1979).

NATHANAEL WEST (1904–41)
The Dream Life of Balso Snell (1931); *Miss Lonelyhearts* (1933); *A Cool Million* (1934); *The Day of the Locust* (1939).

EDITH WHARTON (1862–1937)
The House of Mirth (1905); *Ethan Frome* (1911); *The Custom of the Country* (1913); *The Age of Innocence* (1920); *Hudson River Bracketed* (1929); *The Writing of Fiction* (essays, 1925).

WILLIAM WHARTON (1925–   )
Birdy (1978); *Dad* (1980); *A Midnight Clear* (1982).

EDMUND WHITE (1940–   )
A Boy's Own Story (1982); *The Beautiful Room Is Empty* (1988).

JOHN EDGAR WIDEMAN (1941–   )
The Glance Away (1967); *Sent for Your Yesterday* (1983); *Fever* (stories, 1989).

JOHN A. WILLIAMS (1925–   )
The Man Who Cried I Am (1967); *!Clicksong* (1982); *The Berhama Account* (1985).

TENNESSEE WILLIAMS (1911–83)
The Roman Spring of Mrs Stone (1950).

THOMAS WOLFE (1900–38)
Look Homeward, Angel (1929); *Of Time and the River* (1935); *You Can't Go Home Again* (post., 1940).

TOM WOLFE (1931–   )
The Kandy-Kolored Tangerine-Flake Streamline Baby (journalism, 1965); ed., *The New Journalism* (1973); *The Bonfire of the Vanities* (1988).

TOBIAS WOLFF (1945–   )
Hunters in the Snow (1982); *The Barracks Thief* (1984); *Back in the World* (1985).

RICHARD WRIGHT (1908–60)
Native Son (1940); *The Outsider* (1953).

RUDOLPH WURLITZER (1938–)
Nog (1969); *Flats* (1970); *Quake* (1972); *Slow Fade* (1984).

RICHARD YATES (1926–)
Young Hearts Crying (1984).

Select Bibliography

MODERN American fiction has, of course, been very extensively treated in criticism. For an overall perspective on American literature, see Emory Elliott (ed.), *Columbia Literary History of the United States* (New York, 1988), and Malcolm Bradbury and Richard Ruland, *From Puritanism to Postmodernism: A History of American Literature* (London, 1991). The list that follows deals with general studies of the modern American novel, thematic and general critical treatments, and studies of various periods. For work on individual authors, Lewis Leary's *American Literature: A Study and Research Guide* (New York, 1976) provides brief information that needs supplementing by individual bibliographies. Among the various bibliographies worth consulting are Blake Nevius, *The American Novel: Sinclair Lewis to the Present* (Northbrook, Ill., 1970); Donna Gerstenberger and George Hendrick, *The American Novel: A Checklist of 20th-Century Criticism on Novels Written since 1789* (Chicago, 1961) and *Volume 2: Criticism Written 1960–68* (Chicago, 1970); Irving Adelman and Rita Dworkin, *The Contemporary Novel: A Checklist of Critical Literature on the British and American Novel Since 1945* (Metuchen, NJ, 1972); and Gary M. Lepper, *A Bibliographical Introduction to 75 Modern American Authors* (Berkeley, Calif., 1976).

The best general studies of twentieth-century American fiction largely belong to the 1940s and 1950s, when concern to establish the 'modern tradition' was strong. Key books are Alfred Kazin's early, powerful, but nationalistically oriented *On Native Grounds: A Study of American Prose Literature from 1890 to the Present* (New York, 1942), which can be usefully supplemented by the same author's *Contemporaries: Essays on Modern Life and Literature* (New York, 1962; London, 1963) and *Bright Book of Life: American Novelists and Storytellers from Hemingway to Mailer* (New York, 1973; London, 1974). Also nationalist and naturalist in orientation is Maxwell Geismar's coverage in his four volumes: *Rebels and Ancestors: The American Novel 1890–1915* (Boston, 1953); *The Last of the Provincials: The American Novel 1915–1925* (New York, 1947); *Writers in Crisis: The American Novel 1925–1940* (New York, 1942); and *American Moderns: From Rebellion to Conformity* (New York, 1958). A fuller historical study with an excellent modern section is Leslie Fiedler's *Love and Death in the American Novel* (New York, 1960; rev. edn., 1967); supplemented by his *Waiting for the End*

(New York, 1964; London, 1965) and *The Return of the Vanishing American* (New York/London, 1968). Other good studies are Frederick J. Hoffman's *The Modern Novel in America* (Chicago, 1951) and Joseph Warren Beach's *American Fiction: 1920–1940* (New York, 1960). Though few of these use modern critical methods, they represent founding arguments in the debate. A helpful anthology is *Modern American Fiction: Essays in Criticism*, ed. A. Walton Litz (New York, 1963). For a more modern perspective, see the essays in Thomas Daniel Young (ed.), *Modern American Fiction: Form and Function* (Baton Rouge, La./London, 1989).

Many of the most important studies are thematic, exploring essential themes or tendencies in American fiction. Among the best are Joseph Blotner's *The American Political Novel 1900–1960* (Austin, Tex., 1960); W. M. Frohock's *The Novel of Violence in America* (Dallas, 1957); Blanche Gelfant's *The American City Novel* (Norman, Okla., 1954); *Psychoanalysis in American Fiction*, ed. Irving Malin (New York, 1965); James M. Mellard's interesting if narrow *The Exploded Form: The Modernist Novel in America* (Urbana, Ill./London, 1980), which concentrates on Faulkner, Heller, and Brautigan; Michael Millgate's *American Social Fiction: James to Cozzens* (Edinburgh and London, 1964); Walter B. Rideout's *The Radical Novel in the United States 1900–1954* (Cambridge, Mass., 1956); and David Galloway's *The Absurd Hero in American Fiction* (Austin, Tex., 1966; rev. edn., 1971). For Southern fiction, see Jay B. Hubbell's *The South in American Literature* (Durham, N.C., 1954) and *Southern Life in Fiction* (Athens, Ga., 1960); John M. Bradbury, *Renaissance in the South: A Critical History of the Literature 1920–1960* (Chapel Hill, N.C., 1963); and Richard Gray, *The Literature of Memory: Modern Writers of the American South* (London/Baltimore, 1977). On black American fiction, see Robert A. Bone, *The Negro Novel in America* (rev. edn., New Haven, Conn., London, 1970); *Modern Black Novelists: A Collection of Critical Essays*, ed. M. G. Cooke (Englewood Cliffs, NJ, 1971); and C. W. E. Bigsby, *The Second Black Renaissance: Essays in Black Literature* (Westport, Conn., 1980). On Jewish-American fiction, see Allen Guttman's *The Jewish Writer in America: Assimilation and the Crisis of Identity* (New York, 1971); Irving Howe's monumental *World of Our Fathers* (New York, 1977); and Abraham Chapman, *Jewish-American Literature* (New York, 1974); as well as the works by Leslie Fiedler mentioned above.

For the 1890s and the rise of naturalism, the best studies are Charles C. Walcutt, *American Literary Naturalism: A Divided Stream* (Minneapolis, Minn., 1956) and Donald Pizer, *Realism and Naturalism in Nineteenth Century American Literature* (Carbondale, Ill., 1966). A brilliant evocation of the decade is found in Larzer Ziff's *The American 1890s: The Life and Times of a Lost Generation* (New York/London, 1967); Gordon O. Taylor's *The Passages of Thought: Psychological Representation in the American Novel 1870–1900* (New York/London, 1969) is admirable on the treatment of 'consciousness' in the novels of the period. The continuing impact of naturalism on the progressive novel of the 1900s is studied in Robert W. Schneider, *Five Novelists of the Progressive Era* (New York/London, 1965); Jay B. Martin, *Harvests of Change: American Literature 1865–1914* (Englewood Cliffs, NJ, 1967) and Brian Lee, *American Fiction 1865–1940* (London/New York, 1987) give a broad view of the period.

For the emergence of modernism on the international scene, including the United States, see *Modernism 1890–1930*, ed. Malcolm Bradbury and James McFarlane (Harmondsworth, 1976; rev. edn., 1991), with an extensive bibliography. The topic is explored comparatively, and admirably, in Edmund Wilson, *Axel's Castle: A Study in the Imaginative Literature of 1870–1930* (New York, 1931); interesting, if rather partial and overnationalistic, is Hugh Kenner's study, *A Homemade World: The American Modernist Writers* (New York, 1975). The fundamental changes of style involved have been widely explored in modern criticism, but especially recommended are Wylie Sypher's *Rococo to Cubism in Art and Literature* (New York, 1960) and *Loss of the Self in Modern Art and Literature* (New York, 1962). An important area is covered in Bernard Duffey, *The Chicago Renaissance in American Letters* (East Lansing, Mich., 1954), while a good general background to the cultural changes of the immediately pre-war years is Henry F. May, *The End of American Innocence: A Study of the First Years of Our Own Time 1912–1917* (New York, 1959).

The direct impact of war on modern American writers is examined in Frederick J. Hoffman, *The Mortal No: Death and the Modern Imagination* (Princeton, NJ, 1964); also see Stanley J. Cooperman, *World War I and the American Novel* (Baltimore, 1967). Frederick Hoffman also offers an excellent introduction to the Twenties in *The Twenties: American Writing in the Postwar Decade* (New York, 1949) as well as in *Freudianism and the Literary Mind* (New York, 1977). Malcolm Cowley's *Exile's Return: A Literary Odyssey of the 1920s* (New York, 1934; rev. edn., 1951) is a key book of memoirs and analysis; also see the valuable critical essays in his *A Second Flowering: Works and Days of the Lost Generation* (New York/London, 1973). *The American Novel and the 1920s*, ed. Malcolm Bradbury and David Palmer (London, 1971), offers essays on the period and the main authors, with general bibliographies.

An admirable historical survey of the period is William E. Leuchtenburg, *The Perils of Prosperity* (Chicago, 1958).

On the 1930s and the rise of proletarian fiction see Daniel Aaron, *Writers on the Left* (New York, 1961) and Leo Gurko, *The Angry Decade* (New York, 1968). Kazin's *On Native Grounds* and Geismar's *Writers in Crisis*, cited above, also provide valuable material. The reaction of the 1940s is best found in Chester E. Eisinger, *Fiction of the Forties* (Chicago/London, 1963); also see John W. Aldridge, *After the Lost Generation: A Critical Study of the Writers of Two Wars* (New York, 1951), Marcus Klein, *After Alienation: American Novels in Mid-Century* (Cleveland, Oh., 1962); and Sidney Finkelstein, *Existentialism and Alienation in American Literature* (New York, 1965).

The best general survey of the post-war American novel is Tony Tanner, *City of Words: American Fiction 1950–1970* (London, 1971); a broader but less analytical portrait is to be found in the *Harvard Guide to Contemporary American Writing*, ed. Daniel Hoffman (Cambridge, Mass./London, 1979). Three useful collections of essays on the post-war American novel are *Recent American Fiction: Some Critical Views*, ed. Joseph J. Waldmeir (Boston, 1963); *Contemporary American Novelists*, ed. Harry T. Moore (Carbondale, Ill./London, 1964); and *The American Novel Since World War II*, ed. Marcus Klein (New York, 1969). For a more detailed study, see Ihab Hassan's very useful and central *Radical Innocence: Studies in the Contemporary American Novel* (Princeton, NJ, 1961). Howard M. Harper, *Desperate Faith: A Study of Bellow, Salinger, Mailer, Baldwin and Updike* (Chapel Hill, N.C., 1967); Nathan A. Scott, *Three American Moralists: Mailer, Bellow, Trilling* (Notre Dame, Ind., 1973); and *Five Black Writers: Essays on Wright, Ellison, Baldwin, Hughes and LeRoi Jones*, ed. Donald B. Gibson (New York/London, 1970); deal well with major figures.

On the fiction of the 1960s, see Tony Tanner, cited above, and Raymond Olderman, *Beyond the Waste Land: The American Novel in the 1960s* (New Haven, Conn., 1973). Other useful studies are Jonathan Baumbach, *The Landscape of Nightmare: Studies in the Contemporary American Novel* (New York, 1965); Max F. Schultz, *Black Humor Fiction of the Sixties* (Athens, Oh., 1973); and Richard B. Hauck, *A Cheerful Nihilism: Confidence and 'The Absurd' in American Humorous Fiction* (Bloomington, Ind./London, 1971). Also valuable are Jerry H. Bryant, *The Open Decision: The Contemporary American Novel and Its Intellectual Background* (New York, 1970); Josephine Hendin, *Vulnerable People: A View of American Fiction Since 1945* (New York, 1978); John R. May, *Towards a New Earth: Apocalypse in the American Novel*

(Notre Dame, Ind., 1972); Frederick R. Karl, *American Fiction, 1940–1980: A Comprehensive History and Critical Evaluation* (New York, 1983); and Patrick O'Donnell, *Passionate Doubts: Designs of Interpretation in Contemporary American Fiction* (Iowa City, 1986).

On postmodernism a key source is the various books of Ihab Hassan: *The Dismemberment of Orpheus: Towards a Postmodern Literature* (New York, 1971), *Paracriticisms: Seven Speculations of the Times* (Urbana, Ill./London, 1975); and *The Postmodern Turn* (Columbus, Oh., 1986). Also see the volume edited by Ihab and Sally Hassan, *Innovation/Renovation* (Madison, Wis., 1983). Another good collection of essays on experimental fiction internationally is Raymond Federman (ed.), *Surfiction: Fiction Now and Tomorrow* (Chicago, 1973); Sally Sears and Georgiana W. Lord (eds.) offer a still broader view in *The Discontinuous Universe: Selected Writings in Contemporary Consciousness* (New York/London, 1972). Other important titles on postmodernism are John O. Stark, *The Literature of Exhaustion: Borges, Nabokov, Barth* (Durham, N.C., 1974); Robert Alter, *Partial Magic: The Novel as a Self-Conscious Genre* (Berkeley, Calif., 1975); Robert Scholes, in *The Fabulators* (New York, 1967) and his later revision, *Fabulation and Metafiction* (Urbana, Ill./Chicago/London, 1979); Mas'ud Zavarzadeh, *The Mythopoeic Reality: The Postwar Nonfiction Novel* (Urbana, Ill./London, 1975); David Lodge's very useful *The Modes of Modern Writing: Metaphor, Metonymy and the Typology of Modern Literature* (London, 1977), with an important section on postmodernism; Manfred Pütz's *The Story of Identity: American Fiction of the Sixties* (1979); Christopher Butler's international study of modern artistic experimentalism, *After the Wake: An Essay on the Contemporary Avant Garde* (Oxford, 1980); Linda Hutcheon's *Narcissistic Narrative: The Metafictional Paradox* (Waterloo, Ont., 1980) and her *A Poetics of Postmodernism: History, Theory, Fiction* (New York/London, 1988); and Philip Stevick's *Alternative Pleasures: Postrealist Fiction and the Tradition* (Chicago/London, 1981).

More recent important studies of the topic are Maurice Couturier (ed.), *Representation and Performance in Postmodern Culture* (Montpellier, France, 1983); Alan Wilde, *Horizons of Assent: Modernism, Postmodernism and the Ironic Imagination* (Baltimore, 1981); Charles Caramello, *Silverless Mirrors: Book, Self, and Postmodern American Fiction* (Tallahassee, Fla., 1983); Patricia Waugh's short and handy *Metafiction: The Theory and Practice of Self-Conscious Fiction* (London/New York, 1984); Allen Thiher's *Words in Reflection: Modern Language Theory and Postmodern Fiction* (Chicago, 1984); David Porush's *The*

Soft Machine: Cybernetic Fiction (New York/London, 1985); and Brian McHale's interesting study *Postmodernist Fiction* (New York/London, 1987). In Europe, Manfred Pütz and Peter Freese have edited *Postmodernism in American Literature* (Darmstadt, 1984), which reflects the good German scholarship in this area. Also see two volumes in the continuing series on postmodern writing edited by Douwe Fokkema and Hans Bertens, *Literary History, Modernism, and Postmodernism* (Amsterdam/Philadelphia, 1984) and *Approaching Postmodernism* (Amsterdam/Philadelphia, 1986).

On the overall concept of postmodern culture, see Jean-François Lyotard, *The Postmodern Condition* (Manchester, 1984); Jean Baudrillard, *Amerique* (Paris, 1986); Steven Connor's highly useful *Postmodernist Culture: An Introduction to Theories of the Contemporary* (Oxford, 1989), which looks at the arts generally and has a fine bibliography; David Harvey, *The Condition of Postmodernity* (Oxford, 1989); Scott Lash, *Sociology of Postmodernism* (London/New York 1990); and Fredric Jameson's *Postmodernism* (London, 1991). Two important books on feminism and postmodernism are Alice Jardine's *Gynesis: Configurations of Women and Modernity* (Ithaca, NY/London, 1985) and Meaghan Morris, *The Pirate's Fiancee: Feminism, Reading, Postmodernism* (London, 1988). Also see Mary Allen, *The Necessary Blankness: Women in the Major American Fiction of the Sixties* (Urbana, Ill., 1976). For some interesting and important alternative views challenging postmodernism, see the two contentious studies by Gerald Graff, *Literature Against Itself: Literary Ideas in Modern Society* (Chicago/London, 1979) and Charles Newman, *The Postmodern Aura* (Evanston, Ill., 1985).

Many of the key statements about the state and nature of the modern and postmodern novel (including those by Roth, Bellow, and Barth) are collected in Malcolm Bradbury (ed.), *The Novel Today: Contemporary Writers on Modern Fiction* (rev. edn., London, 1990), which puts these developments in an international context. There are also interesting interviews and commentaries in Nora Balakian and Charles Simmons (eds.), *The Creative Present: Notes on Contemporary American Fiction* (New York, 1963); L. S. Dembo and Cyrena Podrom (eds.), *The Contemporary Writer: Interviews with 16 Novelists and Poets* (Madison, Wis., 1973); and Heide Ziegler and Christopher Bigsby (eds.), *The Radical Imagination and the Liberal Tradition: Interviews with English and American Novelists* (London, 1982). There are important essays by writers in William H. Gass's *Fiction and the Figures of Life* (New York, 1970), *On Being Blue* (Boston, 1976), and *The World Within the Word*

Index